FUTURETELLING

BY
PATRICIA TELESCO

THE CROSSING PRESS
FREEDOM, CALIFORNIA

Copyright © 1998 by Patricia Telesco
Cover Design by Tara M. Eoff
Cover photograph by Art Montes DeOca / FPG International
Interior Design by Victoria May and Tara M. Eoff
Tarot card illustrations by Pamela Coleman Smith
Composition by Phyllis Beaty
Book set in Janson and Baker Signet

For information on bulk purchases or group discounts for this and other Crossing Press titles, please contact our Special Sales Manager at 800-777-1048.
Visit our Web site on the Internet: www.crossingpress.com.

Library of Congress Cataloging-in-Publication Data

Telesco, Patricia. 1960–
    Futuretelling / Patricia Telesco.
        p. cm.
    Includes bibliographical references.
    ISBN 0-89594-872-9 (pbk.)
    1. Divination. I. Title.
BF1751.T45   1998
133.3--dc21   98-5019
                                                                                CIP

Table of Contents

"Among the notionable dictes of antique Rome was the fancy that when men heard thunder on the left the gods had somewhat of a special advertisement to impart. Then did the prudent pause and lay down their affaire to study what omen Jove intended."

—*The Dangers of Mortal Life*
Sir Eustace Peachtree, 1640

Introduction

*"Let it be discovered by divination, or let a divinely
inspired man declare it."*
—Hittite prayer of Mursil II

As a new millennium dawns, interest in divination and fortune-telling is growing steadily. Since reason and religion are not always adequate to answer humankind's troubling questions, divination systems have tremendous appeal, offering the gift of insight. Around the world, millions of people consult astrology columns, tarot decks, the *I Ching*, palm readers, and psychic hotlines, believing them to be meaningful spiritual tools for coping with the uncertainties of daily life.

A curiosity about the future and what it holds naturally developed alongside humankind's understanding of time and awareness of tomorrow's inevitability. Because of life's harshness, our ancestors had nagging questions and concerns about their fate. So they observed nature's signs and experimented with different predictive techniques, trying to take better control over fate's whims. No prophetic method that could possibly offer help and hope was overlooked.

Exactly how each divination method was developed and applied depended heavily on when and where it appeared. For example, natural omens were among the first prognostic systems early humans devised, requiring little more than old fashioned observation on the part of the diviner. By 1400 B.C.E. healers in China examined the patterns formed in cracked animal bones and shells to determine a patient's chances for recovery. Greek and Roman augurs listened to the sound of the wind through sacred oaks or looked to the movement of birds to help them decide when to wage wars. In Tibet it was the job of select diviners to find the new incarnation of the Dali Lama.

All these individuals rendered a basic service, using culture, tradition, and common sense as a guide. Once a diviner established the validity of a portent or technique as a basis for correct predictions, their familial or village storytellers and scribes preserved this information in oral and/or written histories to benefit everyone. Many of these records have been passed down from generation to generation in nearly unchanged form. Consequently, many of the divination systems we presently use are actually hundreds or even thousands of years old.

So it is that individuals in different eras and settings honored the diviner's art by seeking it out, sharing its lore, or learning and using the methods themselves. But, as with many metaphysical techniques, the public has had an ongoing love-hate relationship with fortune-telling, depending on the religious and sociological climate of the times. During periods when mystical or occult studies were repressed, divination systems found a safe haven among the folk traditions and sayings from which they grew. Many of them are preserved there today.

Early diviners acted in a role similar to a modern counselor. Their task was to provide alternative perspectives and hope. Also, most diviners, soothsayers, and fortune-tellers were everyday folk who used their abilities to help family, friends, and neighbors with common needs, like determining the best time to sow crops. The modern seeker should remember this. Divinatory arts are not now, nor ever have been, limited to an elite group. Anyone with the right intention and concentration can learn to tap effectively into the collective unconscious and allow fresh insights to come through. These arts don't have to be fancy to yield impressive results. In fact, the spontaneous, heartfelt approach is frequently best, because it comes directly out of your experience and environment.

Each of us faces very difficult questions and struggles daily. Divination is one instrument that can help us examine those issues objectively. Yet, many people have justifiable doubts and concerns about this art. That is precisely where this book can help. The first section in Part One examines some of the most commonly asked questions about divination, including how it works, how new divination systems evolve, and what are some of the ethical guidelines. Building on this foundation, the second section provides instructions for choosing or designing a divination system and using it successfully.

Beyond this, the lion's share of this book constitutes a divination encyclopedia that investigates the world's fortune-telling methods from historical, cultural, and practical vantage points. The encyclopedia goes on to review plausible contemporary applications and adaptations for many of the techniques or tools discussed. With these modified approaches, an ongoing examination of your living space and everything in it is conducive to your spiritual, emotional, or mental growth and understanding. From this perspective, the mundane world and the esoteric find a commmon ground that is generated by your own hands and vision.

Following this narrative, Appendix A lists some gods and goddesses strongly associated with the divinatory arts. Many diviners choose to call on a divine being to bless and direct their work. If you wish to do likewise, refer to this section for ideas.

Finally, Appendix B assembles emblems and pictographs together with potential interpretations. Some divination systems rely on symbolic content, such as cloud or crystal gazing and tea leaf reading. Think of this section as a pictorial resource when unfamiliar symbols appear in such a reading, or when an image doesn't immediately make sense.

Despite our technology-dependent society, the importance of the divinatory arts to humankind should not be underestimated. Divination opens a spiritual window through which we can see our present situations more clearly and peek into possible futures. In those moments when you find the world around you moving too quickly, when life seems chaotic and incomprehensible, or when you feel you need a different outlook, consider divination as a possible helpmate. Turn to the methods used by our ancestors and many people today, and find one that's meaningful to you. Then cast your stones, read your cards, scry a bonfire, or interpret the wind. In the process, your understanding of, and appreciation for, the simple truths evidenced in everything from the trees to the stars will grow proportionally, alongside your questing spirit.

PART ONE

The Art and Practice
of Divination

CHAPTER ONE

Isn't It Divine? The Basics of Divination

"The future cannot be hidden or obscured from the intelligent soul, but this perfect knowledge cannot be acquired without divine guidance."

—Nostradamus

In reviewing the questions that arrive daily in the mail and my discussions with spiritual seekers around the U.S., it seems that nearly everyone at sometime struggles with the concepts and practices of divination. Our sense of logic and concrete thinking makes it difficult to remove the mental wall that hides future potentialities. Too much rationality also creates doubt, which then becomes an additional stumbling block.

This chapter, therefore, reviews some basic information about the diviner's art and its workings to guide in the breaking down of those mental walls. Knowledge is a powerful hammer. Commonly asked questions are examined here, as well as both ancient and modern thoughts on the subjects. Alongside this historical exploration are reflections drawn from my personal studies of, experiences with, and beliefs about prophetic arts and practices.

Should you still find yourself in a quandary about divination after reading this chapter, try skipping forward to the encyclopedia of systems and tools (Part Two). History is a potent mirror for us, reflecting who we were as a people and where we are going together. These pages contain insights from hundreds of individuals, just like yourself, who have sought and found answers through the diviner's art. With a better understanding of the rich tradition that divination represents, you can then reread this chapter for more detailed or alternative insights, and then move on to finding or making a divinatory tool that's right for you in the next section.

1. What does divination offer me spiritually and mundanely?

The most popular reason for consulting a diviner is to gain insight into future possibilities. Knowing what could happen given the present set of circumstances has tremendous value. A consultation provides a setting for the examination of potential problems or opportunities that might not otherwise be obvious. This often motivates the querent to make dynamic efforts toward positive, empowering changes.

Another reason for consulting a reader is to gain perspective on a difficult situation or to find the solution to a problem that's been particularly evasive. For example, a young woman came to me about eight years ago, very distraught, and asked for a psychic reading. After the reading revealed that her dearest wish was a good goal for her, she set about the task of making that dream into a reality. In this case, divination provided a nudge at the right time to help things along. This is the type of positive effect that any sensitive, balanced reading offers.

Most people really do know, deep down, what is best for them. Accessing that knowledge is the hard part. By utilizing traditional or personally formulated divinatory tools, or by consulting a professional reader, we give ourselves a way of stepping back, becoming observers, and finding previously elusive answers, thanks to the alternative perspective that divination offers.

2. Why are there so many different types of divination?

Everyone relates most strongly to life through one of their senses, or perhaps a combination of several. Our relationship with the spiritual dimension is no different; we seek input in some sensual manner. Consequently, each divination system appeals to one predominant sense. For example, tarot cards usually attract visually oriented people, while runes or stones fascinate tactile individuals.

Beyond this sensual dimension, the vast assortment of divinatory tools speaks directly of humankind's diversity and creativity. Because each person is distinct, with likewise distinctive ways of interpreting the universe's mysteries, a variety of fortune-telling systems developed that reflect historical, cultural, and personal experiences. For example, ancient Chinese monks cast yarrow stalks on the ground and read the resulting patterns, because yarrow was a respected plant of their civilization. This particular branch of botanomancy (divination using plants) evolved into the *I Ching* later in history. A gypsy wishing to honor family tradition can learn tasseography, the art of reading tea leaves, from his or her grandmother.

Individuals without a familial or cultural heritage to draw on may instead devise a system that suits the moment. A Victorian farmer with a question weighing heavily on his or her heart might have concentrated on that question, randomly picked an herb or vegetable, and discerned their answer from that plant's symbolism.

The gypsy, monk, and farmer in these examples all made the same basic inquiry through different rituals and mediums that suited their social environment, current needs, and the tools readily available to them. This is the beauty of divination—its capacity to reflect human originality and insight. Like all the aforementioned people, you will soon be considering what tools are best to enhance your own latent talents for divination. There is indeed a diversity of divinatory methods from which to choose!

3. **How do people create new divination systems, or adapt those that already exist, like all the different types of Tarot decks?**

Just because something has ancient origins doesn't mean that it's outmoded or lacking in usefulness today. However, the original symbols and mechanisms of some divinatory arts don't always fit into contemporary social, religious, or personal ideals and restrictions. For example, contemporary outlooks on eco-spirituality regard the use of animal parts in religious practice as generally abhorrent. Yet, divining the remains from sacrificed animals was a common practice among the Mesopotamians, Greeks, Romans, and some Druidical sects. In those eras and settings, people considered the animal sacred once sacrificed and accepted by the Divine, and believed that the gods left messages for worshippers amid the creature's remains.

The difference between these two outlooks reflects the growth and transformation humankind has experienced as a species. Some of the ways we thought and acted as "children" became quite inappropriate in an "adult," cultured setting. So when a person considers creating a divinatory system, he or she looks to historical or cultural practices as a starting place for ideas, then adapts those ideas to societal ethics, daily realities, and the guidelines of personal beliefs.

To cite a personal example, several years ago I found myself fascinated with the Victorian flower language and a divination system known as flouromancy. After researching this, I patterned a floral deck on thirty three-by-five cards using that language. While it would have been more historically appropriate and visually appealing to make a pressed flower or decoupage deck, I just didn't have the time or artistic ability. So instead I took photocopied images, hand colored each, and sprayed them with a protective coating. This simple tool traveled everywhere with me, and regularly exhibited surprising accuracy. The *Victorian Flower Oracle*'s success resulted from several factors, the primary two of which were the personal energy invested in the making, and my enthusiasm for something that had specific meaning for *me*.

I hazard to guess that there never has been, nor ever will be, a divination system invented solely for the purpose of appealing to the general public. Instead, the creator(s) of a system works to the best of her or his ability to make a self-functioning tool, hoping that other people with similar ideals and interests will be able to use the finished product effectively.

This explains why almost everyone, except the creator(s), will find one or two symbols they just can't relate to in *any* prophetic method. The reaction to each image is an expression of individuality. This is also why people decide to make their own divination systems. The resulting tool vibrates agreeably with that person's path, vision, and energy.

4. **So are there any historical or personally invented divination systems that don't have merit?**

No, although there are tools that require more caution than others. For example, people who use the *Ouija* board often report negative experiences. In modern times, the *Ouija* board has become a parlor game. This casual association lessens the respect with which people approach the tool. Additionally, the *Ouija* in its present form also carries few, if any, safeguards in its instructional materials, meaning an untrained individual can end up playing with powers that he or she does not truly understand. These observations lead me to believe that one should carefully consider the merits and drawbacks of this system before consulting it yourself or with the aid of a professional.

Despite this type of precautionary illustration, you could potentially use anything as a divination tool as long as you approach that object respectfully. It is not the implement of divination that makes a difference in the reading, but the reader and querent themselves. Our ancestors proved this by successfully prognosticating with everything from bird feathers to dust!

Truthfully, a diviner doesn't need any tools whatsoever to do readings, but they may want them. A divinatory medium acts as a support system for a reader, helping them discern the undercurrents of a situation. It also gives the querent something concrete upon which to focus his or her attention during a session.

5. Why are divinatory tools treated so specially?

Divination is a sacred art when used properly, and the tools someone uses for readings are similarly sacred. Before this concept puts you off, remember that one engenders holiness through attitudes and actions. A diviner who respects his or her tool shows this in the way that implement gets handled. This special treatment is not far removed from the way a lumberjack respects his or her axe and acts on that reverence by cautiously cleaning and storing it away after each use. Both the diviner and the lumberjack know the inherent power and responsibility for their tools and treat them accordingly. The only difference is the setting.

Another reason for having special pouches or containers for divinatory tools is random energy. Every person gives off a certain amount of good, bad, or neutral vibrations when they enter a room, and especially when they handle objects. For example, when a friend is sad or depressed you may notice yourself feeling heavy-hearted after they depart. That's because some of your friend's stray negative energy was left behind. A responsible reader does not want this kind of uncontrolled energy inhibiting or prejudicing their work, so they take protective precautions.

Some people who use stones wrap them in a white silk cloth (the color of purity) in between readings and cleanse them using saltwater as a purifier. Owners of Tarot decks or runes often keep them in colored pouches or cedar boxes. The choice of protective measures is purely personal, so long as it results in safeguarding the tool from everyday dirt and unwanted, untrained, or overly playful hands.

The more a reader works with a system, the more it becomes attuned to them (and they to it), like two radio stations slowly adjusting to the same frequency. Consequently, some fortune-tellers seem almost superstitious about people handling their tools outside the setting of a reading. Such interactions may unintentionally interrupt the rapport they've developed with that tool.

Additionally, a novice who randomly draws a few cards or runes might find themselves quite confused or frightened by the reading because they misinterpret the images. In a Tarot deck the Death card worries the uninformed. An adept reader knows that Death, in this case, is more figurative than literal, symbolizing drastic changes and personal transformations, but a "novice" would not know this. So by properly storing his or her tool, the diviner protects the querent too.

6. What is the difference between a medium or channeler and someone who reads cards or runes?

To answer this question, let's look to history for examples. In ancient Greece, people traveled from miles around to consult the Oracle at Delphi. They came to hear missives from the *Pythia*, a female prophetess. Apollo spoke through the *Pythia* when she uttered predictions. Similarly, the Japanese had village oracles called *Takusen Matsuri*. Individuals sought council with the *Takusen Matsuri* for important forecasts regarding the annual rice crop. In both instances, it was not the individual themselves nor the collective unconscious being consulted, but rather a guiding spirit, god, or goddess that the prophet channeled. Referring to this type of spiritual position as an "oracle" indicates that divination was a sacred calling. Oracle comes from the Latin term *orare*, to pray.

This relinquishing of the self, in whole or in part, is the important difference between becoming an oracle and *reading* an oracle. Zolar, a popular writer on the Occult arts, once said that every atom was a medium for the expression of spiritual force. A medium or prophet, therefore, temporarily adjusts every cell in their body to the frequency of a guiding spirit, angel, or deity during a reading. She or he then broadcasts the message received like an inter-dimensional radio, putting the ego aside momentarily so the communication remains clear.

Divination stems from the Latin word *divus*, meaning "from god," or "belonging to a deity," and the suffix "-ation," also from Latin, translates as "condition of being." So the diviner is striving to perform a function analogous to that of a medium by becoming a conduit of divine or universal energy during a reading. The way this energy is applied, however, is vastly different than with mediumship or channeling.

The diviner uses the sensual input from their chosen medium to tap into psychic impressions. In the process, the tool becomes a vehicle for discerning specific thought-forms on the astral plane, then communicating those ideas. This reading does not involve spirit possession in any way. Instead, the diviner remains in control, listening to and watching the appropriate "station." They then tell the querent about what they see and hear, and its interpretive value.

This distinction between mediums and readers is a very important one to remember while reading this book and in your personal experiences with divination. If one accepts the immortality of the soul, then the spirits communicating through mediums may still need to reincarnate to finish their earthly lessons. The spirit contacted may have a personal agenda and prejudices even as a living person does. Therefore, a medium must take care in who they allow to speak through them, and the information received from a medium must be considered with these possibilities in mind.

In many tribal societies the shaman is the prophet for the entire community. Shaman comes from the Tunquso-Manchurian word *saman*, meaning "one who knows." This connotation for the healer-seer-priest remains. We turn to diviners, mediums, and shamans because they "know" how to become an effective conduit for mystically obtained information, and can teach us how to do likewise.

7. What exactly does a diviner do before and during a reading?

Every diviner I know performs a personal ritual before a reading begins. This ritual's procedure may or may not have strong "religious" connotations. Some readers simply wash their hands, others lay out a special cloth, some meditate or pray, and still others light candles and incense. Whatever the approach, these actions have distinct purposes.

First, the preparation time creates a quiet ambiance that improves the quality of any reading. Second, this gives the reader a chance to adjust their ways of thinking and communicating to a different level than that of everyday conversations. Third, these rituals encourage a semimeditative state of mind in which the reader becomes more receptive to messages from Spirit. Fourth, this gives the querent a valuable moment to settle her or his mind and decide on the question to be asked.

During the reading, the diviner looks for specific patterns and signs within the divination system being used. If scrying a candle flame, for example, high, bright, active flames are viewed as a positive portent. With the Tarot or runes, the specific emblems on the stones and cards provide the starting point for interpretation, though it doesn't stop there.

Next, the reader considers how each symbol interacts with the others and what this means to the querent. In the process, any knowledge about this person must be kept out of the picture, along with any personal opinions on the question posed. The reader also tries to remain open to fleeting images or feelings received from the universe. Needless to say, this balancing act isn't always easy. Readers are people, too, with human failings. Consequently, it is always wise to maintain a little skepticism and listen closely to your inner voice when considering what information, if any, you accept as "truth" from a reading.

8. Why do some readers ask for your question before hand, and others don't?

There is nothing wrong with a reader asking about your question at the inception of a session. The choice not to do so stems from a difference in philosophy among professional readers. A reader who knows your question is better equipped to interpret the enigmatic symbols in a reading because the question provides a frame of reference. Additionally, the reader can then explain the interpretation more specifically as it pertains to your query.

On the other hand, having foreknowledge of the question may taint the accuracy of the session, especially if the reader knows the querent intimately. How does this happen? First, in an effort to relate an interpretation directly to your question, a diviner may inadvertently "seek out" a comprehensible answer that might not exist within the given symbols. Second, the diviner may unconsciously "fill in" parts of the reading with her or his own opinion or feelings based on recent experiences. If, for example, the querent voices a question about entering into a deeper relationship with a new "significant other," and the diviner is just getting over a nasty divorce, there may be a tendency to interpret more negativity in the reading than really exists. This is quite understandable, but it does not make for an unbiased, objective session.

A reader who chooses not to know your question up front is trying to maintain a neutral position in their job. This individual will likely ask about your question at the end of the session so further clarification can take place.

9. From where do the answers given in a reading originate?

This question, more than any other in divination, depends on how you believe the universe works and on the divination system itself. In the case of mediums or channelers, sources include departed souls, spirit guides, and even devic energies (see question #6). In other forms of divination, if you believe in the Great Spirit (or any of its manifestations), then the information presented in your session originates at that source. If you believe instead in the collective unconscious, which pools all of the experience and knowledge of humankind, then your reading pours from that wellspring.

I have met very few fortune-tellers who credit themselves for the insights in a reading. Most feel they are an implement or servant of some higher authority for the duration of a reading. For the purpose of this book, I will designate this authority simply as Spirit—the unifying power behind all space, time, and dimensions.

10. How accurate is the information from a reading, and how much of it should I take to heart?

The answer to this question changes with each session and each reader, and unfortunately it is one only you can determine. Diviners are not gurus sitting on some remote mountaintop, able to explain all the mysteries of the universe. That's not their job. They are helpers, people who give us an extra set of eyes with which to review our situation and where we may be headed.

Unfortunately, because New Age products and services have become quite popular, opportunists look at divination as one way of making an easy profit from people's curiosity or needs. However, there are some warning signs that will help you recognize a misinterpreted, erroneous, or wrongly motivated reading. Watch for a reading:

- in which you feel frightened, persecuted, or oppressed by what you hear.
- in which the diviner tells you that something will 100%-for-sure happen. Humans are creatures of habit, but we all create our futures every minute of every day.
- in which the diviner strongly suggests doing something that goes against personal taboos or beliefs.
- that makes no sense whatsoever with regard to your question or any other circumstances in your life (still jot this one down—it may bear out in the future).
- that is overly "doomsday-ish" without providing any positive, constructive alternatives to help the situation.
- that seems rushed or hurried along without any time at the end to ask questions about the information.

If any of the aforementioned warning signs occur during a reading, treat that session skeptically. Readers do have off days, that doesn't mean they're "bad" people. However, if these problems recur with the same individual, I suggest finding another diviner to consult and sharing your negative experience with others. Word of mouth is still the best way to find good readers and keep other seekers away from fortune-tellers whose motivations are suspect.

11. If I get a really accurate reading from a stranger, why does this happen, and what role do I play in the process?

Strangers are sometimes the best people to have read for you. They know nothing of your personal situation and can therefore be far more objective. Realize that accomplished diviners are adept people-watchers, whether consciously or unconsciously. They pick up a lot of nonverbal information, and having done numerous readings they are able to identify patterns. On a purely psychological level the diviner's observational skills go a long way toward providing an accurate reading.

On an esoteric level a great deal more occurs. Divination involves an energy triangle, the first point of which is located within the reader's aura. The second point of the triangle resides within the divination tool, and the final point is within the querent's aura from which the vibrations of the question emanate.

Thoughts take form as a wave of particle energy. This wave moves out from your mind, changing the texture of your aura. This textural shift then interacts with the divinatory tool on a quantum level, transforming the energy patterns in the tool in response to the question. The reader then reviews and interprets those changes as they manifest in the layout, casting, or whatever.

For example, as you think of a question, the reader hands you a set of stones to hold. Your aura carries your question into the stones. This changes the stones' normal vibrations, which is why they might start feeling warm in your hands. Energy always follows the line of least resistance and the most natural progression. So when you cast the stones from your hands, the "pattern" created by the question directs their motion. The diviner then ascertains the meaning of pattern in which the stones have come to rest.

Extending this concept a little further, this also explains why readings done through the mail lack the accuracy of person-to-person sessions. Some of your energy dissipates from the paper and gets muddled as numerous people in the postal service handle it. By the time the letter arrives at its destination, the core of your question remains, but other random energies have altered it.

No matter the setting, your role in this process is vital. Without providing a question, the stones have no pattern by which to fashion an answer. When you have no specific question, the resulting reading will be generalized, describing the current major circumstances in your life and the most plausible outcomes from those circumstances.

12. Why do I sometimes get answers in a reading to questions that I haven't asked about?

In the greater scheme of things, what we think is important and what really *is* important can be quite different. Consequently, Spirit sometimes whacks us with a proverbial two-by-four to get our attention. Such awakenings sometimes come through psychic readings, especially when you've been trying to avoid an issue.

As a case in point, when doing a young woman's reading at a conference, I kept coming back to physical concerns, specifically how she needed to better manage her health. She just shook her head, saying she was very healthy, and left thinking that divination was nothing more than "bunk." Three months later I received a call telling me this woman had just had emergency bone spur surgery. Apparently, she lifted heavy boxes every day at her bookstore, causing physical damage! In this instance the universe tried to step in with good advice, but it went unheeded.

Another illustration of this came to me with a mother and daughter in Georgia. During their reading, I kept seeing a close, negative spiritual influence that needed attending. When I shared this with them, the woman said, "That has nothing to do with my question, but how did you know? We think our house is haunted!" The discussion that followed was very enlightening, and the two went home to begin taking protective measures appropriate to their faith. Here, Spirit offered a gentle nudge to take care of a lingering spiritual problem.

Besides answering unexpressed and sometimes urgent needs, unusual readings may also be motivated by stray thoughts. Humans rarely think of just one thing at a time. While we ponder a question, our brain must still control things like breathing, digesting, and blinking. With all this activity, minor musings can easily cross our mind without ever being noticed. Divination tools have the capacity to pick up that random thought and reveal it during the reading. Quite frequently, this thought has *some* incidental connection to the question anyway. In any case, when these answers come, there is usually a very good reason for it. Take the time to consider what the universe or your own subconscious is trying to tell you.

13. Why do some readers pull extra cards or runes at the end of a reading?

The answer to this question varies from reader to reader. Generally, it is because (*a*) something went amiss in the session and the reader wants to confirm the information, (*b*) a few details seemed to be wanting in the session and there was a need to fill in the gaps, or (*c*) some of aspects of the reading didn't fit together neatly. In this last instance the reader draws extra symbols to provide cohesion. Finally, some readers pull extra cards at the end of a session as you ask questions. This helps provide answers that complete the portrait of the whole reading, like putting together the last pieces of an intricate jigsaw puzzle.

14. Are there any ethical guidelines that govern divination?

Nothing is carved in stone, but there does seem to be a generally accepted code among responsible readers:

- If they cannot put aside negative feelings toward the querent, they will not read for them.

- If they are ill, out of sorts, angry, or otherwise ill-disposed, they will gracefully decline to do readings until they are physically, emotionally, and spiritually at their best to so do.

- They find "good" ways to share "bad" news, i.e., they offer constructive criticism and advice, not just "gloom and doom."

- They always remind the querent that the information obtained from divination systems is not 100% accurate nor certain, and that the individual should seriously ponder any reading before accepting it.

- They take precautions that the session won't be interrupted.

- They often offer barter or sliding-scale fees.

- They always take time at the end of a session for the querent's questions.

Beyond this, it is important to know that the civil laws governing divinatory arts vary from city to city, and state to state. In our area, for example, a reading must be accompanied with the disclaimer, "For Amusement Only." Since one of the purposes of this book is to help you find and use a divination system of your own, please be advised to check applicable regional laws during your studies.

15. Why do some people charge for readings, others offer barter systems, and yet others do them for free?

Divinatory skills, once honed, are a spiritual gift that should be honored. Diviners have a tremendous capacity to help others, and consequently their talents may be taken for granted. For example, friends will periodically "volunteer" my time without asking. I don't mind helping out now and then, but there are days when it's just too taxing. Setting oneself up in a professional capacity deters one's friends from causing these awkward situations.

I have noticed that while my friends appreciate the readings I do for them, those who come to me professionally *really* pay attention. They tape their sessions, take notes, ask tons of questions, and generally make the most of their time. I suspect that is because they appreciate it more. Something about our society encourages us to value those things for which we must work or pay.

Some readers use divination as a means of supplementing the family income. Most of us have to wear more than one "hat" these days to get by, and readers are no different. However, I do not personally agree with the exorbitant prices being charged by some channelers. Nonetheless, it is up to you to decide how much money you feel comfortable paying for divinatory services. And remember that there are no "satisfaction-guaranteed" promises associated with most readings.

Readers who offer bartered or free sessions may have several reasons. They feel the size of someone's wallet should not deter the quest for spiritual knowledge and insight. Just as many early diviners worked on a barter system, many modern diviners honor this tradition by asking little or nothing for a reading. Some believe divination should be given as a community service, in which making one person's Path less long or less difficult offers a greater reward than money.

Again, just because someone asks a high price for their time does not guarantee the accuracy of their work. For that matter, the "freebie" may turn out to be a waste of time too. So, whenever possible, get a personal recommendation for a reader from someone you trust. Usually, word of mouth is the best starting point.

16. Some people seem to go to readers religiously. Is this common, and is it something I should consider?

I do not believe it is healthy to consult divination systems endlessly. There can be "too much" of a good thing. Ultimately, each individual needs to learn to be their own best council and trust in their heart. People who constantly depend on psychics for decision making, or those who seek out flashy spiritual "experiences" cheat themselves out of the growth that comes from making everyday decisions and mistakes on their own.

This doesn't mean that periodic readings won't prove helpful. It does mean that you—not your psychic—are responsible for your life and what you make of it! So try your best first. If you feel perspective is lacking or you just can't seem to get a handle on a situation, then try the psychic. Listen to the reading carefully and take in what is most helpful. Leave the rest by the wayside or in a notebook. If it is truth for your life, it will always come to you through several unrelated sources.

17. Can anyone learn how to read for themselves or others?

Yes, definitely. Everyone has their own learning pace, however, so be patient with yourself. With time, practice, a positive outlook, and a loving heart as a guide, you can learn to use divinatory arts as an effective tool for obtaining perspectives on everything from health and work to spiritual pursuits. The only limits to divination are those determined by your faith, those inherent in the tool (dependent on the number of potential symbols and interpretations), and those that come from the workings of the universe itself.

Consider the diviner's art as a wonderful medium for exploring a new facet of your mind, opening a window to the tomorrows, and reconnecting with Spirit today. There is a wealth of information waiting for you, to enrich and empower every moment of living.

CHAPTER TWO

Developing and/or Adapting Divination Systems

"And many ways of prophesy I put in order..."
—Aeschylus

The growing public interest in esoteric and metaphysical studies betrays itself with the wide spectrum of divination systems available. On the less complex end, people flip coins and draw straws for decision making. On the other end, New Age publishers provide hundreds of artistically impressive Tarot decks and other fortune-telling tools. With so many vastly different divination systems, it's hard to know which is the best choice for your personal use.

This chapter will help you make a sound decision about which divinatory system is right for you. Please remember that there is no rule stating you must always use one and only one divinatory technique. The only real guide to follow religiously is that you should always use a divination system that appeals to your higher senses and path. Remember, if a divinatory tool has a lot of emblems that don't make sense, ones that seem out of sync with your vision, or symbols in which you have no confidence, then it will not function well for you. If you follow this simple guideline, you will always be more successful.

Ten Steps for Choosing a Personal Divination System

1. Review the systems in Part Two; note those of interest.
2. Narrow down the list compiled in step 1 to four or five choices.
3. Appraise the difficulty of each system.
4. Put your preferences in order.
5. Review, test, and feel out each system under consideration and make your choice.
6. Obtain the necessary tools to work with your chosen method.
7. Give the technique a trial period of 3–6 months minimum.
8. Expand your knowledge of the chosen system or try a new one.
9. Do trial readings for family and friends.
10. Consider working with a new system after drastic life changes.

Numerology or tea leaf reading? Runes or stones? Dice or natural omens? The list of divination methods to choose from seems endless. So how does a person decide?

(1)

Start by going through Part Two with an open mind, writing down all the systems that intrigue you.

(2)

Review the systems noted in step 1 again. This time, focus on narrowing down the list to four or five choices by considering how each system measures up to your cultural or familial traditions and personal ideology. Ask yourself questions like:

- Do any of the preferred techniques appeal specifically to my spiritual vision or cultural traditions?
- Did my ancestors practice any of these arts?
- Do any of the systems have imagery or instructions that make me uncomfortable?
- Do any of the systems have imagery or instructions that hold tremendous appeal?

The answers to these questions often eliminate some choices, and accentuate others.

Next, consider the sensual impact of each technique, bearing in mind what you respond to most strongly. If you're a very tactile person, for example, runes made from wood might be a good option because of the textural quality of this medium. If you are a highly visual person, weigh what styles appeal most to your higher senses. Do you respond to literal or symbolic imagery? This will make a tremendous difference if choosing between a Tarot deck and, for example, hydromancy (interpreting ink or wax patterns on water). The Tarot contains more literal portraits, while hydromancy requires the ability to "see" form in an ambiguous shape.

(3)

Appraise each divinatory system's level of difficulty and how long it will take to learn the method. Bear in mind your mundane responsibilities and time constraints. As a beginner it is easier to work with systems that have a limited number of symbols to memorize, like a pair of dice. Two dice have only twenty-one interpretive values to remember. Dice also take far less time to cast than more complex systems, so they appeal to people with hectic schedules.

Keep in mind that dice do not yield overly detailed readings, but it's a good place to start. On the other hand, if you're really drawn to a complex system, just realize that it will take some diligent study to learn to interpret it effectively. It also takes a little more time to complete most readings because of the number of symbols available to you. These considerations are very important in a world where many of us have to juggle jobs, families, homes, and our spirituality with only two hands.

(4)

Place the four or five systems you like in order of preference. Find a friend or local New Age shop that has similar systems that you can review and try. If your location or circumstances don't allow this, write to some metaphysical journals and ask for feedback on those techniques. Alternatively, write to an author you respect in this field and request some input (be sure to enclose a SASE for a response).

(5)

As you review and test the various techniques from step 4, take a moment and breath deeply. Close your eyes and extend your intuition toward that tool. Take your time. This is an important exercise.

Once you feel totally focused on the system's energies, how does it *feel* to you? Is it comfortable, warm, and welcoming? Itchy or sticky? The implements that appeal to your spiritual instincts are also those through which you'll usually get the most accurate readings.

(6)

Obtain the items necessary to begin working with the technique that finally topped your choice list. Some individuals believe divination systems, particularly the Tarot, are best received as gifts, likely due to the positive energy associated with giving. Other people recommend having a friend buy the necessary components or tool for you, even if you provide the funding. If you find out later that you or a companion made the wrong choice, just pass along the system to another curious seeker, and get something different. It may take a few misses before you "hit" on just the right thing. I personally started with runes, went on to the *Victorian Flower Oracle*, and finally settled on *The Sacred Stone Oracle* (distributed by Blue Pearl, 1-800-822-4810).

(7)

Work with your chosen system for at least three to six months by yourself or with a "reading buddy," giving it a fair trial period. Make notes of your successes or failures in a diary. At the end of this period, review these notes and see if you want to continue with that system, or try another.

(8)

If you choose to try something else after the trial period, return to the list you made in step 4, and then proceed with the ensuing steps again. If, on the other hand, you're happy with what you've originally chosen, find a few books on the subject so you can expand your knowledge of alternative ways to work with that tool, and can gain a broader understanding of its symbols.

There is only one caution to keep in mind during this research process. No book should be the final determinant of a symbol's meaning in a reading. That is for your higher senses to discern, even if your interpretive value is different from the norm. Just be certain to use this alternative interpretation regularly to maintain continuity.

(9)

Try doing a few readings for friends and family members who don't mind you practicing on them. At the end of a reading, let them give you feedback. Note the results from these experiments in your diary. Hopefully, you will begin to see a pattern of accurate readings develop. When this occurs, your confidence in your chosen divinatory tool, and your ability to use it, will likewise blossom into maturity.

(10)

Finally, know that at some junctures in life, especially after important personal transitions, your old, faithful divinatory system may loose its appeal. This is quite natural. As we grow and change, be it spiritually, intellectually, or physically, so we must change our figurative shoes. Divinatory tools are no different.

When this happens—and I can almost promise it will—return to Part Two of this book to refresh your memory of all the wonderful divinatory options that exist. Then find the technique that suits both the new person you've become and the ever-growing vision you carry in your heart.

Ten Steps for Making a Personalized Divination System

1. Decide if the system will be based on an existing concept or something new.
2. Consider household and everyday items as potential base mediums.
3. Choose a base medium.
4. Decide on the finished size of the system.
5. Decide if the system is cast, scried, drawn, laid out, or whatever.
6. Decide if the system will include upright and reversed meanings.
7. Decide on layout formats, if any.
8. Detail the interpretive values of your symbols.
9. Enact trial runs to work out the bugs.
10. Begin using and enjoying the system.

Considering that creative individuals at different points in history devised all the divination systems that presently exist, you will certainly have tradition on your side if you decide to make your own tools! Be forewarned, though, that this process can be a huge undertaking, filled with much research and introspection. The result of such explorations, however, are always worth the extra effort. You cannot help but learn much about yourself and "universal" archetypes in the process.

(1)

First, decide whether to base your divinatory system on an existing concept or something wholly new. One person may wish to design a Tarot deck reflecting a unique theme. Someone else with less artistic ability, or little interest in the Tarot, may prefer to cast jelly. Please note that the apparent humor in the second choice does not imply that it cannot function exceptionally well if approached with serious intentions. And, in a metaphoric sense, edible divination tools give the querent an opportunity to internalize the insights physically as well as spiritually.

In considering the foundation for your system, again bear in mind which sense you respond to most strongly and what level of symbolism you prefer. Complex symbolism can be unclear without extended consideration (see Appendix B). If you have a knack for interpreting things like ink blots, symbolic systems will probably work very well for you. If not, I suggest seeking a more direct, candid medium.

(2)

Determine if there are any household or everyday items that could become the base medium for your system. The person wishing to create a unique version of the Tarot might use pictures from magazines pasted on cardboard, food coupons, three-by-five cards with hand drawings, or greeting card covers, for example.

The advantages to this hearthside approach are numerous. For one thing, these items are familiar to you and evoke an immediate reaction that can motivate intuitive interpretations. For another, the familiarity of the system creates a comfortable, de-mystified relationship between you and your tool. Divination implements do not have to look mysterious to effectively open doors to understanding life's mysteries! And, because the medium came from your own home, it is already filled with your personal energy that will naturally improve rapport with that tool. Last, but not least, homemade tools are generally inexpensive. If lost or damaged, it is easily and cheaply replaced.

(3)

If you find no suitable household items, decide on another base medium for your system. Keep your personal constraints in mind. For individuals with children, hectic schedules, and travel obligations, durability, ease of assembly, and portability are prime considerations.

Actually, these are three important considerations for any divinatory system. Find a hardy base medium, or protect more fragile mediums, so that the finished tool doesn't soil or break easily. For example, if you devise a set of hand-colored cards, coat them with a fixative or laminate the surface. Either makes the paper a little sturdier and safeguards your work. Most people grow emotionally attached to personally designed divinatory systems. You will want yours to last a very long time.

Please note that many of the entries for traditional systems in Part Two include alternative and updated base media for your consideration. The number of unusual and unique possibilities from the worlds of nature and technology is practically endless. Here is a small sampling to help get those creative juices flowing:

buttons	nuts and bolts	candies
noodles	beans	ribbon
flower petals	colored pencils	quotes
shells	sliced wood	wax leaves
computer file names	magazine pictures	VCR
license plates	soap bubbles	business cards

Properly cleanse and purify any base medium before using it as part of your diviner's kit. For ideas on different purification processes, see step 5 of "Five Steps to the Care and Treatment of Your Oracle" later in this chapter.

(4)

After determining the base medium, decide how many items you want in the finished system. Generally, I suggest a minimum of twelve or thirteen symbols. This provides enough diversity to represent the major archetypes of human experience. Even tools normally used for yes-or-no questions can be reworked to have twelve options. By way of illustration, a pendulum circle could have twelve markers at the hour points. These marks each indicate something different by the hour's number, or by a symbolic item placed at that location (see Part Two: Pendulums).

Each additional symbol that a system contains allows it to grow geometrically toward more detailed readings. Runes, for example, have twenty-five and the *I Ching* has sixty-four, with the added dimension of change, as one symbol may also transform into another. This does not make one system better than the other, but it does make each system suited to distinct types of questions. Don't anticipate particulars from a divination system that can only provide general responses.

(5)

Once you assemble the symbols, decide how the system will get used. Will it be laid out? Will it be cast (as with bones or witan wands), randomly determined (as with bibliomancy), or drawn (as with runes)? Remember, some divination systems do not lend themselves to being drawn because of the distinctive sizes and shapes in the base medium. For example, if you have gathered tumbled stones or bracelet charms together, you can learn to identify the pieces by their variances. This hampers the randomness of a reading, making it more indicative of your conscious hopes or fears. Conversely, a carefully sized greeting card deck allows for both layouts and drawings, because you cannot feel the difference between the cards.

(6)

If laid out, drawn, or cast, do your symbols have both upright and reversed meanings? Some readers of the Tarot only interpret the cards upright, while others read all the cards as if they were upright when over half the reading is reversed. So you need to determine whether you will have reversals, which doubles your interpretive value, or whether your system even allows for them.

Returning to the example of tumbled stones, it would be hard to figure out, literally, which end is up! In a case like this, consider indicating locations on your reading surface for negative influences and/or obstacles to overcome. I personally like this option for cast tools, because just having a "negative" area doesn't automatically mean anything will land there (after all, not everything in life has to have a "down side"). Creating a region like this on a casting surface lets the energy of the question, and the system, guide the response.

(7)

If your system is laid out, what formats will you use and why? You may certainly adapt layouts that exist for the Tarot, runes, or other techniques, but if possible you should also maintain compatibility with the theme of your method. When I designed the *Victorian Flower Oracle*, I designed the layouts to look like shapes that exist in nature, including a flower layout. Similarly, when designing *The Sacred Stone Oracle*, I made the central casting surface round, like a tumbled stone, with sections corresponding to seasonal cycles.

Designing your layouts with thematic appeal has three purposes. First, it reinforces the symbolism inherent in your divinatory tool. This creates a harmony of format and function that improves the accuracy and conceptual congruity of the readings. Second, a good layout furnishes hints about the meanings of each position. For example, if the layout takes the shape of a diamond, the four points could represent the directions or seasons, each of which has established correspondences that add interpretive value (east—beginnings and hope, south—energy and passion, west—healing and emotions, north—rest and rejuvenation). Finally, the process of creating thematic layouts causes you to think more clearly, and in more detail, about each of the symbols in your divinatory tool and how they will ultimately interact with each other once used in an actual reading.

(8)

Now that you know what systemic elements you have at your disposal and how to employ them, the next step is detailing, in writing, what the results from readings mean. Each symbol's significance should be defined according to its placement in the reading (such as a sequence in drawn systems, or surface location in cast systems, including upright and reversed, if applicable). This is important so that readings maintain a consistency of interpretation, with minor variations as provided by Spirit.

For recording your interpretations, I suggest a spiral-bound notebook with each emblem's interpretation detailed on a separate sheet. This will allow you to make changes, then insert or take out pages until the system is totally refined. You can transfer this information later into something more permanent like a bound diary.

The time spent on definition and delineation has an additional benefit. It acts as a mnemonic device. Coherence provides a valuable side effect, too. Each session increases the latent power of a symbol because it then becomes more and more associated with its defined meaning. This recognition infuses it with the energy of its interpretive value.

(9)

Once assembled, test your system on yourself and a couple of friends. See if any important experiential representations seem to be missing. As you discover gaps, or find that symbols don't "feel" quite right as originally conceived, add symbols or adjust the interpretive values accordingly. Repeat this process several times to calibrate and hone the system as much as possible, while committing the symbols and their meanings to memory.

(10)

In the process of creating your tool, I can almost guarantee that your understanding of and appreciation for the diviner's art will grow tremendously. With this outlook, new or increased intuitive abilities will quietly flourish. It is time to enjoy the manifestation of your hard work! Allow your personalized divinatory system to become an extension of your growing spiritual insight. You will not be disappointed.

Five Steps to the Care and Treatment of Your Oracle

1. Blessing
2. Dedication
3. Charging
4. Choosing suitable storage
5. Regular maintenance

As mentioned in the first section of this book, divination tools deserve some special care and attention in order to keep them free of random energy and sanctified for their function. The idea of sanctity need not be stuffy or frightening. We are all sacred beings, and a divinatory tool properly applied for our spiritual growth and awareness is likewise holy. The way you treat your oracle should reflect this.

To make each of these five steps personally meaningful, adjust them so that they better reflect personal beliefs and traditions. This personalization can be accomplished by using prayers from your faith, calling on a specific deity to aid your work, burning specially chosen incense and candles, playing thematic music while you work, and so forth.

(1)

Blessing. Blessing invokes divine approval and favor, not only for the divination system, but also for the user of that system. Each reading opens a window into all the cumulative knowledge, wisdom, and foresight available in the collective unconscious. Your divinatory system is about to become an instrument of universal energy, as are you. Consequently, a diviner can use all the spiritual guidance they can get!

Taking a cue from the world's great religions, the extension, or laying on, of hands is one way to channel divine power and blessings. After preparing yourself, perhaps by quiet meditation, take your tool in hand and ask Spirit for its sanctification using whatever manner feels comfortable. A brief prayer (silent or out loud), visualization, chanting, dance, or song are all options. Continue until you feel confident that the special spark of the Divine has imbued your instrument.

(2)

Dedication. Dedication ordains, commits, and consecrates your divination tool to a specific function. The breadth and depth of this function is up to you. For example, perhaps you've chosen to use this system only when reading for yourself. Your dedication would then indicate the personal nature of this implement. One option would be to add a few words to your blessing, like "I dedicate this tool to personal growth, awareness, and empowerment. May I always find truth herein."

Remember, neither your blessing nor your dedication has to be great poetry. There is no one to impress here; this is between you and Spirit. What's most important is having honest motivations and allowing your heart to guide your words.

(3)

Charging. Think of charging your divination tool as similar to charging a battery. Once a divination system has been created, it holds tremendous potential that can be augmented and actualized by adding energy. To achieve this goal, the diviner "hooks up" the tool to a spiritually significant source of power and infuses it with that energy prior to its use. There are several ways to do this.

The most common means of charging is placing the tool in the light of the sun or moon for a specific number of hours or days. Sunlight accentuates the conscious, logical, and traditionally masculine symbols of the system, while moonlight empowers the intuitive, emotional, and feminine. The amount of time you expose the tool is purely personal. Some people use numerological correspondences in making this decision. If charging the tool for a reading about relationships, for example, the diviner might charge it for two hours in moonlight, two being the number associated with partnership. A question about an important financial decision benefits from exposure to sunlight for four hours, the number four having correspondence with earthly matters (see Numerology in Part Two). If charging the tool for general use, however, setting it in both types of light is very beneficial. This encourages a balance between Spirit and earthliness, insight and conscious thought, emotions and action in all the readings to follow.

A second type of charging is done with the aid of visualization. For this, the diviner holds her or his hands over the tool while envisioning a pure, sparkling white light pouring down from above, through the hands, and into the tool. This continues until the diviner senses that the tool is filled to overflowing. There is no definitive way of explaining this awareness. It comes to different individuals in different ways. For example, the tool might become warm or hot to the touch. You will have to try this method yourself to find out what indicates to you that the charging process is complete.

A third type of charging is very symbolic, and it is worth considering if your implement might be damaged by long-term exposure to light, or if you are not comfortable with either of the first two approaches. This technique uses smoke, soil, water, or sand (the elements of air, earth, water, and fire, respectively). Being careful to wrap it so it won't get damaged, immerse the tool in one of the mediums. Let your instincts guide you for the duration of the immersion. Choose a medium appropriate to your question. The air element emphasizes the mind, movement, and whimsy. Earth accentuates solid foundations and good common sense. Water adds healing, nurturing energy, while fire (the sand) purifies and energizes. As with the solar/lunar charging technique, you may also employ all the symbolic mediums to improve the tool's sympathy for general readings.

If you're not familiar with the concept of magical sympathy, think of it as the difference between receiving a clear radio station signal and getting only partial reception. The elemental charging approach fine tunes your tool to one question by delineating the specific "frequencies" involved. This eliminates spiritual "static," and consequently improves the reading's accuracy.

Please note that charging can be done anytime, anywhere. It should be performed once right after the tool's creation or purchase, then again any time the diviner wishes. The extra benefit here is that charging indirectly helps keep the tool free from random energies (see also step 5, Regular Maintenance).

(4)

Choosing Suitable Storage. There are several ways to store your divination system when not in use. If using a fabric wrap (such as a scarf), I recommend natural fiber over manmade. Natural fibers have more positive connotations and energies associated with them. Other options include finding a special box, making a pouch, or using a cedar-lined dresser drawer. Whatever your choice, make certain the item's container protects it, and that it somehow reflects the tool's significance. One example is using white fabric, the color of purity, as pouch lining and embroidering a personally significant, mystical emblem on the pouch's exterior.

An interesting benefit of having a special place to store your diviner's kit is mental preparation and termination. The removal of the tool from its protective container becomes part of a ritual that separates the reading from mundane reality (see "Personal Preparation for Readings"). When the tool is put back, the diviner can then "remove the seer's mantle" and get back to the business of everyday life.

(5)

Regular Maintenance. Any tool requires regular maintenance and cleansing, and divination tools are no different. After each reading take a moment to purge any lingering energy. Also remember to do this for yourself. It is easy to pick up residual energy from readings. One of the simplest techniques to remove it is simply to flick the energy off of your hands like shaking off excess water.

Good old-fashioned soap and water is an effective cleanser for tools that are waterproof. Crystals in particular benefit from a saltwater soak to purify their energies. Move cards and other moisture-sensitive items through the smoke from a purgative incense like frankincense, myrrh, sage, or cedar. Both the liquid and the smoke collect then transfer unproductive energy away from your divinatory system and dissipate it into the earth or air.

As you work with this implement more frequently, you will begin noticing times when the responses seem flat or really off. This either indicates that you're not in a good "space" to do a reading or that the tool needs an energy infusion (see *Charging*). Always place your implements back in their honored place at the end of a reading until you need them again. As you do, take a moment to thank Spirit for its assistance and insight.

Learning to Use a System Effectively

Whether you've made your own divination system or purchased one, become intimately acquainted with it. This means lots of practicing, fine-tuning your interpretations, and exposing that tool to your personal energy. The first few weeks, and possibly months, of using a new divinatory system is rather like courtship. You will discover everything you love and hate about the way you interact with the system you've chosen.

These discoveries are very valuable. They help in choosing future divinatory systems and/or refining the current one. This applies to a prepackaged system too. Just because you don't like 100 percent of its symbolism doesn't necessarily mean that a purchased tool should be abandoned. It may simply need minor tweaking to better suit your criteria. Don't be afraid to make adjustments, as long as they maintain the integrity of the overall system.

During the "courtship" period, try to be patient. Realize that practice is integral to becoming proficient in any art. You cannot expect to be totally proficient with a divination system after just the first few days or weeks of trying it. Also, take your time and become adept with one system before trying to work with others. Divination, as any spiritual endeavor, is not a "fast food" buffet; you can't nibble at one technique, move on to another, then sip at a third, and hope to be truly satisfied by any.

The time you spend exploring any system will not be wasted. Learning more about your tool and how it works is a very constructive way to also learn about divinatory procedures in general. This is an excellent opportunity to sharpen your spiritual senses and think more deeply about universal symbols as they pertain to your life and the lives of those for whom you read.

Personal Preparation for Readings

I cannot overstress the importance of being properly prepared mentally, physically, emotionally, and spiritually for each and every reading you perform. A mentally unfocused person makes an ineffectual reader no matter how experienced. Physical limitations lead to distractions. Someone who is emotionally overwrought, worried, or angry will find it difficult to separate personal feelings from the images in a reading. Finally, one's spiritual motivations and attitudes for fortune-telling need to be sincere, not guided by personal agendas or idle curiosity.

Every diviner has different ways of knowing if and when they are in the right space to perform a reading. Many people have special rituals to help put them in a more receptive, selfless frame of mind. These rituals aren't usually elaborate. In fact, most rituals go wholly unnoticed by the querent. The actions that accompany this preparation process include but are not limited to:

- washing one's hands before handling the divinatory tool
- laying out a special surface on which the reading takes place, and always doing so in a prescribed fashion (part of effective ritual is routine)
- stopping to breathe deeply for a moment, or say a prayer
- meditating briefly with the querent to help establish a unity of mind, spirit, and purpose
- anointing one's hands or chakras with aromatic oil to adjust the body's auric vibrations away from the physical and toward more esoteric functions
- invoking the presence of a spiritual guardian, either mentally or verbally
- fasting for a number of hours before the reading, if physically feasible, to create a clearer channel through which information can flow freely.

You may choose any number of these, alone or in combination, and test them out to see which ones help you prepare most effectively. Alternatively, consider creating a preparation ritual all your own. In any case, do not go forward with a reading until you feel ready, willing, and able.

Working Atmosphere for Readings

Similar to the preparations that create an appropriate spiritual atmosphere within your heart before a reading, the area in which you work should also have a special ambiance. In developing this atmosphere, consideration should be given to the querent's comfort and ability to clearly see the divinatory device in use. Set up seating so that eye contact is easily maintained for effective, positive lines of communication. And provide the querent with a tape recorder or pen and paper with which to chronicle the experience. This way, the person can return to the recording or notes at a later date for additional insight and significance.

Beyond this, there are a number of general preparations that can improve the overall atmosphere of any spiritually centered working area. As with your personal preparation ritual, mix and match the following suggestions to find just the right blend, suitable to your environment and chosen divinatory tool:

- lighting candles to encourage a meditative state of mind on the part of all participants
- playing specially chosen instrumental music to improve the mystical mood
- burning incense that heightens psychic and spiritual awareness (good choices here include sandalwood, lotus, rose, and/or pine)
- dimming lights so that the focal point is the reading, not the setting and its fixtures (be sure the candles provide enough cursory light so the querent can see clearly)
- turning off the phone, placing pets and/or children in another area, and putting up "Do Not Disturb" signs so that the reading can proceed peacefully without unnecessary interruptions.

Doing Readings for Yourself

Many people ask whether it's all right to do readings for themselves. Simple questions with which you have little emotional involvement work best for self-directed, personal readings. For example, pulling one card, stone, or rune to get an overview of the day or week ahead should yield a reasonably accurate reading.

More important concerns that are self-presented to the divinatory tool can carry your unconscious hopes, wishes, or anxieties. As a result, the reading could easily make a bad situation look good, or an improving situation look bad, just because you are too close to the issue to maintain perspective. For some people this causes serious errors in their decision making, as their hopes or fears lead them to act in ways that a more realistic, balanced outlook wouldn't.

I remember one time when I was terribly worried about my employment situation. I spent an entire weekend agonizing over job security. Finally, I grabbed a Tarot deck and did a brief reading, which looked absolutely hopeless. Being the terminal optimist, I had someone else do a reading for me after my own. The results were quite different. The second reading issued caution, but the outcome looked very positive. The reading I performed for myself was clouded with apprehension; I wouldn't have seen good news at that juncture if it bit me on the nose!

So I advise caution in reading for yourself. Always remember that being human means having human failings, not the least of which is a certain myopia with regards to yourself and your own situation. For the really important questions in your life, find a psychic buddy—someone with whom you can exchange readings when serious issues crop up. These readings should prove to be far more accurate.

Doing Readings for Others

Inevitably, once someone becomes proficient with divination, people come out of the woodwork to ask for readings. Before you automatically say "yes," however, stop for a moment and consider the following:

- Are you in the right frame of mind for a reading? If not, politely decline and set up another mutually agreeable time to meet.

- Does this person have a real need? Is he or she just looking for a flashy experience, or possibly trying to debunk your abilities? You alone can decide if you want to put forth the personal energy to perform a reading under potentially dubious conditions. But you serve no one by allowing divination to become a crutch or a sideshow. Some people leave a reading with very different outlooks on both the process and their predicament, while others will never lose their cynicism. So listen to the guiding voice of Spirit.

- Do you have enough time to do a good reading? Or do you expect that this session might be interrupted due to other obligations? If your time or privacy is limited, ask the individual if they want a brief overview that you can return to and expand on later. Otherwise schedule another meeting.

- Are there any negative or harsh feelings toward the querent that you cannot put aside for the duration of the reading? If the current relationship is too rocky for you to maintain perspective, gently decline and wait until you're more centered.

After examining the circumstances, if you decide to move ahead with a session, it is important to remember that each time you say "yes" to giving a reading, you are also saying "yes" to the Universe's request for community service. Never forget that a diviner bears the responsibility for his or her words. Your reading can affect the querent tremendously, so choose your manner and modes of communication accordingly. The old rule of "do unto others" is a good one to follow here. Divine with the same sensitivity as you would want when going to a professional reader yourself.

In addition to the aforementioned guidelines, follow these steps regularly in your reading sessions:

- Determine ahead of time whether or not to have the querent voice their question at the outset of a reading.

- Before proceeding with your interpretation of the symbolic values, take a moment to remind the querent that readings are not infallible or unchangeable. How tomorrow unfolds cannot be totally known until it happens, thanks to our free will.

- Finally, at the end of the session, give the querent time to ask questions about things that are bothersome or messages that seem nonsensical. This step is very important as it aids understanding and integration. If time simply runs out, have the individual review the tape or notes and get back to you with questions at a mutually agreeable time. The benefits of this review far outweigh any minor inconveniences. Without this opportunity, the querent could be just as frustrated, uncertain, and confused as before the reading.

Divination with Groups

I have been conducting experiments in group divination methods throughout my travels. In group divination, an entire assembly becomes the focus of a reading and the interpreters of the results! Thus far, I have found two effective ways of coordinating group fortune-telling efforts.

The first approach uses a set of tiny tumbled stones. You need about two cups of stones, each about one-sixteenth inch across, and a large white sheet of paper. Talk the members of the group through a meditation in which they focus all their energy on one personal question. Pass the container of stones around to each person in the group and allow each to direct a question into it.

Next, have them open their eyes and gather in a circle around you while you carefully pour the stones out over the paper's surface. From where they stand, each person then scries the resulting pattern like interpreting an ink blot. In fact, if you can't find stones or crystals for this exercise, paints or markers work nearly as well. For this alternative, each person randomly picks a paintbrush or marker with eyes closed (this diversifies the color), and then draws a stroke on the paper while meditating on a question. The final pattern is interpreted after everyone has taken their turn with the paints or markers.

If the same group has a question that concerns them all, this exercise is still very effective. Follow the same procedure, only have everyone whisper the question at hand while meditating. Upon pouring the stones or revealing the painting, each person in the group gives an interpretation of it, followed by a discussion of the results.

The second exercise I've used successfully requires nothing more than equal-sized slips of paper and pencils or pens. Have the group breathe deeply in unison for about five minutes while each person formulates a question. Guide a visualization in which everyone imagines a huge bubble in the center of the room into which is placed his or her question. Then ask all of them to clear their minds and breathe in unison again for two to five minutes. Guide the visualization once more, having them imagine the universal light of knowledge and wisdom filling the sphere. Once it's filled, have them scan it for images, feelings, or words that emerge from the flowing light, and write them on the slips of paper.

After bringing the group members back to a normal level of awareness, have them fold the papers in half, and place them in a large bowl. Shake this up well, and have each person draw out a fortune! Discussions should follow, noting levels of success and analyzing messages that don't immediately make sense.

The results from the second exercise are always interesting. Sometimes literal answers come. For example, a person who asks whether he or she will have the opportunity to travel soon may receive paper with the word "boat" written on it. The indication here is that a sailing trip is on the horizon.

Symbolic answers can be baffling at first, but often yield much food for thought. In one case, a woman asked about her spiritual path. The paper she got back had the image of an owl on it. This could lead to several different interpretations. The owl is a companion of Athena, which might indicate a Hellenistic path. But owls are also important in several shamanic traditions. While the universe provided an answer, it was one that still required the querent to make a decision and listen to her heart.

If you wish to use the second exercise for a communal question, follow the exercise as given. At the end, however, lay out like a jigsaw puzzle all the impressions pulled from the collective unconscious. See if words go together to make a sentence or if pictures relate to one another, then discuss the possibilities.

Helpful Hints and Insights for Success

Always conceptualize or verbalize your question concisely. Vague questions yield vague answers.

Remember that each divinatory system or technique determines how detailed your question, and its potential answer, can be. Don't expect more from the diviner's kit than is realistic, considering these constraints.

Failure of a reading to answer your question or accurately predict the future does not necessarily mean failure of the system or the reader. Remember that the Universe may have important messages that have nothing to do with the original question. Likewise, remember that each individual always has the ability to change his or her future.

A diviner's job is to relate what is seen to the best of his or her ability, and with kindness. Beyond that, how the reading is interpreted, utilized, and integrated is totally up to the querent.

Never be tempted to peek into another's fate without permission. No matter how good your intentions may be, this is a breach of privacy.

Be careful to phrase what appears to be bad news in such a way that it is constructive and helpful. Never leave a querent frightened, upset, or feeling hopeless.

If you get an unclear answer, it is acceptable to repeat any reading for the same question three times. Compare the results. If the information is still confusing, it means that the lines of fate are tangled around the querent. He or she will have to depend on personal insights and instincts to find the best solution, or wait until the oracle provides clearer answers.

Remind yourself and the querent that not everything in life has to have spiritual significance. I had a friend who once, in the spirit of fun, wrote a series of odiferous omens. Unfortunately, some people actually become too dependent upon divination, expecting omens, signs, and prognostications to tell them how to live every moment of their life.

No matter what symbols a reading places before you, always remain open to the signals from the Universe, Spirit, or Nature as an important guide to interpretation. Clarify to people what information is coming directly from the reading, and what information you "sense" from these sources. This allows them to determine validity for themselves.

Don't let your talents be misused. People will often volunteer your time and skills without consulting you first. They are so excited about what they experienced that they want everyone else to experience it too. While very well intentioned, such individuals should be taken aside and told to ask first. This will usually solve what I call the "sideshow" syndrome, in which you begin feeling like a trained seal performing readings on cue.

Last, but certainly not least, always read with loving heart, interpret with open mind, and maintain a healthy portion of skepticism. This will help you to serve the community honestly, gently, and with a balanced viewpoint that recognizes the important difference between fact and faith. We cannot prove that divination works; we can only prove its results. May yours always be positive and life-affirming.

PART TWO

The Encyclopedia
of Divination

CHAPTER THREE

How to Use The Encyclopedia of Divination

"How can I tell the signals and signs by which one heart another heart divines?"

—Henry Wadsworth Longfellow

"In today already, walks tomorrow."

—Samuel Taylor Coleridge

Seers and sages, farmers and feudal lords—all, at one time or another, turned to divination in hope of gaining insight into the future. Each person's fortune-telling approaches were different, reflecting individuality, communal beliefs, and sociological constraints. Consequently, some of the approaches in this book may seem odd, if not totally ludicrous, to our modern minds. Despite this spiritual "generation gap," each technique was valued in its setting, and should be considered accordingly.

To make this encyclopedia more effective for your personal research and reflection, please bear in mind the following:

(1)
The divination encyclopedia is set up alphabetically by the common name of the predominant tool or technique in question. For example, Ornithomancy is written up under *Birds* because it bases its forecasts on the observation of birds. Geomancy can be found under the heading *Earth* as it bases its observations on land masses, earth sounds, and dirt casting.

(2)
Divination systems with broad-ranging applications have more than one listing. The first listing is found under the technical name (like *Scrying*), with a brief definition or cross-references. The secondary listings and descriptions can be found under the media used for

that method (like *crystals*, *fire*, or *water*). This allows you to review the technical variations in a system and decide which medium you find most interesting.

(3)
The number of omens found in the natural world is nearly endless. In the interest of providing an overview of these, natural omens are listed in alphabetical order under general headings like *Animals*, *Plants*, *Trees*, *Insects*, and *Weather*. These listings are by no means complete. There is much more information on this subject available in collections of superstitions and folklore, if you wish to research further.

(4)
Underneath many entries you will find cross-references for similar systems described in this book. These allow you to easily compare your options more fully.

(5)
There are some divination systems whose origins were unclear. Entries with no reference to documentation or with a reference only to hypothetical origins are those for which research yielded little other than sketchy instructions on the methods, or those which simply listed the omens without source material.

(6)
Many divination techniques explored in this text could be and have been subjects of entire books themselves. Astrology is a perfect example. Thus, some entries will not contain enough details for a serious student of that system. Consult the bibliography provided at the end of this book for possible resources of further research.

(7)
Some divination methods are strongly interconnected with specific cultures, religions, or both (for example, the *Dafa* of Santeria). We cannot pretend to understand the full meaning of such systems without a full understanding of their cultures or paths. Consequently, approach these techniques with care. Either take the extra time for self-education, or adapt the system in a way that a "traditional" practitioner will not find offensive. Realize that people can be very sensitive about their heritage and traditions. Those feelings need to be considered in the spirit of building respect and tolerance.

(8)
Finally, the entries here will assist you in finding and using divination systems suited to your ideals. They can also prove valuable in interpreting the missives from nature and the universe that might otherwise go by unappreciated. When an odd happenstance occurs— a bird taps your window, you find a unique stone at your feet, or you notice an image in a frosty window—consider what questions have weighed heavily on your heart. Then turn to the pages of this encyclopedia and see if the time-honored art of divination has recorded a special message to help meet the needs in your life.

•ABSTINENCE

Many ancient divination rituals prescribed that the augur abstain from meat, alcohol, or physical pleasure for a specific period of time beforehand. This act was an offering and also served to cleanse the diviner, making him or her a purer receptacle.

Related Systems: Offerings, Ritual

Adaptation: Before asking important questions, one might choose to abstain from a well-loved food or drink or fast, if physically feasible. Fasting should be undertaken with care, however, and never exceed three days without a physician's consent.

•AFTERBIRTH

Folk traditions link the afterbirth with the soul, character, and future of a baby. Siberians attached the afterbirth to a bow and arrow to endow the child with good hunting skills as they grew up. Pomeranians attached the afterbirth to a tree to ensure that the child would be as vital as the tree. In British Columbia, parents fed the afterbirth to ravens, believing it gave the child foreknowledge. In fact, they believed if any animal ate the afterbirth, the child would possess that creature's most positive attributes.

In old England, mothers sometimes burned the afterbirth from a child. The number of *pops* it made in the fire predicted the number of future children the mother would have.

Related Systems: Amniomancy, Birth Omens, Burning

•AIR (AEROMANCY)

Divination by atmospheric phenomena such as cloud formations, wind directions, storms, and the like, is called Aeromancy. It was originally based on the idea that everything in nature, particularly elusive things like the wind, represented a powerful spirit that could reveal truths. One knowledgeable in this art could predict the weather (among other things), which was valuable in agrarian communities.

Related Topics: Clouds, Lightning, Rainbow, Thunder, Weather Omens, Wind

Adaptation: Learning to read nature's signs is as valuable today as it ever was. The approaches and symbology reviewed in this text may be a little outdated, however, considering modern technology. For example, seeing the image of a boat moving through the sky in a cloud formation once portended travel by sea. Today this could represent a journey by any number of vehicles.

• ALCHEMIST, THE

The Alchemist is a contemporary system that bases its values on the ancient symbols and ideals of alchemy. Fifty-two cards on rings, divided into four subgroups are the basis for interpretations. The querent tosses four color-coded dice, then turns the guide to the indicated cards to read their fortunes.

Related Systems: Cards, Deva Disks, Dice, Dominoes, Medicine Cards, Runes, Tarot

Adaptation: This system is available on CD.

• ALECTROMANCY

(see Roosters)

• ALEUROMANCY

(see Flour)

• ALOMANCY

(see Salt)

• ALPHITOMANCY

(see Bread)

• AMNIOMANCY

In amniomancy, a predictive system thought to have originated in the East, a diviner examines the condition and placement of a baby's caul to determine the child's future. For example, a baby born with the caul over his or her eyes is expected to grow up able to see spirits.

Related Systems: Afterbirth, Birth Omens

Adaptation: It is interesting to note that the afterbirth from a baby is still examined today for medical reasons.

•ANGANG

Angang is a term used by folklorists to describe divinatory insights gathered from random encounters with people or animals while traveling. For example, meeting a horse while traveling, especially a white one, is a lucky sign in Germany. Meeting an old woman or priest, on the other hand, is unlucky. What the person or animal is doing during this chance meeting may also be considered in the interpretation.

Related Systems: Animal Omens and Signs, Random Divination, Spontaneous Divination

•ANIMAL OMENS AND SIGNS

Indigenous creatures have been valued by indigenous peoples for a variety of reasons for thousands of years. For example, cats were honored in numerous countries because they caught and killed pests like rodents. Consequently, seeing a cat in these areas was a favorable omen (see *Cats*).

Animals have always been valuable as a source of food. With this in mind, ancient people sacrificed animals to their deities to gain favor. In Rome, augurs took this one step further with extispicy, divination by sacrificial animals, based on the belief that the gods would express their wills through any sanctified creature accepted on the sacred altar. This is covered in more detail under *Entrails* and *Offerings*.

Thankfully, this practice fell into disfavor with humankind's evolution, and augurs began observing live animals instead. From these observations there comes a literal plethora of forecasts, some of which interpreted chance meetings (see *Angang*). This form of divination is sometimes called apantomancy. Here is a list of a few traditional animal omens and signs:

Animal Coats: Thicker animal coats predict a harsh winter is ahead (see *Weather Omens*).

Camel: Arabs considered meeting a camel, the bearer of water, a very fortuitous sign.

Dog: Prognostication based on the howling of dogs is called ololygmancy. Most often, howling is considered a bad sign for the person hearing it, especially if they are embarking on some type of partnership. In this case, the dog's cry reveals hidden agendas and possible deceit.

According to Hittite tradition, a dog coming into your house and immediately lying on the bed foretells the acquisition of new possessions. Among Arabs, a black dog indicated bad luck was on the way.

Babylonian high priests used the color of a stray dog's fur as an omen. A white dog entering the temple, for example, indicated a long wait or enduring effort. Red symbolized renunciation or the need to abandon a project. Gray revealed a loss, and yellow warned of devastation or blight. If any dog was to get into the throne room and lay upon the monarch's seat, it meant that special care should be taken against fires in the palace.

Donkey: Meeting a donkey warns of trouble or unexpected burdens (see *Donkey*).

Fox: In most cultures, seeing a fox at the start of an endeavor is a very bad sign, except among the Welsh who regard it as a positive omen.

Frog: In Babylon, hopeful lovers left a frog in the sand for seven days to die. Afterwards, the carcass was tossed into a river. If it sank, this predicted a loveless relationship.

Gazelle: Arabians believed that meeting a gazelle was a very bad omen, especially if it crossed your path from left to right. To counter this bad luck, you were supposed to shout "Gazelle, gazelle, let misfortune vanish as well."

Goat: In Europe, encountering a goat predicted improved fortune.

Hare: Seeing a hare early in the morning is taken as a warning to be cautious all day.

Horse: Meeting a horse is a good sign, often preceding excellent news. A horse frolicking on a newly sown field portends an increased yield (see *Horse Divination*).

Lamb: Seeing a lone lamb indicates peace, joy, and love. In England, the direction the lamb faces when first sighted in spring also indicates specific things. If the creature looks at you, your year is supposed to be prosperous.

Lizard: A lizard is a sign of forthcoming disappointment. According to some Eastern beliefs, if one runs across a young person's hand, she or he will grow up to be a skilled needleworker.

Mice: Seeing mice generally warns of danger or difficulties ahead. In France and Germany, the appearance of many mice warns of war. Conversely, in Bohemia seeing a white mouse was regarded as a sign of better luck. Divination based on mice is called myomancy.

Mole: A mole hole in your garden foreshadows a move to a new residence.

Mule: Meeting a mule is a bad sign for business. This is also true of hogs and hares.

Ox: Babylonian diviners sprinkled water on the forehead of an ox three times while it was lying down. The diviner monitored the creature's reactions, seventeen of which had interpretive value. If the ox snorted and rose immediately, this was a very positive sign for the querent.

Pig: Europeans have a belief that a pig forewarns that worries are on the way.

Sheep: Meeting sheep and goats signifies financial gain.

Weasel: If you respectfully ask a weasel about its health, this kindness wards off any negative luck headed your direction. Seeing a weasel on a trip is a bad omen, and near the house it warns of domestic discord.

Related Topics: Angang, Birds, Bull, Cats, Donkey, Insects, Omens, Signs, Weather Omens

Adaptations: Birds, insects, and small wild animals that have not been driven away from urban environments can be considered for their symbolism when they appear suddenly or in unusual spots or formations. Consider not only the animal for its meaning, but also its movements and location.

Pets can be excellent prognosticators once you learn how to read their clues effectively. To illustrate, if your dog or cat begins eating a lot more and grows a thicker coat around September or October, you may interpret this as a sign of an early or unusually cold winter.

Medicine cards are a set of forty-four cards and an accompanying book written by Jamie Sams and David Carson (see Bibliography for publishing information). The system is based on Native American totemism and the idea that guiding animal spirits can be protectors and teachers of humankind. Each card contains a beautiful illustration of one animal, such as a Hawk, Snake, Otter, Turtle, and Moose, and text describing the meaning of each card in both the upright and reversed positions. The cards can be drawn individually or in one of several recommended layouts, including understanding your life's path or the outcome of a particular project. Alternative layouts can be used from other cartomancy systems.

• ANTHROPOMANCY

When human sacrifice was still used to appease the gods, both the behavior of the sacrificed person and the remains were studied. This system of divination is known as anthropomancy. The Mesopotamians read human entrails, and Roman emperor Heliogabalus used a similar method for insight into various matters of state.

The Druids used the bowels of prisoners for prognostication, meting out a rather unique form of justice, and looked for blood patterns created during the accused's execution. Sometimes humans were burned as offerings, and their screams interpreted.

Related Systems: Blood, Entrails, Offerings, Rituals

• APANTOMANCY

(see Animal Omens and Signs)

• APPLES

Apples appear in numerous myths, remedies, and magical procedures. In some settings the apple tree was considered the "Tree of Life," and in others the "World Tree." The apple itself was considered a powerful fruit and an obvious choice for divinatory efforts since it was readily available. Some traditional beliefs were:

- Peel an apple making an unbroken spiral strip and ask a yes-or-no question. Toss the peel over your left shoulder. If the shape formed when it lands is an "O" or "U," the answer is "no". This was common in rural England during the Victorian Era and in America around the same time.

- Hold an apple in your left hand and twist the stem with your right while concentrating on a question. With each twist, alternate saying "yes" and "no." The one spoken when the stem finally breaks is your answer. The stem can also be twisted off while reciting letters of the alphabet. This is to determine an initial in the name of a person central to your question.

- European tradition instructs a querent to cut an apple in half on the night of the full moon. Eating half before midnight and the remainder as the clock strikes twelve brings precognitive dreams.

- On Halloween, dunk for apples. The larger the apple you get, the better it bodes for the coming year. In some traditions getting a large apple also equates to long life.

Related Topics: Ball, Bread, Fish, Food, Nuts

Adaptations: Consider choosing your fruit so that it corresponds more closely to the question at hand. For example, if you ask about love, twist a strawberry stem instead. For questions of devotion and loyalty, peel an orange.

• APPLE BLOSSOMS

On a spring day, go beneath an apple tree and wait for the wind to scatter some petals. Each petal you catch before it reaches the ground indicates a month of joy and luck to come. Please note that the petals must be released by the wind and not shaken free forcefully or this system will not work. After gathering the petals, dry and carry them as a charm to encourage good fortune in and around your life.

Related Systems: Dandelion, Flowers, Leaves

Adaptations: Flowers have a language all their own. Each blossom carries a different meaning. If you have a specific need or question, consider using flowers related to your query. One example is collecting cherry blossoms for improved vitality or fertility (see *Trees*).

•APPLE SEEDS

Our pragmatic ancestors did not allow much to go to waste. Apple seeds were used in fortune-telling just like the rest of the apple. Here are some examples and their traditional interpretations that you can try:

- Cut an apple in half while concentrating on a question. If the number of seeds revealed is even, your answer is positive. This is especially true for questions pertaining to relationships. If any seeds are split by the cutting, however, trouble awaits you, even if the answer was "yes."

- Cut an apple in half and count the number of seeds you see. If there are 13, you will soon have a new friend or be offered some type of partnership. If there are 14, you will soon receive a kiss.

- Throw apple seeds onto a fire while thinking of a question. If the seeds pop and fly, this is a positive omen. Flying to the left reveals that your hopes will come to fruition, but not without some difficulties. To the right, smooth sailing lies ahead. Should the apple seed fly away from you behind the fire, you will have a period of waiting before manifestation occurs.

Related Systems: Ashes, Fire, Food, Seeds

Adaptations: Any type of seed will work for the third method given, many of which can be purchased at a gardening shop. Choose the seed so that it corresponds to the theme of your question. Examples include using carrot seeds to determine the correctness or incorrectness of a viewpoint; cauliflower seeds for matters of intuition, creativity, and other traditionally feminine qualities; periwinkle seeds for questions about a friendship; and sunflower seeds for questions about leadership, strength, and other traditionally masculine qualities.

•APRONS

During the Victorian Era, if a woman's apron dropped off it was an omen of something impending. In Britain, it was interpreted as a sign that the woman would have a baby within a year.

Related Systems: Clothing, Dressing, Rings, Shoes

Adaptation: Today this might be comparable to losing a piece of jewelry or dropping a button suddenly. Its significance may be interpreted by noting any images on the item itself, the direction in which it falls, its color, etc.

•ARITHMANCY

Arithmancy is an ancient form of numerology, also known as Gematria, used to divine number and letter significance. One example, *Temurah*, comes from the Hebrew tradition. *Temurah* transposes or regroups the letters in phrases or words anagramatically to yield meanings like in a giant word hunt. Most often the words or phrases used come from the scriptures.

Related Systems: Hebrew Letters, Names, Numerology

Adaptation: If you are pondering a question and a random word or phrase suddenly comes to mind, write it down. If it has no immediate significance, then try regrouping the letters in the word or phrase to make other words (use each letter only once). Alternatively, reduce the word or phrase to a number and interpret that (see *Numerology*).

•ARROWS (BELOMANCY)

Divination by arrows appears in the traditions of Korea, Greece, Rome, Mexico, and Arabia, probably as a result of their use in hunting and warfare. Additionally, the symbolism of "hitting one's mark" was not overlooked by the ancients. For example, the king of Babylonia used a loosely described method of arrow divination to make sure his timing was accurate before he proceeded to invade Judah.

In Tibet, divination with arrows is called *Md-mo* or *Dahmo*. The diviner used two arrows, one tied with white cloth and the other with black. These represented the intrinsic polarities of all things. A white wool cloth was laid on a table with a heap of barley on top. The arrows were then thrust into the barley while the querent sat in front concentrating on his or her question. Eventually, the arrows began to move. They might fall together, apart, or hit each other. This movement provided the foundation for the interpretations given.

Another type of arrow divination appears in Islamic tradition. For many years, there was an idol in Mecca placed outside the Ka'bal. The region near the idol was specifically set aside for divinatory work. Here a *Sadin* (custodian of sorts) received seven arrows to shuffle for a determination on the matter in question. Each arrow had words or emblems inscribed on it that were appropriate for the question undertaken. Exactly how the divinatory method worked is uncertain, but linguistic hints exist. The Islamic word for "shuffle" literally translates to mean "strike." Perhaps one arrow was randomly drawn by the *Sadin* and cast to the ground before the parties.

Another version of this Islamic tradition employed only three arrows for determining personal actions. The arrows were always marked with words or emblems that meant "prohibit," "command," or "wait." Essentially, this translates as "no," "yes," and "not now," respectively! The *Kahin*, a type of divinatory magistrate, used this approach to resolve differences between two opposing parties. The *Kahin* conducted background investigations, and when all precursory efforts were completed, the arrows were cast. The *Kahin* recited rhymes that cleverly hid wise observations under the guise of a cryptic oracle. In some cases, actual divination may have been involved here, but this particular approach seems more like a play to alleviate any dissension caused by a negative outcome.

In the Western world, common approaches to belomancy included shooting an arrow up into the sky. The arrow's flight and where it landed revealed the future. Perhaps this is related to the little poem "I shot an arrow into the air." Alternatively, arrows were shot or dropped against a hard surface. Afterward, the nicks and scratches on the arrowheads were interpreted for meaning.

Related Systems: Systems that are cast like witan wands, runes, and stones

Adaptations: A variation on the Tibetan method uses wooden sticks placed into straw, sand, or loose dirt. Another, easily performed at home, uses colored toothpicks in mashed potatoes or a similarly "earthy" medium. Potential interpretive values:

• The two falling together toward the querent indicates a partnership or harmonious group effort.

• The two falling apart in opposite directions indicates division of purpose, energy, or loyalties.

• Both falling to the left indicates a negative or "no."

• Both falling to the right indicates a positive or "yes."

• Both falling away from the querent indicates a time of waiting and no quick answers or help.

• The two falling in odd positions that look like a specific time on a clock can be used as the foundation for an interpretation (see *Numerology*).

For those readers who enjoy archery, you may wish to make an interpretive target for yourself. Paint it with symbolic images, and set it up with a protective back behind it. Take aim, but close your eyes just prior to releasing your shot. Release the arrow with your question in mind. Whichever symbol it lands closest to on the target is your answer. If the arrow misses altogether, no response can be given at this time.

• ASHES (SPODOMANCY, TEPHRAMANCY)

Divination by ashes grew out of pyromancy, the observance of sacred fires both during and after a ritual. Spodomancy pertains specifically to soot, while tephramancy is divination by ashes, often those of tree bark. One approach recommends scattering some ashes evenly on the ground to the left and right of a querent. If the first wind blows the right side of the ashes away, the answer to the person's question is yes.

During the Victorian Era people adapted tephramancy, using the hearth fire as a source of signs. If a spark popped from the hearth, it was allowed to lie and cool. The shape of the ash then became the foundation for interpretation, such as a heart for impending romantic interests or marriage.

Other omens derived from ashes included:

- Ashes that fly out of the fire predict the arrival of a guest or a friend.

- In old England, soot dropping down the chimney portended both wealth and the coming of bad weather (see *Weather Omens*).

- On the Isle of Man, ashes were used to divine a child's protective spirit or god, though I could not find the actual procedure used.

Many other superstitions surrounded the hearth, as it was considered the true "heart" of any home.

Related Systems: Burning, Fire, Wind

Adaptation: Out of consideration to the earth, make sure to use wood ash (not charcoal, which is often chemically treated). If possible, choose the wood so that it corresponds to the focus of your question, such as pine for determining the potential longevity of an effort, or oak for questions about vitality.

• ASTRAGALOMANCY

(see Bones)

•ASTROLOGY

"What the thief has missed, the astrologer carried off."
—Arabian Proverb

Astrology is considered a branch of natural omen interpretation with origins as far back as 2000 B.C. Records from around 1700 B.C. indicate that the Babylonians believed the gods moved celestial objects to reveal forthcoming events. Around 1620 B.C. tablets with over 7,000 astrological omens were assembled into a collection called *Enuma Anu Enlil* (sky omen collection).

Mesopotamian priests connected the sun, moon, and planets with specific deities, believing that each represented a facet of the universe's order and structure. Slowly, Mesopotamian ideas spread into Greece, Egypt, Syria, and India. The earliest surviving horoscope appeared around 410 B.C. on the Cylinder of Gudea from Babylon, which now resides at Oxford. It recounts a dream where a goddess studies a map of the heavens, giving brief positive and negative predictions based on her observations.

By 300 B.C. the astrologer's art had been refined to the point where the sky was divided into twelve sections. During this century, Aristotle developed the principal philosophies for more methodical approaches to astrology. By postulating that heavenly bodies influenced actions on earth, Aristotle promoted the axiom of "as above, so below" and encouraged further studies.

Generalized writings on celestial influences circulated throughout the Mediterranean world. Aristotle's efforts were followed three centuries later by Greek physician and writer Galen (A.D. 130–200), who strongly believed in validity of astrology and celestial omens such as meteors. Alexandrian astronomer Ptolemy, living in the second century A.D., similarly detailed in *Tetrabiblos* how celestial objects affect human life in complex ways. He did not feel their power was absolute, however.

Early astrology focused mostly on being an effective sky map for travel, farming, and healing rather than predicting individual futures as we see today. Actually, the concept of natal astrology was not introduced until around 5 B.C. A Greek astronomer, Eudoxus, reintroduced the idea in the fourth century A.D., but it was not taken very seriously until much later in history.

Astrological correspondences were originally based on a five-planet system consisting of Mercury, Venus, Mars, Jupiter, and Saturn. Astrologists also based their observations on the moon. Its appearance and phases became the foundation for timing everything from hair cutting to planting cycles. This tradition was still common in the early 1900s in the U.S., as evidenced in the *Farmer's Almanac* and among certain French agrarians who followed this celestial drummer's rhythm in their daily tasks.

Europeans and Americans were by no means the only ones to show a continued interest in astrology. For example, in Islamic tradition, the astrologer was known as the *Murajjim*, who taught the children how to pray for a "true star" to govern their future. The *Murajjim* often had an elaborate astrological instrument called the *za'irajah*, which was like a compass with ciphers, sciences of the world, astrological signs and degrees, and the numerical values of letters. To devise a prediction, all of these bits of information were compared with celestial objects and their placement at the time of the inquiry.

Turning our attention away from ancient to modern ideas about astrology, most of the traditional symbolic elements have survived into our times, though a far stronger emphasis is now placed on personal fates or one's horoscope. The word horoscope comes from the Greek *horuos skopos*, meaning "time observer." The heavens are still divided into twelve sections, or houses, each of which has an associated sign and correspondences. Depending on when one is born, each sign of the zodiac, the arrangement of the houses, and the celestial objects in the individual's horoscope chart predicts aspects of personality and even the fields in which he or she will be most successful. A comprehensive explanation would require more space than is available here, so please bear in mind that the following overview is a broad generalization.

Houses and Their Associations

1st: Aries and personality

2nd: Taurus and material possessions

3rd: Gemini and intellect and communication

4th: Cancer and home and security

5th: Leo and children and play

6th: Virgo and service and health

7th: Libra and relationships, music, and the arts

8th: Scorpio and matters of sexuality and spiritual responsibility

9th: Sagittarius and learning, science, and travel

10th: Capricorn and honor, goals, and personal standing

11th: Aquarius and friendship, loyalty, and maturity

12th: Pisces and hidden matters, enemies, and retribution

Planetary Influences

Mercury: Versatility; the ability for reasonable thinking; communication

Venus: Sensitivity; the ability to love; enjoyment of pleasure; morality

Mars: Competitiveness; physical centeredness; strong, enterprising leadership ability

Jupiter: Optimism; philosophical outlooks; kindness and open-mindedness

Saturn: Sagacity; responsible goal-orientation; honesty

Uranus: Service; creative ability; mysticism; willfulness

Neptune: Emotion; idealism and religiousness; mysteriousness

Pluto: Hidden matters; introspection; independent thinking

The Sun's Influence in the Signs

Aries: Strong will and pioneering spirit

Taurus: Tenacity and faithfulness

Gemini: Diversity and sociability

Cancer: Cautious, creative and home-body

Leo: Courage and pridefulness

Virgo: Rationality and sense of duty

Libra: Harmony and beauty

Scorpio: Ingenuity, determination, and competition

Sagittarius: Liberality, outgoing energy, and extravagance

Capricorn: Devotion, practicality, and discipline

Aquarius: Eccentricity, originality, and idealism

Pisces: Flexibility, generosity, and caring

The Moon's Influence in the Signs

Aries: Dominance, zealousness, and pridefulness

Taurus: Devotion, resolve, and even temper

Gemini: Insightfulness, diversity

Cancer: Dedication and prudence

Leo: Charisma and passion

Virgo: Insecurity

Libra: Courtesy and ambivalence

Scorpio: Depth of emotion and reservedness

Sagittarius: Imaginativeness and perceptiveness

Capricorn: Sensitivity

Aquarius: Detachment and anxiety

Pisces: Instinctuality

The Zodiac Birth Signs

Aries (March 21–April 19): Arians are fiery, authoritarian people with tendencies toward violence. Strong masculine attributes evidence themselves in this sign. Aries make good leaders, explorers, and inventors. Romantically, the Aries-Libra combination is volatile, while Aries-Leo or Aries-Sagittarius are more harmonious. Famous Aries include Bach, Descartes, Wordsworth, Joan Crawford, and Doris Day.

Taurus (April 20–May 20): Taureans are very earthy people with strong feminine attributes, who tend to like the night and remain somewhat aloof. Professionally, Taurus excels in the arts. Famous people born under this sign include Shakespeare, Browning, Barbra Streisand, Shirley Temple, and Dante Gabriel Rossetti. In love, Taurus should avoid Scorpios and look to those born under Virgo or Capricorn.

Gemini (May 21–June 21): Geminis are restless, active people who sometimes have difficulty being understood and typically exhibit a lot of nervous energy. Geminis profit from careers like teaching and journalism. In love, Gemini and Sagittarius are ill-matched, while relationships with an Aquarius or Libra are better. Famous Geminis include Walt Whitman, Pascal, Gladys Knight, Cyndi Lauper, and Thomas Hardy.

Cancer (June 22–July 21): Cancers are successful gamblers, with shrewd economical sense and long memories. They love nature, especially water. Professionally, Cancers should work with the public. For love, Cancers should avoid Capricorns, but can find very happy, devoted relationships with Pisceans or Scorpios. Famous Cancers include John Jacob Astor, Gilda Radner, Diana Rigg, Ann Landers, and Paul Jones.

Leo (July 22–August 21): Leos are very lucky, especially financially. Leos enjoy refinement and luxury to the point of ostentatiousness. Professionally, Leos work well in predominant positions where they can shine. Famous Leos include Shelley, George Bernard Shaw, John Dryden, Lucille Ball, Madonna, Helena Blavatsky, and Alexandre Dumas. In relationships, Leos should avoid Aquarius, looking to those born under Aries or Sagittarius.

Virgo (August 22–September 22): Virgos are very flexible, keen-witted, somewhat impulsive, and forever thinking deeply about life's questions. Virgos make good philosophers, politicians, and detectives. Romantically, Virgos and Pisceans do not get along well, but they can find happiness with a Taurus or Capricorn. Famous Virgos include Lafayette, President Taft, Anne Bancroft, Lily Tomlin, Agatha Christie, and John Locke.

Libra (September 23–October 22): Libras are humorous, adaptable people. Libras enjoy welcoming surroundings, anything that challenges their intellect, and avoid unpleasant confrontations at all costs. Professionally, a Libra does well in most careers, especially those requiring esthetics. Among their numbers are Lord Nelson, George Westinghouse, Susan Sarandon, Aimee Semple McPherson, and Augustus Caesar. Libras do best with an Aquarian or Gemini mate.

Scorpio (October 23–November 21): Scorpios are people of extremes, very charming, emotional, and introspective. Scorpios usually leave their mark on the world somehow, for boon or bane. Good careers for Scorpio are usually those of an "official" or highly skilled nature. In love, Scorpios can be impulsive, making Pisceans or Cancers their best choice for a partner. Famous Scorpios include Neil Young, Prince Charles, Martin Luther, Jamie Lee Curtis, Pablo Picasso, and Ezra Pound.

Sagittarius (November 22–December 21): Sagittarians are very changeable, yet successful no matter what transitions or transformations are required. Sagittarians enjoy sports and nature, but can also be very prideful. Sagittarians should seek authority positions where they can use their insights and talents and give advice. Thomas Becket, Prince Rupert, Weber, Walt Disney, Agnes Moorehead, Emily Dickinson, and Beethoven were all born under this sign. In love, Sagittarians are well advised to focus their attentions on people born under the signs of Leo or Aries.

Capricorn (December 22–January 20): Capricorns are patient people with an even temperament and strong convictions, potentially unforgiving and jealous. They make good negotiators in business, thanks to a talent for precaution and methodical approaches. In love, the best match for Capricorns is Virgo or Taurus. Well-known Capricorns include Alexander Hamilton, Woodrow Wilson, Faye Dunaway, Isaac Asimov, Betsy Ross, Barbara Mandrell, and Edgar Allan Poe.

Aquarius (January 21–February 19): Aquarians are unconventional folk, though social, idealistic, and adventuresome. There is no predicting what Aquarians will do. They can often go to two different extremes in a very short time. Professionally, Aquarians excel in research or the arts. In mates, they should choose Libra or Gemini. Some interesting Aquarians include Mozart, Mendelssohn, Vanessa Redgrave, Helen Gurley Brown, and Lord Byron.

Pisces (February 20–March 20): Pisceans are kindly and empathetic, "mommies" to many, and potentially overwhelmed by emotion. Pisceans often strive to balance the spiritual with the mundane, but find it difficult to define the exact boundaries that make this possible. Good occupations for Pisceans include anything associated with philosophy, classical literature, and imagination. The best partners for Pisceans are Scorpio or Cancer. Famous Pisceans include Michelangelo, Albert Einstein, Victor Hugo, Bernadette Peters, Dr. Seuss, Lynn Redgrave, and Handel.

Related Systems: Birth Omens, Celestial Omens, Comets, Day Signs, Meteors, Moon, Stars, Sun

Adaptations: There is now computer software that can chart out horoscopes with a fair amount of accuracy. Also, the pictorial representations for each sign may be used in a personally devised divination system for increased interpretive value (see Appendix B).

•ASTROLOGY, CHINESE

Chinese astrology, while based on similar concepts as Western forms, varies greatly in its techniques and interpretive values. An ancient myth tells how Buddha designed the twelve signs in the Chinese system just prior to his ascension. Before leaving the Earth, he wished to see all the animals, but only twelve answered his invitation. The Rat arrived first, loving social occasions. The Ox came next, being very timely in nature. Then the Tiger made an entrance, wishing to be the center of attention. The Cat would have been next had it not been for the distraction of a mouse. Then the Dragon brought excitement and energy. The Snake arrived sixth, hoping to charm all the guests, while the Horse quietly entered seventh, offering assistance. The Goat was eighth and fully planned to be the party's show-off, but the Monkey, number nine, took the center stage with humor and charm. The Rooster reached the celebration tenth, wishing to be late as to get more attention. The Dog, not wanting to rush, arrived eleventh, and finally the Boar, ever the party animal, came last. In gratitude for each animal's participation, Buddha promised to name successive years after them, saying that all people born during those years would bear that animal's traits.

The Chinese Zodiac has one cycle every sixty years, during which each animal rules for five separate years. Each animal also rules different hours in the day. The year of one's birth is the predominant factor in forecasting personality and future potential, but the "hour sign" also contributes partially developed characteristics. Besides determining personality at the time of birth, the animal characteristics for each year influence what a person can expect within that year, depending on his or her birth sign.

To determine your birth animals, use the following two charts, then look below to read more about the creature's talents and demeanor. Keep in mind that the Chinese New Year falls sometime in February, so Western and Chinese calendars do not line up exactly.

BIRTH YEARS	ANIMAL
1936, 1948, 1960, 1972, 1984, 1996, 2008, 2020	Rat
1937, 1949, 1961, 1973, 1985, 1997, 2009, 2021	Ox or Buffalo
1938, 1950, 1962, 1974, 1986, 1998, 2010, 2022	Tiger
1939, 1951, 1963, 1975, 1987, 1999, 2011, 2023	Cat or Hare
1940, 1952, 1964, 1976, 1988, 2000, 2012, 2024	Dragon
1941, 1953, 1965, 1977, 1989, 2001, 2013, 2025	Snake
1942, 1954, 1966, 1978, 1990, 2002, 2014, 2026	Horse
1943, 1955, 1967, 1979, 1991, 2003, 2015, 2026	Goat or Sheep
1944, 1956, 1968, 1980, 1992, 2004, 2016, 2027	Monkey
1945, 1957, 1969, 1981, 1993, 2005, 2017, 2028	Rooster
1946, 1958, 1970, 1982, 1994, 2006, 2018, 2029	Dog
1947, 1959, 1971, 1983, 1995, 2007, 2019, 2030	Boar or Pig

BIRTH HOURS	ANIMAL	BIRTH HOURS	ANIMAL
11 P.M.–1 A.M.	Rat	11 A.M.–1 P.M.	Horse
1 A.M.–3 A.M.	Ox or Buffalo	1 P.M.–3 P.M.	Goat or Sheep
3 A.M.–5 A.M.	Tiger	3 P.M.–5 P.M.	Monkey
5 A.M.–7 A.M.	Cat or Hare	5 P.M.–7 P.M.	Rooster
7 A.M.–9 A.M.	Dragon	7 P.M.–9 P.M.	Dog
9 A.M.–11 A.M.	Snake	9 P.M.–11 P.M.	Boar or Pig

Animal Personality Traits

Rat: The Rat is ever charming and aggressive, bearing a calm exterior that hides restlessness. Rats love people and social occasions, but are selective in friendships. They tend to keep problems to themselves, lacking true security and always fearing failure. However, the Rat is also an opportunist, being very good in financial matters. Their imagination, creativity, honesty and good advice endear them to people easily. Accounting, music, and writing all make good careers for the Rat. In relationships, the Rat does well with the Ox or Dragon. Famous Rats include Shakespeare, Tolstoy, Jules Verne, and Mozart.

Ox: Oxen are quiet, patient, methodical people who inspire confidence in others. They are contemplative idealists, sometimes to the point of bigotry. Oxen must watch that their anger does not get in the way of goals. They can become good leaders, having a strong sense of duty and a good work ethic, but they have some trouble accepting new ideas. Oxen easily slip into dogmatism and stubborn behavior, which makes them devoted mates, but not overly romantic ones. This is an excellent sign for statesmen. In relationships the Ox does well with the Rat and Rooster. Famous Oxen include Hitler, Richard the Lionhearted, Aristotle, and Dante.

Tiger: The Tiger is a rebel with a cause, who will follow that cause with reckless abandon just to test his or her limits. Tigers have a natural air of authority, and if they take the time to think before they act, these people can be very successful. Tigers don't trust others much, but can be generous and sensitive, especially in an introspective mood. Good mates for the Tiger are the Horse, Dragon, and Dog. Famous Tigers include Marilyn Monroe, St. Francis Xavier, Mohammed, and Ho Chi Minh.

Cat: The Cat is a happy, refined, virtuous person, at least on the surface. Dig a little deeper and you will find someone who has ambition, loves to entertain, and may like gossiping. Cats like to show off their knowledge and refinement, yet always stay at a paw's length from real intimacy. They are good with money, handling it conservatively, and keep their balance in difficult situations. Good mates for the Cat include the Goat, Dog, and Boar. Famous Cats are Queen Victoria, Confucius, Martin Luther, and Henry Wadsworth Longfellow.

Dragon: A Dragon is a healthy, vital, direct individual with a definite lack of tactfulness. People born in the year of the Dragon will carry the courage of their convictions stubbornly. They can be quite demanding and idealistic, often putting emotions before logical thought. Nonetheless, the Dragon is gifted and very smart, showing tremendous ability when they complete a task. In love, the Dragon is somewhat of a hermit, afraid of vulnerability. Good mates for the dragon include the Rat, Snake, and Rooster. Freud, Joan of Arc, Lewis Carroll, and Immanuel Kant were all famous Dragons.

Snake: People born in the year of the Snake exhibit wisdom, good will, humor, and tremendous charm. They like to dress everything up to appeal to the public, including personal knowledge and philosophies. Snakes follow through on their commitments, make firm decisions, and have luck with money, which they spend wisely. In love, they can be possessive and jealous, making the Ox or Rooster the Snake's best mate. Among Snakes we find Copernicus, Gandhi, Charles Darwin, Pablo Picasso, and Audrey Hepburn.

Horse: Horses are physically appealing people who love sports and socialization. They exhibit upbeat, funny personalities and are always popular. Once a Horse gets an ambition in his or her head, however, they can trample those who stand in the way. People born under this sign have sound financial ability, but don't take advice very well, and they will sacrifice everything for love. Goats, Dogs, and Tigers make the best mates for the Horse. Some of the world's famous Horses include Cicero, Charlemagne, Isaac Newton, Leonard Bernstein, Sean Connery, and Theodore Roosevelt.

Goat: Very elegant and charming, Goats love nature and always seem to seek those "greener grasses." Goats graze lazily under the sun, often losing track of time or procrastinating so much as to become a nuisance to others. Even so, the Goat has wonderful manners, fits well in many different social situations, and has a natural interest in the supernatural. The best mates for a Goat are the Cat, Pig, or Horse. Goats include Laurence Olivier, John Ford, Alexander Graham Bell, Mark Twain, and Jane Austen.

Monkey: Monkeys are full of mischief, playfulness, and energy. Children born in this year exhibit good memories, social behavior, and astonishing inventiveness, all of which are easily distracted by anything new or interesting. Monkeys become dramatic and clever opportunists who tend toward vanity and deviousness. To balance this, the Monkey should marry a Dragon or Rat. People born under the Monkey include Homer, Leonardo da Vinci, Milton, and Susan B. Anthony.

Rooster: Roosters love flattery. These people speak their mind to the point of aggressiveness. They are brutally honest, with no idea of how to take a diplomatic approach. Roosters live a life of bold adventure, always building proverbial castles in the air, but rarely putting foundations beneath them. The best mates for the Rooster are the Ox, Snake, or Dragon. Famous Roosters include Maria de Medici, Richard Wagner, Rene Descartes, Rudyard Kipling, Groucho Marx, and Catherine the Great.

Dog: Dogs are worrisome, defensive, alert, introverted, stubborn, and very single-minded. They are always intent on duty and detail, but these attributes can also be their undoing. Dogs hate injustice to the point of developing pessimism about it, but balance this with unwavering loyalty, making sacrifices for those they care about. Horses, Tigers, and Cats are good mates for Dogs, and people born in this year include Socrates, Lenin, Louis XVI, and George Gershwin.

Boar: Boars are obliging to a fault. They can easily be fooled by others due to their naiveté and overt tolerance of people's faults. Among Pig traits are sincerity, honesty, a sense of duty, inner strength, passivity, a hunger for knowledge, and a strong will. Cats are the best mates for Boars. People born under this sign include Albert Schweitzer, Ernest Hemingway, and Andrew Jackson.

Yearly Influences

Year of the Rat: For Rats themselves this is a terrific year filled with joy, love, and success, especially for a writer. The Ox can accumulate money now, at least some of which should be saved. Tigers find themselves at a standstill, while Cats discover their trusts have been mislaid. For the Dragon this is a good year for investments and relationships. The Snake discovers a lot of activity to the point of being over-whelmed. Horses have a bad year, especially in business. Goats don't fare well financially this year either, while Monkeys have a "golden touch" with everything. A Rooster may wish to take a risk, but is well advised to wait. Dogs are bored in Rat years, and Boars experience success with money and love.

Year of the Ox: Rats will have to work very hard this year to keep what they gathered in the previous. Oxen continue to reap the rewards of hard work. Tigers should take no risks; this is a very bad year for them. Cats find the Ox years enhance their ability to land on their feet. The Dragon has problems with authority figures, while the Snake has tons of work in store. Horses will find they have a good business year, but difficulty in relationships. Both Goats and Dogs would rather this year never happened, while the Monkey and Rooster both fare well. Finally, the Boar will have to adapt somewhat and keep his or her temper under control.

Year of the Tiger: Rats and Oxen both feel insecure and anxious this year, while the Tiger shines brightly in the limelight. Cats, who prefer a quiet pace, find themselves uneasy and in the midst of many changes. Dragons don't mind all the busy-ness, focusing on their goals, often quite successfully completing one or two. The Snake will find this year tiresome but also educational, while the Horse takes advantage of transitional times, finding something new. The Goat is lost in all this commotion, the Monkey thinks all the fuss is amusing, and the Rooster just plain hates it. The Dog, however, displays devotion and finds happiness, and the Boar, as usual, adapts with the changes.

Year of the Cat: As one might expect, Rats need to be very careful this year, watching for well-hidden Cats with personal agendas. Oxen find that things seem to be getting a little better, and the Tiger rests on the laurels attained in the previous twelve months. Cat have no troubles in their own year, being able to enjoy both leisure and business at their own paces. Dragons like the ambiance right now and shine even more brightly, while Snakes take much needed breathers and discover some success. For the Horse, this is a good year for both romance and careers, and the Goat finally gets a little attention for his or her hard work. Monkeys find this a terrific year for business, Roosters are still recuperating from the previous year, the Dog rests contentedly, and the Boar has a good year in all areas except legal.

Year of the Dragon: This is generally a pleasant year for the Rat. Oxen have to be cautious to build their dreams with solid foundations. Tigers enjoy this year; it's full of pomp and circumstance. Cats prefer to be homebodies and watch everyone else's activities now. Dragons revel in their own year, and the Snake finds peace. The Horse will be quite satisfied with life, and Goats and Monkeys both have a lot of fun in store. The Rooster may discover the perfect mate this year, while the Dog wants to retreat to a quiet cave alone. Boars stay to their own kind.

Year of the Snake: Rats should use this year for contemplation or writing and just stay away from business. Oxen may have trouble in the home that requires keeping their temper under control. The Tiger feels the need to explore and find adventure, Cats experience a good year, and Dragons just keep shining in the glory of the previous twelve months. This is the Snake's year; they can do anything! The Horse is tempted to give up all for love, but this would be a mistake. For the Goat, an interesting year awaits, and the Monkey hears opportunity's knock. Roosters have some problems in the roost, and Dogs spend this year thinking and discovering new things. The Boar has a great business year, but alas will not find love.

Year of the Horse: This is a year full of debts for the Rat, while the Oxen seem to inherit the Rats' success at business. Tigers want to start something new, and Cats will enjoy themselves quite a bit. Dragons can be very successful this year, some becoming leaders. For the Snake, disappointment in love awaits, and the poor Horse can't find anything whatsoever about his or her own year to relish. Goats have a fun year, Monkeys compete for and get good jobs, Roosters move smoothly ahead, Dogs are restless and irritated, and Boars get organized, though still experience troubles.

Year of the Goat: Rats will begin to recoup this year, while the tables turn on the Oxen. Tigers need to get out of town because trouble awaits. Cats have some disappointments, and even Dragons may find difficulty if they get too involved. Snakes yearn for romance this year, while Horses experience a lot of improvements, and Goats finally discover their potential. The Monkey plots and plans, the Rooster falls into many predicaments, and the poor Dog is totally discouraged. Boars, however, are hopeful, seeing that both their love life and career goals are finally moving ahead.

Year of the Monkey: Rats are now happy and back in balance, while the Oxen continue to have lousy luck. Tigers have lots of energy and ideas, not all of which are sound, while Cats pace themselves quietly. Dragons should not be in the forefront this year or they may find themselves tarnished from the exposure. Snakes use wisdom and learn to cope, while Horses display political savvy. Goats become proverbial wallflowers again, and Monkeys have nothing less than the times of their lives. The Rooster becomes moralistic and pompous, the Dog rushes in where angels fear to tread, and the Boar has a fine year, especially with his or her mate.

Year of the Rooster: Rats continue successfully and can now enjoy a little social breather. The Ox's life gets back on track now, while the Tiger rebels quite loudly. Cats are discontent, Dragons can shine, but only by being cautious, and Snakes have a very hard year. Horses and Boars both achieve success through hard work, while Goats take the year for personal recreation. The Monkey is no longer reveling in his or her victories of the previous year. The Rooster, of course, has everything under control, while the Dog experiences disappointments.

Year of the Dog: Rats need to focus wholly on business now, Oxen have a gloomy year, and Tigers embark on great causes. Meanwhile, Cats are uneasy and take precautions, Dragons can achieve almost anything, and Snakes want to make changes, but refuse to put any energy toward their goals. Horses continue to work for personal pleasure, Goats feel neglected, and Monkeys bide their time until financial constraints end. The Dog has a modestly good year, knowing that effort and service have their own rewards. Boars have a quiet year with steady finances.

Year of the Boar: Rats begin to plan for the future, Oxen come out of the dark clouds, and "lady luck" visits Tigers with a flourish. The Cat regains contented composure, the Dragon's shrewdness provides financial gains, and the Snake tries to roll with this year's punches. Horses have money and can begin to realize their dreams, Goats and Monkeys both experience profits, but Roosters work very hard for little gain. The Dog stays close to home, and rightfully so, while the Boar turns anything and everything into fortunes.

Related Systems: Birth Omens, Day Signs, Medicine Cards

Adaptation: Pictures of these animals could easily be used to create a set of divinatory cards akin to a Tarot deck, with the animal's predominant traits central to interpretive value. For example, the upright Rat might mean financial gains through skill, while reversed, losses.

•ATRAMENTAMANCY
(see Ink)

•AUGURY

An augur is anyone who can foretell the future, prophesize, or read omens and signs. Every culture has had different terms for this person, who was very often a spiritual leader. Among tribal societies, the medicine man or shaman held this position (see *Shamanism*). Among the Aborigine, the augur is called *Mekigar*, and in New Zealand they are known as *Tohunga Makutu*.

The best-known augurs were those in Rome, and they wielded tremendous political clout. They could suspend various affairs by declaring an unfavorable omen. Besides a *littus* (a divining rod and symbol of the augur's art), the Roman augurs were distinguished by a purple striped toga called a *trabea*. They would often be accompanied by a magistrate who observed a particular rite, then helped enforce the augur's message.

Related Systems: Clear Sight, Omen Observation, Oracles, Signs, Shamanism

•AURORA BOREALIS
(see Celestial Omens)

•AUSTROMANCY
(see Wind)

•AUTOMATISM

Automatism is a diverse field of parapsychology commonly associated with mediums. In it, an individual contacts the astral realm in some manner and asks a spirit for a message. This message may be written, as in automatic writing or psychography, drawn, painted, or channeled. The purpose of this procedure is to divine answers regarding a present situation or to foretell the future.

Related Systems: Key, Necromancy, Ouija, Pearl, Pendulums, Table Tipping

Adaptation: The methods recommended for automatism, while normally associated with a temporarily indwelling spirit, also have the capacity to help people tap into their own intuition. Find an artistic medium through which you feel comfortable expressing yourself (clay, paint, music, writing, or whatever). Gather what you need for it around you and begin meditating. Release all your tensions and try not to think of anything other than your question. When feelings or images begin to emerge, express them through your medium. Afterward, look to what you created for answers and insights.

•AX (AXINOMANCY)

Two types of axinomancy predominated. The first was tossing an ax randomly into an open region. The way it landed and how long it stayed upright in the ground became the foundations for interpretation. The second technique, with Hebrew and Greek origins, required that an ax be heated until red hot, then placed on the ground with the sharp edge upward. Three times an agate was placed on the ax's edge. If the stone fell in the same direction all three times it meant treasure was close by. People also used axinomancy to divine the direction in which one should search out a thief or the best location for a child's birth.

Related Systems: Arrows, Binary Divination, Fire Tongs, Knife

Adaptation: Any cutting implement might be substituted for an ax, with proper precautions. Agates are readily available at most stores that sell stones and crystals, including children's science shops.

•BALLS

A ball is used in a child's method of divination by bouncing it against a wall. The number of rebounds foretells either the number of years until something specific happens (like marriage) or the number of children that person will have. By relating this number to a letter of the alphabet, the first or last initial of a future mate can be predicted.

Related Systems: Meteorites (or other counted systems), Moon Scrying, Stones—skipping, Trees—cherry

Adaptation: Use the numerical correspondences given under Numerology instead.

• BAMBOO STICKS

Chim, a Chinese divinatory system practiced in the temples, uses bamboo sticks with numbers or symbols, which may be drawn or cast. There are sixty-four sticks in a cylinder, which is usually shaken until one falls out. Each of these sticks correspond to a specific entry in a book of verse, which a priest reads in answer to the inquiry. If there is any question as to the accuracy of the *Chim*, then *Chiao Pai* may be used to confirm the answer (see *Blocks*).

The favorite time of year for bamboo rod divination is during the Feast of the Hungry Ghosts, which takes place on the fifteenth day of the seventh moon. In this instance, the rod that the querent draws corresponds to an answer of a piece of paper. This paper is burned, and its ashes are added to tea and consumed by the querent. This indicates acceptance of the answer to the question.

In Burma, green bamboo stems are heated until small fibers stand out along the stem's edge. This is eaten by a diviner, believing it will endow him or her with future sight. This ritual technique is known as *Ning wot*.

Related Systems: Casting, Food, Lots, Rods, Wands

Adaptations: A handful of carved twigs, doweling, or even painted "pick-up-sticks" might work well here. The number of sticks in your version may be symbolic or personal. For interpretive meaning, use the instructions for arrow castings, *I Ching* hexagrams, or other sigils (see Appendix B).

• BAY LAUREL (DAPHNOMANCY)

Divination using bay laurel likely originated in Greece where the herb was considered sacred to Apollo. When a bay tree withered in Rome, it was considered a negative portent for the entire community, preceding things like fires and floods (see *Trees*).

One divinatory technique prescribes taking five bay leaves (or branches) and burning them while thinking of a question. If they burn noisily, the answer is "yes." If they smolder silently, the answer is "no." Flames rising up together are a positive sign. Three points on the flame reveal a harmonious conclusion, one point, single-mindedness. Two points indicate either a distraction or the need of aid from friends.

Another tradition suggests crossing two bay leaves under your pillow and sprinkling them with rose water to dream of your future loves.

Related Systems: Botanomancy, Burning, Dreams, Flowers, Herbs, Plants

Adaptations: If your question is about something other than relationships, focus your attention on it while anointing the bay leaves with an appropriate tincture. Examples include a lettuce tincture for financial questions or a lily tincture for questions of truthfulness and sincerity. Then go to sleep and see what answers your dreams bring.

•BEANS

A favorite divination method in Greece used an equal number of black and white beans in a deep vase and a small piece of lead. The querent dropped the lead into the jar and shook it while voicing a question. Then, without looking, the lead was retrieved with a single bean, a white one indicating a positive response.

Another type of bean divination with origins in rural Europe uses three beans. One is left as it is, the second is partially peeled, and the third, totally peeled. These are hidden by a friend on Midsummer's Eve. If you find the unpeeled one first, it portends money. The stripped one predicts poverty, and the partially peeled one, mixed blessings.

Related Systems: Colors, Findings, Food, Lots

Adaptations: Small dry seeds or other uniformly shaped objects can replace beans for either of the aforementioned systems. Use variegated colors to increase the interpretive values.

•BELLS

Bells were used in many ancient religious rituals. They were frequently added to houses of worship as a protective measure. As part of the diviner's art, bells fall into the category of omens and signs. For example, bells are believed to toll of their own accord to warn of impending calamities, especially the death of a notable person in a community. It is also believed that any bell maker who uses stolen metal to make one for religious purposes will see no end of troubles.

Related Systems: Drums, Tambourine

•BELOMANCY

(see *Arrows*)

• BENGE

Benge is a type of poison used for divination in Africa. Usually, a medicine man or shaman administers a nonlethal dosage to an animal. The creature's reactions and fate then determine the question's answer. Because the animal consumes only a small amount of poison, people believe it chooses life or death in service to the spirits.

Related Systems: Animal Omens and Signs, Entrails

• BIBLE

(see Books)

• BIBLIOMANCY

(see Books)

• BINARY DIVINATION

Any type of prognostication that results in a yes-or-no answer uses a binary system. Good examples include coin flipping, bay laurel burning, and pendulum work. Some people include systems under this category that also allow for a "maybe" answer, as with blocks.

Related Systems: Ax, Beans, Blocks, Coconut, Fan, Tea Kettle, Tug of War

• BIRD AUGURY (ORNITHOMANCY)

Ornithomancy is divination by the appearance, number, movement, and cry of birds. The Greeks favored eagles, crows, and vultures for observation, while the Celts preferred crows, eagles, and wrens. Italian diviners sometimes charged minimal fees to querents to have parakeets choose among slips of paper with fortunes written on them.

The Hittite version of ornithomancy was the forerunner to Roman *Auspicium.* In 1330 B.C., over twenty-seven species of birds and their movements in various environments were cataloged for interpretation. A specialist called a Bird Watcher was entrusted with observing the birds, often taking up to three days to note the movements and associated omens.

Roman augurs not only adapted this earlier system, but went on to design a ritual around bird-watching. The augur would sit on a hill in a special robe and circumscribe an area of the sky with his *littus*, or divining staff, which was supposed to have no knots or bends in it to distort revelations. He would then watch this region of the sky for birds to determine a yes-or-no answer. Generally, the appearance of one or two birds was a good sign, while more than that was negative. Alternatively, an odd number of birds signified a "no," and an even number meant "yes."

In Germanic regions the practice of ornithomancy continued well into the Viking age. The most popular birds for augury were crows, eagles, and ravens, all of which were observed by travelers and warriors for omens. For example, a raven met before a battle portended a victory. Ravens also were said to guide travelers, especially sailors, to their destination.

The use of birds for divination in this region probably originated with the overall reverence for these creatures. In the Norse language, the term *galdra* was used to describe both a magical incantation and the cry of birds, implying that birds and magic were linked. Certain archeological studies have uncovered evidence of a cultural belief that wandering souls sometimes appeared as birds and that their cries were communications from the dead.

In Tibet, bird divination was known as *Bya-rog-kyi-skad-brtag-pa*, and it relied predominantly on crows. As messengers of the gods, these creatures were trusted to communicate answers to seekers. The querent would go outside and voice a question. Hearing the cry of a crow in response from the southeast meant an enemy was en route, and from the south, it indicated a visit from a friend. A cry from the west portended great winds, figuratively or literally, and a cry from the southwest was a sign of unexpected profit. In all cases, the time, direction, place, and intensity of the cry was important to the interpretation. Also included in the Tibetan texts are ways to interpret crows encountered on a journey or discovered in a nest.

The Aztecs used bird divination to determine the future location of Mexico City. When an eagle was spied sitting on a cactus holding a snake, this was considered most fortuitous. Stones were laid on that very spot, and the construction of the city begun. The image of an eagle perched on a cactus with a snake in its mouth appears on Mexico's flag, honoring the bird's valuable assistance!

Here are some bird signs and omens collected from various sources:

Blackbird: Blackbirds are considered a good omen.

Bluebird: Bluebirds foretell of happiness.

Chicken: The Romans released chickens to piles of feed (see *Corn; Grain*), and if they scattered the grain or refused to eat, it was regarded as a bad time to engage in battle. Ovid relates that many Roman generals took chickens with them on campaigns to help determine the best possible actions or inactions for each day.

Cock: Meeting a cock portends visitors soon to follow.

Crane: In Zulu tradition, meeting a blue crane forewarns that you will have to sacrifice something or be very brave to endure the days ahead.

Crow: A crow cawing overhead is an ill omen, announcing sickness or tragedy. If you hear a crow cawing on your righthand side, be very cautious in all you do that day. If the first crow you see in spring is flying, a trip is forthcoming. Crows leaving an area is a very bad sign. In Maine, some people believe that seeing one crow prefaces a sad time, that two come before joy, and three before a letter. Zulus have always regarded crows as a very lucky sign, because crows clean up the world.

Cuckoo: According to a tradition that originates in the southern United States, you should listen for the first cuckoo cry in May. If it comes from the north, there will be tragedy; from the south, a good harvest; from the West, luck; and from the east, romance. When you hear a cuckoo on your right side in the spring, the summer months will be good. But if the cuckoo sings before a swallow, this portends a year of sorrow.

Dove: The dove reveals peace and joy for the querent.

Duck: In questions of love, seeing a duck indicates a stable relationship.

Eagle: Seeing an eagle reveals that you will succeed in your hopes through strength and personal ability.

Flock: Seeing a flock of birds on your wedding day is a sign of fertility in European tradition.

Gull: Gulls presage travel according to old Seafaring lore.

Hawk: If a hawk flies over your head, you will experience a victory or a successful outcome from a contest or decision. Low flying hawks foretell that rain will be followed by a rainbow.

Heron: In New Zealand, the heron is sacred and a very welcome sight. For the person spying a heron, it means blessings and luck on the horizon.

High-flying bird: Seeing birds high above after you voice a question to the winds is a very favorable omen.

Hummingbird: A hummingbird bears fidelity, love, or fertility on its wings.

Magpie: In England, one magpie portends an argument, two indicate forthcoming joy, three presage a wedding, four are a sign of forthcoming good news or a birth, five or six precede the arrival of money, and seven flying together indicate secret matters.

Owl: In ancient Greece the owl was Athena's messenger. In New Zealand, seeing an owl flying over the house or hearing one call out three times at night foretold the passing of a loved one. If the bird instead landed on a gate or window ledge, it indicated news was en route. Among the Zulus, the owl is a bird of mystery, and seeing one is a bad omen for anyone other than the medicine man or healer of the tribe.

Peacock: A peacock is an omen of happiness.

Pigeon: A pigeon flying into a house warns of sickness; two, however, predict a wedding. Zulu tribes regard three pigeons as a harbinger of guests; six, of forthcoming romance; and seven, of a letter or other message forthcoming. Pigeons flying in a circle over water foreshadow rain (see *Weather Omens*).

Quail: A quail is generally a bird of good fortune.

Raven: Bird augury was strictly condemned by Mohammed as a pagan practice. Even so, in Islamic culture people still consider the raven a harbinger. When flying in pairs, ravens portend good fortune; alone they warn of trouble. Meeting a raven when embarking on a new project signals that the effort will not succeed.

Red bird: A red bird indicates a wish coming to fulfillment, especially if it flies upward or east.

Robin: Sighting a robin first thing in the morning means visitors are coming that day. A robin nesting near your house indicates you're in for some luck. Should you hear a robin singing in a bush, expect bad weather by the end of the day.

Sparrow: Sparrows signify peace at home, but are a bad omen for lovers. When one nests on your window, expect a trip of some type.

Stork: In Europe, a stork is a very auspicious bird, foretelling the arrival of important news or a significant event.

Swallow: During the Victorian Era, if swallows built their nests high, it was considered the sign of a dry summer. Low nests revealed an excellent season ahead for planting and harvesting. When they fly near the ground, expect rain (see *Weather Omens*).

Woodpecker: Hearing a woodpecker indicates that your efforts will be successful.

Wren: Sighting a wren means your future prospects are improving.

Related Systems: Alectromancy, Animal Omens, Feathers, Insects, Omens, Signs, Weather Omens

Adaptation: If you live in a region where it is highly unlikely that you would ever see any of these birds in an outdoor setting, consider instances when the bird's image in art or advertising strikes you strongly. Consider both the bird and its placement or surrounding images for interpretive value.

• BIRTH OMENS

One divination method based on birth omens, whose written origins can be traced to Europe, employs a thirty-day cycle beginning at the new moon. Each of the thirty days portends something specific for a child born that day.

Day 1: The child will be lucky and live a long life.

Day 2: The child will thrive.

Day 3: The child will have good fortune thanks to the support of authority figures.

Day 4: The child will have political talent.

Day 5: The child will be vain.

Day 6: The child will have a shorter life span but become an excellent hunter (in a figurative or literal sense).

Day 7: The child will have a troubled life.

Day 8: No birth omen given.

Day 9: The child will have both wealth and honor.

Day 10: The child will travel, tend toward a gypsy spirit, and never be at peace.

Day 11: The child will have a spiritual nature.

Days 12–15: No birth omens given.

Day 16: The child will be unfortunate and ungrateful.

Day 17: The child will tend towards foolishness.

Day 18: The child will be courageous but also face many hardships.

Day 19: The child will have an ill disposition.

Day 20: The child will have difficulty being honest.

Day 21: The child will be quite strong but will grow up selfish and tend to take whatever they want.

Day 22: The child will have a gentle character and be well-loved by all.

Day 23: The child will be temperamental and have the soul of a wanderer.

Day 24: The child will be heroic.

Day 25: The child will meet dangers in life.

Day 26: The child will be rich and esteemed.

Day 27: The child will be sweet.

Day 28: The child will be delightful but may live a rather short life.

Day 29: The child will face hardships but always have good outcomes.

Day 30: The child will exhibit talents in the arts and sciences and will be happy throughout their lives.

Other birth omens, most of which originated in and around England, include:

New moon: Children born at the time of a new moon will experience health and wealth and will always be safe from wolf attacks.

Nighttime: A child born at night will be able to see ghosts and fairies.

Midnight: A child born right at midnight will be filled with intelligence and poetry.

With a caul: A caul is a sign of great fortune and happiness.

On Whitsunday: To be born on Whitsunday is bad luck.

Days of a month: The sixth, ninth, and twelfth of the month are all lucky days on which to be born.

With teeth: Teeth portend selfishness. Among Slavic people, being born with teeth is a sign that the child will grow up to be a sorcerer. In Italy and France, it's considered a wonderful omen.

With one hand open: In some parts of the rural U.S., an open hand is an omen of a generous nature.

On New Year's: A child born on New Year's will bring prosperity to the home (see *Holiday Omens and Signs*).

Twins: In Mesopotamia, twins were a troublesome omen. If both children were male, this meant a natural disaster in the offing. Twin girls represented trouble in the home, and one of each sex portended a battle.

Cesarean section: A child delivered by C-section will be strong and possess the ability to find hidden treasures. This idea originated in Rome with Julius Caesar, purported to be the first person ever successfully delivered this way.

Related Systems: Afterbirth, Amniomancy, Astrology, Day Signs, Moon Signs, Names

•BISBA

Bisba is a fairly modern system of divination that observes the shape, size, and other features of a woman's breast to determine character traits.

Related Systems: Ears, Eyes, Facial Features, Feet, Hands, Moles, Palmistry

•BLOCKS

A system known as *Chiao pai* in China uses two blocks, each of which has one curved side and one flat. A priest tosses the blocks on the ground while the querent poses a question. If both blocks land flat side up, the omen is positive. Both flat sides down is a negative answer, and one of each is a neutral answer. Note, however, that there are some regional variances in interpretation.

Related Systems: Coconut, Lots, Sortilige, Tiles, and most binary divination methods, especially those that are cast

Adaptation: Take two square pieces of wood 3" by 3" by 1/4". Paint the top side of each black and the bottom white. Cast them as above. Pieces of cardboard will also work, but use them indoors so the cardboard doesn't fly away in the wind. Another alternative is homemade bean bags of two different colors of fabric.

•BLOOD

Blood has a long history of ritual use in most early civilizations, including some divinatory practices. In the Middle East, for example, hemomancy entailed scrying a drop or two of blood held in the hand similar to the way it is done with ink. This approach was also used by the Maori of New Zealand (see *Scrying*).

During the Middle Ages, someone experiencing a nose bleed could interpret it either as a warning of bad luck or as a sign that they had unwittingly become the object of the affections of someone of the opposite sex. Much later in history, the Japanese devised a system of determining a person's characteristics by their blood type. This system became quite popular during the 1980s but has since fallen out of favor.

Related Systems: Anthropomonacy, Entrails, Offerings, Omens, Ritual, Signs

•BOARDS

In Tanzania, special divinatory boards called *bao* are used to determine the future. These boards are 3" wide by 8" long, with a groove carved along the length. The diviner fills the groove with water and floats a wooden cylinder in it. Throughout the procedure the diviner chants and calls out the question at hand. The board is tilted back and forth causing the cylinder to slide up and down the length of the groove. As the water spills from the groove, the cylinder eventually stops sliding due to lack of moisture. Its final position in the groove determines the interpretive value.

A similar Zairean system is called *Diwa*.

Related System: Tablets

•BOILING

Some North American Indians believe that if a pot boils over or if the water boils completely away, it is a sign that a hero is in danger. This particular type of sign is considered a "life token" that people can look at to know if a loved one fares well. Other types of life tokens include candles, rings, and plants.

•BONES AND SHELLS (ASTRAGALOMANCY, SCAPULIMANCY, PLASTROMANCY)

The use of bones and shells was very common in ancient divinatory practices. Arabs and Romans placed sheep bones in hot coals and observed the resulting cracks. The Celts had a similar procedure using the shoulder bone of a pig. In some North American tribes, caribou bone was used.

Plastromancy specifically originated in China around 3500 B.C. The general procedure entailed heating a poker or other metal tool, then applying it to the surface of a bone until random cracks appeared on the surface. The length, direction, or pattern of these cracks determined the interpretive value.

It was not until 100 B.C. that precise instructions appeared in written form for scapulimancy, most commonly detailed for use in the Chinese imperial court. By far the most popular medium was a turtle shell, bearing a geometric emblem that figures heavily in Chinese religion and mythology. Sometimes questions were written on the surface first, as if to encourage a more accurate response.

In Japan a similar technique, called *Kiboku*, was developed. It began around the seventh century A.D. and continued in popularity until the mid 1800s. While *Kiboku* sometimes used the shoulder bone of a deer, the Chinese influence on this system can be seen in its predominant use of turtle shells. By far, the best known workers of *Kiboku* were the *Jingikan*, who were religious ministers of all Shinto ceremonies. The rite of *Kiboku* required a special setting for the divination to be effective. Additionally, in the writings of a Shinto scholar named Ban Nobutomo, we discover that turtle shells collected from specific communities were preferred for the *Jingikan's* use.

Generally, the *Kiboku* ritual followed a pattern. First, since the diviner was consulting a specific deity, *Saniwa-no-kami*, they abstained from strong meat and vegetables for seven days prior to consulting the oracle (see *Abstinence*). Second, the *Jingikan* carefully avoided any potential contact with blood, as this would nullify their ability to perform the rite.

The ritual tools consisted of bamboo stalks grown on the *Jingikan* property in the Izu region, cherry twigs approximately 1/4" in diameter, a knife for preparing the bamboo, and a chisel to carve the shape of a symbol in the shell. Using these tools, the *Jingikan* cut the shell into a pentagonal form, then carved an emblem on the back. This symbol, called a *machi*, consisted of a vertical line, *tami*, one line on the bottom right, *kami*, and one line at the top left, *ami*. Following this, the cherry twig was heated until red hot and placed in the crevices, first along the vertical line, then along the two horizontal lines. This was repeated until cracks began to appear. Then the wet bamboo sticks were shaken, sprinkling water across the back of the shell, enhancing the cracking effects. Finally, the *Jingikan* poured ink over the shell to further pronounce the lines for the reader.

Cracks upward, straight, and to the right were considered positive. Cracks downward, left, or crooked were considered negative. This process was still used in the fourteenth century to find a virgin to represent the Emperor at the shrine at Ise, to locate the proper imperial messengers, and even to decide where to plant holy rice.

In addition to the use of bones and shells in creating patterns of cracks for interpretation, bones were also a popular medium for lots. In Greece, diviners cast the knuckle bones of sheep, which may have been the forerunner of modern dice. Zulu tribes used eighteen pieces of bone, thirteen of which bore numbers and the remaining five, symbols. The Bantu used seventy-two bones with symbolic representations for their castings.

Among South African shamans, bones were used singularly or with other symbolic items for a casting. Some used four objects made of bone, ivory, horn, or wood, allowing for sixteen combinations when tossed. Each combination also had an interpretive poem that was recited to the querent (see *Ifa*). Alternatively, each item in this system was part of a pair, the smaller of the two representing the feminine and the larger, the masculine. Tradition recommended casting during the new moon, and no specific instructions were given for interpreting the bones' patterns. It was up to the individual shaman. Here is a list of some of the objects used and their basic interpretive values:

Chicken leg bones: The cupped side of the bone reflected "grasping at straws" or trying to hold on, while the flip side represented strength and power.

Abalone shells: These were for financial questions. The shiny side symbolized prosperity and abundance to come. The rough side indicated forthcoming trouble with money. When both shells landed with the rough side up, one would be advised to hold off on any important decision that could affect finances.

Cowrie shells: These represented a person's wisdom and decision-making capacity. When both of these faced up, the decision was a good one (or a "yes" response). When both faced down, the omen was negative. When one shell's back (looking like an eye) faced up and the other down, the advise was to hold off until you had more information.

Spiral shells: As a symbol of time, the closer together the shells came to rest, the less time was involved in the question at hand. When touching, the matter was supposed to resolve itself within a week.

Chicken wing bones (one large, one small, and one marked): The marked bone represented a person who might not have your best interest at heart. This could also symbolize an obstacle, usually embodied in a person's attitudes and opinions. The other two bones represented people who would somehow affect the outcome of your question.

Pine cone scales: If these touched the other objects in a casting, or separated them, this was a sign to listen closely to your inner guidance. Otherwise, they reflected the achievement (or not) of a goal, the rough sides usually indicated a "rough ride."

Tiger eye stones: These revealed difficulties, sickness, and other troubles that could deter a positive outcome. The other objects that landed adjacent helped provide more specific meaning.

Related Systems: Dice, Pebbles, Rods, Shells, Stones, Wands

Adaptations: Shells found at the beach are fairly safe for the first method in this section, but they should be rinsed off before use. Alternatively, carefully sanded pieces of old china or pottery might be a substitute for bones, which may carry disease.

Note that these traditions and others like them were the forerunners to the modern Thanksgiving tradition of splitting the turkey's wishbone.

• BOOKS (BIBLIOMANCY)

Think of a question, then open a book and read the first sentence to meet your eyes for an answer. The first mention of this appeared in Greece, where Homer's writings were used. This is why the practice of bibliomancy was sometimes called Homeric Lots. In Rome, people preferred Virgil, and in the Middle Ages people opened the Bible to a random page and verse using a golden needle.

Islamic tradition instructs a querent to pray, then randomly open a book three times. The seventh line of the left page is noted all three times, then compared for an answer.

Another version of bibliomancy, called rhapsodomancy, uses random passages of poetry. When using any form of bibliomancy, if the sentence you picked does not make sense, count the number of letters under your finger. An even number of letters indicates a negative response.

As an interesting aside, before books were bound by machine, bibliomancy was called stichomancy, referring to the technique of sewing books together.

Related System: Random Divination

Adaptations: Choose the book so that it is related to the central theme of your question, or use one that you personally consider sacred. For a technological approach, randomly stop a movie in your VCR and listen to the first phrase that's spoken after this point, or turn on a radio and note the first sentence heard. Another option is writing singular words or short phrases on *Rolodex* cards. Spin the *Rolodex* while thinking of your question, then pick one and read your fortune.

• BOTANOMANCY

Botanomancy is a form of divination that employs plants. The plant may be employed in numerous ways: by placing it under a pillow to invoke a prophetic dream; by making a pendulum with it; by floating it in water and observing its movement; by observing the growth of several plants at the same time; by picking a random flower or plant and interpreting its meaning; by burning parts of a plant and observing the flames; and by observing the first blossom of a specific plant in spring (or on a Holiday) for a specific portent.

This type of divination originated with our ancestors who worshipped the spirits in nature. It should be noted that certain plants, like peyote in Mexico, became sacred mind-altering substances ingested during divination rituals (see *Intoxicants*).

Related Systems: Bay Laurel, Burning, Fern Stalk, Fig Leaf, Flowers, Grass, Herbs, Leaves, Plantain, Plants, Rose, Trees, Victorian Flower Oracle

• BOW

To obtain answers to questions, Siberians listened to the sound made by a bow string as the tension was changed. Alternative uses for a bow included looking down the length of a bow string into a fire and scrying, and balancing the bow at its center point and observing its swing.

Related Systems: Ax, Fire, Scrying

Adaptation: Any stringed musical instrument might replace the bow. In this case, think of your question, then randomly pluck the string. If the sound is long and full, it indicates a positive answer. A short, interrupted, or sour note is a negative response.

• BOWLS OR DISHES (LECANOMANCY)

The ritual of lecanomancy often entailed pouring water, a combination of oil and water, or water and flour (aleuromancy) into a special bowl or dish, so that the mixture formed specific patterns. There were six tablets found in the Akkadian language of Babylonia describing this technique and its interpretations. For example, the oil might split into two parts: if you were asking about war, this meant your camp would be divided; if you were inquiring about someone's health, this meant a difficult recovery. If the flour formed the shape of a lion on the east side of the bowl, it meant a spirit was possessing or influencing a situation in a negative manner.

A different type of bowl divination is called chalcomancy. This system entails striking brass or copper bowls and listening to the sounds. More than likely, this procedure is Tibetan in origin, due to the use of similar bowls for meditative purposes in this region.

A third version of lecanomancy required the querent to fill three bowls with three types of liquid—one to represent favorable conditions, one unfavorable, and one uncertain. With closed eyes, a question was asked. After the eyes were opened, the container with liquid that was rippling or moving in a clockwise direction indicated the answer. If none, then no answer was presently available.

Related Systems: Flour, Ink, Oil, Wax (for the first method). Bird Augury (cries), Earth (noises), and other auditory systems (for the second).

Adaptations: Try using oil tinted with one or more hues of food coloring, different shades of wax, or rice that has been dyed instead of plain oil. In terms of the dish used, choose pottery or earthenware, both of which are more natural. Keep in mind, a bowl with a smooth inner surface allows for easier scrying.

• BREAD (ALPHITOMANCY)

Bread, a primary food substance in many cultures, has been valued and honored. Consequently, it was often used for divination. Here are some examples:

- If bread tossed into a well floats, the weather at sea will be calm.

- Bread that falls buttered side down foretells of hungry guests that will soon be arriving (see *Falling*).

- "Blessed" bread, often prepared from wheat or barley, was used during the Middle Ages to divine the guilt or innocence of an accused. If the accused could swallow the bread without choking, he or she was released. Sometimes communion bread was used instead, being symbolic of sacredness (see *Ordeal*).

- In Greece, *Vasilopitta* containing twelve coins is often baked for the New Year's celebration. If someone finds a coin in a piece, it's a sign of very good luck for the coming year (see *Food, Holiday Omens and Signs*).

- In Italy, if two loaves of bread are joined together during baking, this indicates a wedding in the near future for some member of the baker's family.

- If you accidentally cut bread unevenly, you're to watch your speech for the rest of the day lest you tell white lies.

- In Russia, having a loaf of bread crumble in your hands while serving it foretells arguments.

Related Systems: Cheese, Food, Wine

Adaptation: Think of a question while baking a loaf of bread. Focus your attention on the question during the entire preparation process. If the bread rises evenly, the omen is a positive one. If it rises unevenly, expect mixed results. If the bread falls, this is a negative omen.

• BREAKAGE

Most people lament the breaking of a glass, plate, or similar item, but apparently our ancestors found a way to take advantage of it by using random breakage as a type of augury. Examples include:

- If you break two dishes in one day, you might as well break a third as it will happen anyway.

- Breaking two eggs is a good omen for love, but breaking one is a sign to be careful all day (see *Eggs*).

- If a needle breaks in two while sewing a garment, it brings improved fortune to the person who wears it (Victorian Era). If it breaks in three, a marriage offer is forthcoming, and if it breaks in a machine, you will soon receive news from afar (see *Clothing*, *Needles*).

- If you break a bottle, it brings bad luck, but not so much as breaking a mirror (England).

- Breaking green glass portends a forthcoming disappointment; breaking red glass precedes trouble and anxiety.

- Breaking one side of a pair of scissors predicts a quarrel in the home.

- In Japan, breaking chopsticks is a very bad omen.

Related Systems: Random Divination, Spontaneous Divination

Adaptation: The next time you break something when you were thinking about a specific situation, look at the pattern the breakage created before cleaning it up to see if any messages lie there for you.

• BROOCH

In the Estonian epic, *Kalevipoeg*, we find an example of divination that used a brooch, a thread, and an alder beetle. The brooch was suspended on the thread while the alder beetle's flight was observed. If the beetle moved to the south, it was a favorable omen. The brooch and thread were probably a type of empowering tool that guided the insect or gained its aid.

Related Systems: Bird Augury, Insects

•BULLS

The Celts used a divinatory system called *Tarbfeis* (Bull Feast) as a means of obtaining name of a future king. A bull was ritually sacrificed to the gods. Afterwards, the diviner ate some of its meat, drank some of its blood, and went to sleep wrapped in the bull's hide. This was said to bring prophetic dreams.

Alternatively, a white bull was used at winter solstice, but only the meat was eaten. The diviner then slept or went into a deep trance, after covering his or her left eye with the right hand, and the right eye with the left hand. Holy people nearby would chant as the diviner slept to encourage prognosticative dreams. This method was known as *Imbas forosnai*. When bulls were not available, an ox was considered a suitable substitute in both methods.

Related Systems: Animal Omens, Calfskin, Entrails

Adaptations: It would be unseemly for the modern diviner to undertake such a ritual. However, seeking out prophetic dreams holds merit. One might substitute a small glass of red wine for the blood, using it as both a libation and ritual beverage. Invocations and chanting can help focus the energy. A leather or suede jacket from a secondhand shop might suffice as a substitute for the skin. And since the ancients ritually cleansed, purified, and perfumed the sacrificial creature before use, you might take time before going to sleep to bathe and anoint yourself with psychically enhancing oil, like peppermint.

•BURNINGS

Many divination systems give instructions to burn specific items and watch the results for omens. For example, a European system recommended saving mistletoe after Yule and burning it. If it crackled, it revealed a bad temper hindering the querent's goal. If the flame was steady, faithfulness surrounded the querent. In another similar method, the querent tossed pounded peas on a fire. If the flames rose up quickly, the response was positive.

Another illustration originated with the Druids. On the night before Beltane (April 30), they would burn green oak, dried oak, and agaric together to divine if all present were innocent of crimes such as theft and adultery. If the flame blazed high, it indicated the purity of all assembled.

Related Systems: Bay Laurel, Botanomancy, Candles, Fires, Food, Hair, Herbs, Plants, Smoke, Torches

Adaptation: This system is fairly functional as stands, except that I would recommend burning an item that is earth-friendly, and one that somehow represents your question. If using paper, make sure to write your question on it, or draw a representative symbol of the matter at hand for improved results. Make sure to observe the shapes in the fire and the smoke's movements for added interpretive values.

•BUTTER LAMPS

Known in Tibet as *Sman-gsal-mar-me-brtag-pa-ldep*, butter lamp divination was first discovered in a cave by Lama Sangye Lingpa in 1364. Its instructions and interpretations are very precise and detailed. The diviner works on the eighth or tenth of the month, or at a full or half moon. The procedure begins with a sliver of wood taken from a yew-leafed fir tree, which is wrapped in cloth to act like a wick. The make-shift wick is placed in a lamp surrounded with butter and ignited. The diviner then studies the movement of the flame.

The interpretations of the flame movement are very lengthy as is customary in Tibetan divinations, but here are a few examples:

- If the flame is pale like clear fruit, there are problems being caused in your life by karma.

- If there is black smoke, your vision is obscured and you may not be seeing the truth.

- If the flame is likened to a crescent moon, peace and tranquillity will be yours.

- If there is a pleasant smell to the smoke, it is a sign of success.

- Long-burning flames signify good fortune.

- Flames shaped like banners mean the attainment of a goal.

- If the flame is dark red and black, there are emotional conflicts in your current situation.

- If the flame is ugly, it means ill health and loss of energy.

- If the fire sparks frequently, someone is wishing you evil.

Related Systems: Candles, Fire, Lamps, Torches, Wax, Wicks

Adaptation: Replace the butter lamp with a simple oil lamp.

•CABBAGES

Divination using cabbage is an offshoot of botanomancy. While thinking about your future, randomly pick a cabbage stalk at midnight on Halloween. Its appearance predicts how things will fare and possibly reveals characteristics about a future mate. For example, a straight, sturdy stalk could reveal that your future health looks good or that your mate will be strong and truthful. Additionally, finding two shoots on a single root is an omen of good luck.

Related Systems: Botanomancy, Food, Plantain

Adaptation: Apply this basic technique to any vegetable like carrots or turnips. Small carrots may be grown in window boxes if you don't have a yard. This edible tool will naturally be charged with energy from the sun and the moon.

•CALFSKINS

Sakhas shamans smeared an oval ring of calfskin with fat. Then they held it near a fire until the fat melted and glowed. This was to awaken the spirit within the skin, which represented the hunt. Afterward, the shaman tossed the skin in the air. If it landed face upward, it predicted a successful hunt.

Related Systems: All binary systems

Adaptation: Cover any flame-resistant surface with wax (rather than fat), and think of a question related to finding or obtaining something specific. Hold the wax-coated tool near a source of heat until the wax begins to melt, then toss it in the air. If it lands wax side up, the omen is positive. The cooled wax images can also be scried for further insight.

•CANDLES (LYCHNOMANCY)

There are numerous forms of candle divination, most of which developed with their common household use. In Ireland, people chose a specifically colored candle for its significance to a question; green for money, red for love, and yellow for business. Additionally, candle divination has traditionally been performed at midnight during the time of a waxing or full moon.

One basic procedure requires lighting a candle in a room far away from drafts and observing its movements. Some standard forecasts are:

• If the candle will not light or a halo forms around the flame, a storm is on the horizon (see *Weather Omens*). This may be an emotional storm, too.

- If the candle burns dimly, hold off on any sudden decisions; your timing is bad.

- A bright flame is a positive omen.

- A moving candle flame portends change.

- Sparks in the wick represent forthcoming news.

- Candle wax dripping down the left side is a negative omen, especially for love.

In Europe, another type of candle ritual is performed on New Year's or Halloween. To learn what the coming year holds, you light a candle during either celebration and observe its flame. A brilliant, long flame indicates luck. Dim light is a negative omen, and a candle that goes out indicates very bad news forthcoming, possibly even death.

A third method from the Victorian Era instructed a young woman to light a candle at midnight on Halloween, then look into a mirror. She would then ask, "Who will I marry?" If the candle stayed lit, and the spirit's will was favorable, the young girl would see the image of her future mate peering over her left shoulder in the mirror. This was a method for hopeful young men, too!

Related Systems: Burning, Butter Lamps, Fire, Scrying, Smoke Torches, Wax, Wicks

Adaptation: Other color correspondences for candles include: orange for questions of friendship or a harvest that comes from hard work; yellow for those involving the mind and creativity; blue for queries centering about achieving peace or joy; and purple for spiritual questions. Carve a symbol of your question into the candle, and anoint it with symbolic aromatic oils. This further accentuates the theme of your question and improves the accuracy of the response.

•CAPNOMANCY

(see Smoke)

•CARDS (CARTOMANCY)

The most commonly recognized form of cartomancy is the Tarot, which is covered in its own section due to the complexity of the system. However, a regular deck of fifty-two playing cards may be used for divination, too. They are descendants of the Tarot, and, therefore, playing card divination is considered a type of geomantic lot casting. Each suit has a specific focus in the reading: the spades relating to problems and challenges, clubs to business and other pragmatic matters, hearts to matters "of the heart," and diamonds to money and finances. One may use traditional Tarot or rune configurations for laying out playing cards for a reading.

One note of caution: Because these are common gaming devices, you will need to remember to treat with respect the set of cards you use for divination. Consider keeping a separate deck just for this purpose.

Typical representations follow. Note that reversed cards—if there is a differentiation—indicate a lessening of the interpretive value, or a contrary meaning, depending on adjacent cards.

Clubs

Ace: Happiness and prosperity

King: A person who is forthright, open minded, and kind

Queen: A romantic person with charitable tendencies

Jack: A young person who is bright, energetic, and giving

Ten: Improved finances or success

Nine: Unanticipated gain or gifts

Eight: Attention or affection from another that leads to prosperity

Seven: Recovery of some type

Six: Abundance and/or a victory

Five: Social occasions or unexpected news

Four: A setback or disappointment

Three: A fight followed by some type of proposal that brings resolution

Two: The need to be frugal and pinch pennies

Hearts

Ace: Happy missives, especially in love

King: A liberal person

Queen: A gentle, kind person of great attractiveness

Jack: A young person fond of risk and pleasure

Ten: Overcoming the odds; victory

Nine: Fulfillment of personal hopes

Eight: Affection

Seven: Good relationships; peacefulness within

Six: Unexpected turn for the better

Five: Advice from a respected person

Four: Change in residence or work

Three: Troubles ahead

Two: Prosperity, victory, or new friends

Diamonds

Ace: Enjoyment of sports and the outdoors; forthcoming news

King: A temperamental, shrewd, and dangerous person

Queen: Someone who loves gossip

Jack: An unfaithful and deceitful young person

Ten: Change in residence or other movement

Nine: Delays and frustrating nuisances

Eight: Passion and romance

Seven: The need to get back to nature to find peace

Six: Healing or reconciliation

Five: Business success

Four: Forthcoming improvements

Three: Trouble in relationships; legal difficulties

Two: New or refreshed love

Spades

Ace: General pleasures

King: A person who is envious and dishonest

Queen: A loving, single person

Jack: An ill-mannered person who plots mischief

Ten: Bad news followed by sadness

Nine: Worse news, sometimes death

Eight: Very bad luck; plans undone; illness

Seven: Minor troubles and misunderstanding

Six: Reversals

Five: Support from friends during difficult times

Four: Business trouble; struggling relationships

Three: Sadness or separation

Two: Dishonesty, fraud, or treachery

Adjacent Matching Cards

Four Aces: Danger of failure; the need to be wary

Three Aces: Good news

Two Aces: Someone plotting against you

Four Kings: Success, honor, and rewards

Three Kings: Important council or business dealings

Two Kings: Partnership

Four Queens: A social gathering

Three Queens: An unusual phone call

Two Queens: Seeing a friend; a reunion

Four Jacks: A party or group of young people

Three Jacks: Untrue friends

Two Jacks: Malice and hidden agendas

Four Tens: Your efforts yielding success

Three Tens: Immoral or improper behavior

Two Tens: A new job or trade

Four Nines: A surprise

Three Nines: Good health and luck

Two Nines: Small gains

Four Eights: A trip, but a brief one

Three Eights: Wishful thinking about a relationship

Two Eights: A brief tryst

Four Sevens: Trouble, obstacles, and holdups

Three Sevens: Illness

Two Sevens: Fun and frivolity

Related Systems: Dominoes, Mah Jongg, Tarot

Adaptations: Make your own symbolic cards from coupons, hand drawings on three-by-five cards, or adapt those that exist in games like *Monopoly*.

Literally hundreds of divinatory systems currently on the market owe their origins to traditional cartomancy. Among them we find the *Angel Power Cards*, with sixty meditative cards; *Pandora Cards*, a set of fifty-six cards with challenges and solutions; *Bach's Flower Cards* that relate messages from one of seventy-seven floral themes; *The Olympus Self-Discovery Cards* based on Greek archetypes; *Sacred Path Cards* to aid with the quest for personal wholeness; and *Gypsy Fortunetelling Cards* with twenty-five illustrations that create fifty complete pictures for interpretation. Many of these systems are available through U.S. Games Systems, Harper Collins, or Aquarian Press.

• CASTINGS

A cast system is one in which the querent or diviner randomly tosses objects onto a surface. The resulting pattern of the objects becomes the basis for interpreting the cast, using any number of guides. For example, if objects are cast onto a cloth, the cloth may have designs at designated locations. An item landing near, or on, one of those designs reveals some portent with regard to the question. Or a seer may simply use the configuration of the entire throw as a representation, similar to finding symbolic images in tea leaf readings.

Related Systems: Blocks, Bones, Coconut, Nuts, Rods, Runes, Seeds, Stones, Wands

Adaptations: Lots of household items work in a cast system, including different-colored dried beans, buttons, pencils, pick-up sticks, seeds, nuts and bolts, and rice.

•CATS (FELIDOMANCY)

Felidomancy is divination based on the behavior and actions of cats. This type of omen reading may have originated in Egypt where the cat was venerated as the Goddess Bast. Most of the superstitions below, however, originated in Europe or rural America:

Cat washing its face: Visitors will soon arrive.

Cat washing behind its ear: A sign of rain or high humidity (see *Weather Omens*).

Cat washing itself in the doorway: A visit from clergy is forthcoming.

Walking on a cat's tail: Bad luck will follow.

Cat abandoning house: A very negative omen (you might want to move too).

Stray cat coming into home: A very good sign; money follows this creature.

Seeing a calico cat: An omen of good fortune especially for a new endeavor.

Stroking a stray cat: This act of kindness brings fortune.

Black cat crossing a road: The next person passing will have a wish fulfilled.

Cat entering a room right paw first: If you have been thinking of a question, this indicates a positive answer.

Seeing a lioness: In some parts of the world, people regard this as an omen of sterility.

Cat sneezing: Good luck for the house and all that dwell within.

Meowing during travel: A warning of trouble ahead.

Leaping around playfully: Predicts that a gale is coming (see *Weather Omens*).

•CATOPTROMANCY

(see Mirrors)

•CAUSMOMANCY

(see Ash, Fire, Smoke)

•CELESTIAL OMENS

Fortune-telling based on the observation of celestial objects and occurrences was founded on the idea that the heavens could be invoked for guidance or information. The Mesopotamians devised a rather expansive treatise on omens towards the end of the second millennium, filling 107 tablets in all. Many of these omens were celestially derived, including those based on the sun, moon, stars, and eclipses.

Alaskan natives regard the northern lights, or aurora borealis, as joyful spirits, a rather lovely example of celestial omen observation. Anyone seeing them is ensured of good luck the following day. Among Kwakiutl Indians, this phenomenon presages the death of an important figure in the community. The Scots use the northern lights to predict weather. An aurora appearing low in the sky means that the weather patterns will stay consistent, while one up high indicates storms (see *Weather Omens*).

Related Systems: Astrology, Comets, Meteorites, Moon, Stars, Sun

•CELTIC TREE ORACLE

(see *Oghams, Trees*)

•CEPHALOMANCY

(see *Donkey*)

•CERAUNOSCOPY

(see *Wind*)

•CEROMANCY, CARROMANCY, CEROSCOPY

(see *Wax*)

•CHAINS

In West African Yoruba tradition, shamans space eight tortoise shell disks along a chain for divination. The shaman holds the chain at its center point, then lowers it to the ground and observes the movement of the disks to render an interpretation.

•CHALCOMANCY

(see *Bowls*)

• CHANNELING

(see Oracles/Mediums/Prophets)

• CHANTING

Chanting is a common religious activity in many cultures, specifically as a means to achieve heightened states of awareness within which one can gather and relate divinatory information. One example, *Tenm Laida*, originated in Celtic regions as part of elaborate prophetic rituals. The shaman or seer began the ritual by chewing a piece of raw meat, then chanted to prepare spiritually for the journey into inner realms. If this ritual failed, no readings could be enacted that day.

Among Norse and Germanic peoples, runes were sometimes uttered, chanted, or sung by a seer to help provide the right oracular resonance. Once the power of the rune song flowed through the diviner, he or she could provide the requested insights (see *Runes*).

Related Systems: Dance, Drums, Ifa, Ritual, Singing

Adaptation: The modern diviner can use chanting as a type of sacred song with regularly repeated phrases. If you choose chanting as a meditative aid, always be sure to work in a language you understand completely, repeating words or phrases that have meaning to your Path.

• CHEESE (TIRONMANCY)

Tironmancy may have originated in Greece or Rome, where cheese was often used in important community rituals, like marriage. Basically, it requires a querent or diviner to observe milk as it curdles and look for symbols in the final formation.

Alternatively, a block of cheese was sliced and the holes counted to determine how the days or weeks ahead would fare. An even number of holes meant favorable times. The larger the holes in the cheese, the more momentous were the events in store for the querent.

Related System: Food

Adaptation: Swiss cheese anyone? Also look at the patterns formed by holes in the cheese to see if they create a discernible image.

• CHIAO PAI

(see Blocks)

• CHIM

(see Bamboo Sticks)

• CHIN

(see Facial Features, Physiognomy)

• CHIROGNOMY, CHIROMANCY

(see Hands, Palmistry)

• CHRESOMANCY

Chresomancy bases predictions on the sounds made by a person in a fit. It is likely connected to ecstatic dance.

Related Systems: Dance or Movement, Enlightened Manifestation, Gyromancy

• CLEAROMANCY

(see Lots)

• CLEAR SIGHT (CLAIRAUDIENCE)

> *"Who blind, could ev'rything foresee; who dumb could ev'rything foretell."*
>
> —Charles Churchill

Clear sight is the ability to discern the answer to a problem or foretell the future without the aid of tools. Sometimes called second sight, people who have this gift often fear its accuracy. The Scottish believe that individuals who lead simple lives and eat sound diets will exhibit this talent more readily than others. For such people, the signs of what's to come appear in inexplicable sensual occurrences. For example, one person might smell rotting fish just before something bad happens, even though there are no dead fish around. Alternatively, a seer might envision a shroud around a person who is close to death.

In New Zealand, a person gifted with clear sight is called *matakite*. The Maori say that such a person sees the consequences of actions, specifically those that break the laws of sacredness. Upon receiving a vision, the *matakite* sometimes dances to obtain further information on how to make proper appeasement to the offended higher powers.

In Trinidad, a person gifted with the sight is called a *lookman*. This individual can see illnesses, cures, future obstacles, calamities, and ways to ensure the success of an upcoming trip or a new endeavor. Sometimes the *lookman* interprets dreams and makes protective charms like a shaman. In Trinidad, it is a paid vocation.

The Celts called this divinatory ability *Deuchainn*, meaning first sight; however, the approach was slightly different. A seer might think of a question and walk with eyes closed. When he or she stopped and opened them, the first thing gazed upon provided a symbolic or literal answer (see *Frith*).

Related Systems: Direct Revelation; Oracles, Mediums, Prophets

Adaptation: Most people with clear sight feel the gift is transmitted through family lines. So if your Aunt Sadie or Uncle Bill had an unnerving knack for knowing what would happen, you may find yourself experiencing clear sight once you open your spiritual vision.

• CLEDONISM

Cledonism is a type of random divination that takes accidentally overheard words and phrases as omens and portents.

Related Systems: Random Divination, Speaking, Spontaneous Divination

• CLERDOMANCY

(see Keys)

• CLOTH

The following cloth-based system may have originated in Rome. Begin with seven scraps of equal-sized, different-colored fabric (seven is the number of completion). Put these in a box while thinking of a general question. Close your eyes and choose your fortune. To diversify the response, place one piece of cloth to your left for negative influences, and one on your right for positive ones. Here are some potential positive and negative interpretive values for the colors:

Red: Success, energy, love, victory; anger, hostility

Yellow: Creativity and mental keenness; cowardice or fear

Blue: Health, happiness, and peace; melancholy or depression

Green: Abundance in literal or figurative form; jealousy

Black: Rest and retreat; sadness, troubles, or a waiting period

Orange: Abundance and friendship; numerous trifling problems

Gray: Balance; delay and uncertainty or lack of self-assurance

Purple: Improvements in position and increased spiritual focus; bruised feelings or ego

White: Truce, pure intentions; sickness or terror

Related Systems: Color, Eggs, Lots, Paper

Modern Alternatives: This system is fine as is, but if you do not have fabric, try squares of paper instead. To remember the symbolic values of the colors, mark the paper with personally meaningful emblems. For example, paint a golden ladder on the purple paper representing the "ladder of success."

•CLOTHING

Numerous superstitions exist about wearing specific types of apparel on specific days, such as new clothes on Easter for luck. An outgrowth of this is using the observation of a person's clothes as a type of prognostication in itself. For example, during the Rice Planting Ceremony in Siam (around April 20), people watched a minister's robes for weather omens (see *Weather Omens*). If the robe reached to the ankle, the portended year would be dry. A knee-length robe indicated rain or flooding, and a midlength robe forecast a good year for crops.

Related Systems: Apron, Color, Dressing, Shoes

Adaptation: Building on the old saying that "clothes make the man," consider using clothing as a way of improving your future fate by allowing your choices of colors and style to reflect your goals.

•CLOUDS (AEROMANCY, NEPHELOMANCY)

In China, philosophers taught that clouds follow specific universal patterns. These patterns could be observed and interpreted to answer questions or to determine what was happening elsewhere in the world. During certain times of the year, the clouds also revealed the future. For example, around December 20 (Winter Solstice), red clouds portended a year of drought, black clouds indicated floods, yellow ones presaged plenty, and white clouds foretold of war. This particular system was integrated into what became geomancy around A.D. 220.

Another type of cloud divination, known specifically as nephelomancy, bases its predictions on the appearance of clouds rather than their movements. Among Druids this was called *neladoracht*, and the technique was performed at night on a hillside, using moonlight for illumination.

Related Systems: Aeromancy, Celestial Omens, Geomancy, Moon, Sun

Adaptation: Go outside on a day when the sky is interspersed with clouds. Close your eyes and visualize your question as specifically as possible, directing your mental image toward the sky. Upon opening your eyes, look at the first cloud that catches your attention for a specific shape or image. This will indicate the answer to your question in literal or symbolic form.

•COAL

A relatively modern divination technique prescribed that a querent bury a piece of coal under a mugwort or plantain plant for the three days of a full moon. Afterward, it was removed and put under the querent's pillow to bring prophetic dreams. This method probably became most popular when coal was readily used as a source of heat and power. That was also a time when finding a stray piece of coal was a "lucky" omen (see *Findings*).

Related Systems: Botanomancy, Dreams, Egg, Food, Gems, Lemon

•COCONUTS

A popular system for divination among Africans and Cubans who practice Santeria uses four pieces of coconut shell dropped to the ground from a querent's hand. If all four sides land white side up, this is an affirmative answer. Three light sides portend good luck, two light sides indicate success and achievement, one light side indicates misfortune, and all dark is a negative answer.

In Polynesian cultures, a whole coconut is spun on the ground to determine the identity of a thief. The small, somewhat pointy end of the coconut becomes the pointer.

Related Systems: Blocks, Lots

Adaptation: For the second technique, an old-fashioned game of spin the bottle might work. Place letters or symbols in a circle around the bottle, and voice your question while you spin it. For binary questions, three spins should confirm the results, and with more complex questions, seven is good, being the number of completion.

• COFFEE GROUNDS

Reading patterns in coffee grounds for pictorial representations is a method of divination strongly related to the art of tea leaf reading. It probably evolved from it sometime in the eighteenth century, when coffee began to find popular acceptance in Italy. The Arabs may have also had a system of coffee ground divination, based on their early reverence for this beverage and its use in many household rituals.

To begin a reading, you sprinkle coffee grounds into a white, damp cup. Shake the cup so the grounds disperse, then turn it over and give it a light tap to remove any excess. The patterns within the grounds stuck to the side of the cup provide interpretive values. Symbols that appear close to the rim are timely, while those at the bottom of the cup lie in the future or are less significant.

A few patterns that might appear are listed below with common interpretations. For more ideas look through Appendix B, Symbols and Pictographs.

Anchor: Renewed hope; success in business. If at the bottom of the cup, it signifies constant love, but if clouded, it suggests variableness.

Bird: Trouble will be clearing if the bird is in an uncluttered area of the cup. If "flying" in an area thick with grounds, a journey will be successful.

Cross: Adversity and hardships. If near the rim, this time of difficulty is coming to an end.

Dog: Faithful friends, especially when it appears at the rim of the cup. Toward the bottom, be careful; jealousy may taint this friendship.

Flower: Success in an art or science, or the discovery of a talent for either.

House: A forthcoming blessing. A change for the better when near the rim. At the bottom, an indication that vigilance will be the key to your victory.

Leaf or clover shape: A very lucky omen, especially when near the rim. Clouds nearby, however, speak of luck that is tainted by difficult circumstances.

Letter: The arrival of news. With dots nearby, the news relates to financial matters.

Lily: Near the rim, a sign of true virtue. On the side opposite the querent, a warning of faithlessness.

Moon: Honor. At the bottom of the cup, good luck. If it appears where the grounds are thick, it is a sign of momentary sadness with positive outcomes.

Mountain: Favor with people in authority.

Rings: Cycles or a marriage. Any letters near a ring predict the initials of one's love. Rings that are clear in the center speak of very good relationships, while clouded ones warn of deceit. At the bottom of the cup, a ring suggests separation from a person or object desired.

Roads (straight or windy lines): Movement and change. Those dotted with grounds also suggest that money is coming. Thick or smudged lines warn of reversals.

Serpent: Falsehood. If at the rim of the cup, the querent will overcome this problem through diligence.

Star: Happiness and long life awaits the querent. Several stars indicate the presence of children in whom one has great pride. Note that these "children" can be metaphoric in nature, such as a beloved project.

Tree: Personal health. Several trees portend the fulfillment of a wish.

Related Systems: Ink, Scrying, Tea Leaf Reading, Wine, Wax

Adaptations: Any granulated substance can be substituted if you don't drink coffee. For example, try cornmeal or rice powder, swirling it in a damp cup, clearing the loose matter, then interpreting the remaining patterns. Cornmeal is very suited to financial questions, and rice powder works well for queries about providence and health.

• COINS

Flipping coins is a type of lot casting that originated in Rome, where people used coins to determine the outcome of minor disputes. The Emperor was considered a type of god, thus his image on one side of the coin decided the outcome of the flip. The generally accepted procedure is flipping the coin with one's right hand, and placing it on the left to read the results.

Related Systems: Any binary system, *I Ching* (coin method)

Adaptations: Children's tiddlywinks work well when a coin is not available. Just color one side with indelible marker before flipping to indicate its value. Add other two-sided items with various colors or emblems to increase potential interpretations.

•COLORS (CHROMATOMANCY)

Since ancient times, humankind has been influenced by color. Everyone from healers to philosophers have used color symbolism, trying to tap the sympathetic power that colors have within the human mind. Color consultation and therapies have developed into professions to help us wear flattering, effective, life-enhancing, healthy hues!

In terms of color in divination methods, most forms use colors either as a refinement of interpretive value, or as a symbolic aid. For example, we can observe and interpret the color(s) an individual prefers as an indicator of personality. Correspondences include:

Red: Grit. Someone with an aggressive personality and possibly a flaring anger. In an aura, this reveals nervousness and egocentrism.

Pink: Naiveté. Someone with youthful outlooks.

Yellow: Friendliness. A healthy person who enjoys learning and always strives for self-betterment. These people are socializers, filled with upbeat energy.

Purple: Introspection. Someone who seeks the answers to life's questions and is especially curious about metaphysical subjects. Purple can also be the color of someone who is ambitious and expects much from themselves and others.

Orange: Community orientation. A person of character and confidence. They are also nature lovers and may have a tendency to procrastinate.

Blue: Focus. A deep thinker with creativity and artistic ability who makes consistent progress. Darker blue can reveal moodiness or musical talent.

Green: Peacefulness. A soothing, quiet person. This person naturally attracts others with their compassion. Yellowish-green, however, may reveal deceit or jealous tendencies.

Brown: Practicality. A very grounded person who works hard but progresses slowly. People wearing this color frequently tend to have critical natures.

Black: Perceptiveness. An intuitive, insightful person who exhibits dignity, drive, and self-control.

White: Spirituality. A person who tries to keep everything in symmetry. Creamy tones reveal spirituality balanced with practical, earthy outlooks.

During the late 1940s, an experiment that was developed in Switzerland used these correspondences in testing people's stress levels. The process could easily be adapted for divination. For this, the subject or querent arranges a group of colored squares in order of personal preference, or for divinatory purposes, by intuitive insight. The resulting sequence of colors reveal the answer to the question at hand. For example, if the question related to a love affair, and the color choices began with white, followed by green and pink, the interpretive value might be that the relationship is balanced and peaceful but with some undertones of innocence and potential blindness.

The second type of color divination relates to "found" items. Both the item and its color can hold hidden meanings. One example of this comes from the Seneca tradition. The elders teach that a gift of nature, such as a found feather, shell, stone, or flower, can provide direction if you interpret its color. The correspondences they give include:

Orange: Learn the truth; relate to all aspects of the situation; kinship.

Gray: Honor the truth; use your knowledge and develop yourself.

Brown: Accept the truth; balance your ego, use determination, and be responsible.

Pastels: See the truth; find your inner potential; watch for prophetic dreams.

Black: Hear the truth; strive for personal wholeness and harmony.

Red: Speak the truth; use faith and trust in innocence.

Yellow: Love the truth and use compassion.

Blue: Serve the truth; trust intuition and create.

Green: Live the truth; be dependable and use compassion.

Pink: Work for truth; give service to others and aid the whole.

White/Crystal: Walk in truth; learn to give and receive and use charisma.

Purple: Be thankful for truth; use your talents and strive for healing.

Related Systems: Cloth, Handwriting (ink), Paper

Adaptation: I see tremendous potential in this last system for creating a divining set from natural items that you find. You will need to gather one item of each color and place them in a bag. When you have a question, one of the tokens may be drawn out, or the whole set can be cast and interpreted according to the patterns they create.

Mari Louise Lacy created a divinatory method using twenty-eight color keys, a descriptive book, and accompanying chart. This is available through Aquarian Press.

•COMETS

The Roman naturalist Pliny wrote extensively about comets and their meaning. For example, he believed a comet bearing two flutelike tails portended a global upswing in artistic achievement. In Tyrol, local diviners agreed and stated further that a white comet predicted a time of peace and changes in human affairs. These two positive interpretations were the minority, however. Most cultural groups felt comets predicted disasters. The Chinese, for example, felt that comets preceded a hurricane.

Related Systems: Astrology, Celestial Omens, Meteors, Moon, Stars, Sun

•CORN

In Mexico, querents place thirty corn kernels in a bowl and then randomly scoop out a handful while pondering their question. The handful is then separated into groups of four. If there is an even number of piles and leftover kernels, the omen is favorable. An odd number of piles and leftovers indicates a negative response, and a mixed outcome reveals something hidden or unknown.

Alternatively, the querent may have gone before an image of the god Quetzalcoatl and scattered the seeds before Him. If they landed evenly spaced out, the god's blessing was assured, and the situation in question would work out fine. This particular method was used most frequently to diagnose the duration or outcome of a sickness. If you use this personally, I suggest substituting a divine figure appropriate to your beliefs.

Related Systems: Beans, Grains, Lots, Raisins, Rooster, Seeds

Adaptations: Use any type of dry seeds, like pumpkin, sunflower, or popcorn kernels (see *Popcorn*).

•COSCINOMANCY

Coscinomancy is a very old type of divination that used a sieve, tongs, and shears. It involved the observation of the sieve's oscillation or shaking, but the actual methods and interpretations have been lost over time.

•CRADLES

In Peloponnesus, Greece, there is a church dedicated to the Virgin Mary. Pilgrims used to come here regularly to pay homage and give offerings. One specific offering, that of a coin, was placed in a small silver cradle. This cradle was lifted over the traveler's head three times, then returned to its resting spot. If the cradle rocked after this, it portended many children being born to that family.

Related Systems: Offerings, Omens, Signs

• CRITOMANCY

(see Food)

• CROMINOMANCY

(see Onions)

• CRYSTAL SCRYING (CRYSTALLOMANCY)

Crystal scrying is the method of gazing into a crystal—either the stereotypical ball or sphere, or a flat, polished cross section—to discover images in answer to a question. It is related to other types of scrying, specifically those that utilize a reflective surface like a mirror or polished metal. St. Augustus believed that crystallomancy originated in Persia, where beryl spheres were preferred. Historical treatises indicate this art was also very popular among the Romans, who introduced it to Europe. Divination that uses a polished stone's surface for scrying is also called lithomancy in Western society, and *Me-lon* in Tibet. The Tibetan system instructs the querent to recite mantras while focusing on the stone.

By the fifth century A.D., texts indicate several types of crystals were favored for scrying efforts in Europe, including aquamarine, quartz, and obsidian. In Ireland, beryl was sanctioned. In the 1300s, crystallomancy was used regularly to discover the identity of thieves and uncover their booty. By the 1400s, Swiss alchemist Paracelsus described scrying as "observing rightly" and understanding what one sees.

Magicians developed rituals around this time as well to ensure successful scrying efforts. These rituals often included cleansing, fasting, reciting invocations, placing the crystal in an ornate stand decorated with sigils, and anointing the crystal with olive oil. All this effort invoked the crystal's indwelling spirit, which would then respond.

In the Yucatan, the crystal scryer was known as a *b'men*. They used a *zaztun*, or clear stone, for divinatory efforts, specifically for recovering lost articles. Similarly, Apache medicine men looked to crystals to help them retrieve stolen items. And among the Cherokee, divining crystals were sometimes "fed" deer's blood to keep the spirit of the stone vital.

Yucatan shamans recommended that a scryer sleep with the crystal to increase the sympathy between user and the tool, and that the ball be rubbed with fresh mugwort, passed through copal incense, and dipped in rum prior to use. The diviner was instructed to drink a cup of chicory tea to help in preparing for the rite. Any or all of these suggestions can be added into your personal scrying rituals to enhance the results.

For your own efforts, use a three-inch crystal ball or cross section. This size is comfortable on the eyes and gives you a large surface on which the images can form clearly. Some people recommend a clear crystal, while others prefer one with veils. You can determine which works best for you by trial and error. I personally find that veils aid the process.

Place your chosen crystal on a dark surface, like black or blue velvet, in a dimly lit area (candlelight is a good choice). Accentuate this ritual by working during the time of a waxing or full moon, which symbolizes the intuitive self. Sit quietly, maintain your purpose and attention, and breath deeply. Look into the center of the crystal. Don't worry about blinking, just try to relax. Watch for clouds to form and swirl, or for the veils to begin moving. Be patient. It takes tenacity, time, practice, and a peaceful demeanor to see shapes or pictures.

When you successfully catch glimpses of symbols or images, try not to focus on them too closely. This sometimes stops the movement of the clouds. Just make a mental note of what you see and ponder the significance later. This way, you can receive more input from the crystal. Some of the traditional interpretive values include:

White clouds: A positive omen

Black clouds: A negative omen

Yellow or red clouds: An unpleasant surprise, danger, or trouble

Blue, violet, or green clouds: Happiness, or good news

Ascending clouds: Yes

Descending clouds: No

Symbols: Interpret symbols according to personal vision. Use Appendix B for ideas on unfamiliar or unrecognized symbols.

Related Techniques: Gems, Ink, Knife Blade, Lithomancy, Mirror, Scrying, Stones, Water, Wax

Adaptations: A turned-off computer or television screen is an excellent scrying surface, having the sheen of a crystal. We subconsciously expect to see a picture or words in these places too, which may make the efforts more successful.

Some scryers prefer moonlight to that of a candle to help encourage a more intuitive state of mind.

• CUPS/GLASSES/VASES (SCYPHOMANCY)

The use of cups or vases for divination is most easily traceable to Greece and Rome. After three days of calm weather, as the ritual prescribes, dress in white and prepare the following: a silver vessel filled with wine, a copper one filled with oil, and a glass one filled with water. Pose your question. Movements or images in the silver cup represent the past, in the copper, the present, and in the glass, the future. This reveals which time period is most pertinent to the answer to your question.

In Japan, upsetting a patient's medicine cup portends a speedy recuperation. The *lookman* of Trinidad uses cups to divine cures or determine the outcome of sickness (see *Clear Sight*). For this, the *lookman* places a cup filled partway with water on top of a patient's head and asks questions of the person's soul. If water spills out of the cup, it is a positive response.

Related Systems: Bowls, Ink, Spilling, Water, Wine

Adaptations: To expand the interpretive possibilities, try adding a substance that will swirl and float on top of each glass, like pearly-colored dish detergent. Scry the resulting images for deeper meanings.

• CYCLOMANCY

(see *Wheel*)

• DACTYLOMANCY

Divination based on the examination of fingers and/or the rings on a person's finger(s) is called dactylomancy.

Related Systems: Fingernails, Fingers, Hands, Palmistry, Rings

• DAFA

Dafa is the term for divinatory arts in Yoruban African tradition. Any time divination is used, the spirit of the prophet *Orunmila* is contacted directly for insights and answers (see *Ifa*).

• DANCE OR MOVEMENT (GYROMANCY)

Many cultural groups practiced ecstatic dance as a means of achieving an altered awareness during which they could communicate divinatory messages. The Israelites danced in processionals before the Ark, and prophetic announcements often followed. Arabs danced, drummed, and trumpeted en route to prophetic shrines. Syrians danced to become possessed by Attis, and Gold Coast prophets sang and danced to the gods to prepare themselves properly for oracular tasks.

Among the Whirling Dervishes of Islam and the *Tarahumares* in Mexico, gyromancy is a sacred art. In both settings the dancers spin themselves to become the center of a cosmic wheel, until they fall from loss of equilibrium. At this point, the dancer has achieved an altered state of awareness in which they prophesy for the people gathered.

Related Systems: Chanting, Chresomancy, Drums, Meditation, Singing

• DAPHNOMANCY

(see Bay Laurel)

• DAYS

Foretelling the future by the day of the month or week has strong associations with numerology, astrology, and the observations of the lunar cycle. For example, the first three days after the new moon are fortuitous for those conducting business or signing important papers. The first five days and the twenty-fourth day ensure a positive future for a new endeavor. Other day omens include:

- The seventh, ninth, and twelfth days of the lunar cycle are good days for marriage, presaging happiness. If you wish to be certain that a favor asked will be granted, ask on the fourteenth, fifteenth, or seventeenth day.

- Any letters received on the third, fifth, or ninth days of the month will bring good news and improved luck.

- Tuesdays and Sundays are good days to begin a job. Tuesday is also good for success in legal matters.

- Mondays promise fortune for travel and advertisements.

- Wednesdays are best for buying and selling items and communicating with people effectively.

- Thursday is a lucky day for commercial and financial transactions.

- Fridays are bad for marriages but good for new projects.

- Saturday is the time to complete necessary chores for the best possible outcomes, except for launching a boat or buying a horse.

- Letters received on Tuesday and Saturday are more likely to contain happy tidings, and arrive just before a streak of improved fortune comes your way.

Related Systems: Astrology, Day Signs, Moon, Months, Weekdays

Adaptations: Consider the lunar timing given here when entering into financial agreements, partnerships, or marriages. To encourage better luck when you need it, try mailing yourself a letter so it arrives on a fortuitous day!

•DAY SIGNS

In the Aztec *Book of Fate*, there is a predictive system of day signs that uses a 260-day calendar. Within this system, each day of the calendar receives one of twenty names, moving in cycles of thirteen days. In this manner, each Day Sign appears at the beginning of one of twenty cycles only once in the entire 260-day period. For example, the first day in the first cycle was named 1-Alligator. The days then progressed through 2-Wind, 3-House, 4-Lizard, 5-Serpent, 6-Death, 7-Deer, 8-Rabbit, 9-Water, 10-Dog, 11-Monkey, 12-Grass, and 13-Reed, the last day of the first cycle. The next cycle began with 1-Ocelot. The progression continued through the remaining names, then started over with Alligator, which became day number eight in the second cycle.

For the purpose of divination, a querent would come to a *tonalpoulque*, or reader, and pose a question. The reader would grab a handful of crystals and beans and sort them into piles of four. If the last pile had two or four beans, it was considered acceptable to proceed further with the query. Next, the number of the complete piles was tallied and added to that day's cycle number. So if today's sign was *Reed*, and four piles were made, the question's answer would be divined from the characteristics of *Earthquake*, four names down the list.

The following list gives each Day Sign and its associated characteristics. Note that the sign under which one was born also indicates personality traits like an astrological sign. To use this system yourself, you can calculate forward or backward from August 9, 1992, which corresponds to 1-Alligator.

Alligator: Maternal energy, beginnings, creativity, sensitivity

Wind: Communication, versatility, lofty idealism, irresponsibility, romanticism

House: Strength, resistance to change, organization, hard work, need for security

Lizard: Fertility, achievement, influence, high standards

Serpent: Change, charisma, personal power, knowledge, fanaticism

Death: Faith, obligations and service, politics, materialism, religion

Deer: Meeting, cooperation, peace, generosity, outspokenness, artistry

Rabbit: Conflict, nervousness, humor and strength, intelligent free spirit

Water: Compulsiveness, emotion, psychism, need for self-control

Dog: Guidance, loyalty, team work, thoughtfulness, immaturity

Monkey: Ability, drama, curiosity, fast learner, attention seeker

Grass: Health crisis, kindness, deep feeling, strong work ethic

Reed: Authority, accomplishment, fighter, challenge, morals

Ocelot: Hidden matters, avoidance of confrontation, good listener, spirituality

Eagle: Perspective, independence, logic, strong ambitions and opinions

Vulture: Rejection, seriousness, practicality, hard-heartedness, dominance, criticalness

Earthquake: Balance, logical activity, astuteness, liberality, humor, conflict

Knife: Options, pragmatism, order, manners, social awkwardness

Rain: Cleansing, restlessness, insecurity, philosophy, compassion

Flower: Excellence, good intentions, art, high expectations, devotion

Related Systems: Astrology, Birth Omens, Days

•DEATH OMENS

In earlier times, death at a young age occurred regularly due to the harsher living conditions. Consequently, people paid close attention to any omen or portent that might signal the loss of a loved one, which also could mean the loss of income if it were the head of a family. Some occurrences thought to presage a death include:

- Bees leaving the hive (rural U.S.)

- Birds perching near or pecking on your window (England)

- Black spots found on the blade bone of a sheep (Scotland)

- Clocks that stop for no apparent reason

- Hearing a cuckoo cry when you're fasting (Scotland)

- A dog howling outside the window (Europe)

- Pictures falling to the ground and breaking (see *Breakage*)

In Finland, they made a fire from nine types of wood on Easter (see *Holiday Omens and Signs*). To it they added a porridge twirl stick, a wooden spoon, and brimstone, then watched the smoke (see *Smoke*). If it blew toward the church, this indicated a death in the household before year's end.

Related Systems: Animal Omens and Signs, Birth Omens

•DENDROMANCY

(see Oak and Mistletoe)

•DEVA DISKS

Deva Disks were developed by New Age artist Kama Lee as a means of honoring and connecting with elemental spirits for spiritual growth and insight. This system contains forty-one triangular wooden chips, each one having illustrations that include symbolic colors, emblems, and images. These chips piece together to form a six-sided reading surface (see illustrations on page 106).

Deva Disks are highly adaptable. Use personal insight and vision to create your own layouts and interpretations. Several are suggested but not required. To obtain more information or to order a set write to: Kama Lee, 10 Salena, Bentleyville, PA 15314.

Related Systems: Cartomancy, Dominoes, *I Ching*, Tarot

•DICE (CLEROMANCY)

Homer alludes to the invention of dice, used to help pass the time on the long sea voyages to Troy, around 1260 B.C. There is other evidence that they may have originated in Egypt. What we do know for certain is that divination with dice was common in both Babylon and Assyria. It was a type of lot casting. The original dice were made from bone, and in later years from clay, which was the predecessor to our modern plastic dice. Plastic, however, is not recommended for divinatory purposes.

In Tibet, *So-mo* is an oracle that uses three dice, allowing for sixteen values between three and eighteen. Various texts detail the different interpretations of these values according to the type of question asked. The value eleven, for example, speaks of success if one asked about his or her fortune, but in relation to visitors, it means a friend will be bringing bad news. With inquiries about a lost item, the value eleven suggests to look to the east but warns that recovery may not come without litigation. In legal matters, it portends slow progress. While this system provided an amazing diversity of responses, the diviner had a lot of memorizing to do in order to use the oracle effectively.

In Medieval Europe, rolling three sixes in a row meant you would be getting your desire for one year. Two sixes portended reaching a goal with some associated adversity. These two portents may be added to any contemporary system of cleromancy you choose to adapt or use.

During the late 1800s in America, divination by dice was very popular along with other teatime pursuits. Pamphlets appeared almost everywhere explaining simple procedures for cleromancy, many of which are still used today. These books suggest that the die's message will manifest within nine days and that the best days of the week to consult this system are Monday and Wednesday. Monday may have been chosen due to its association with the moon, a symbol of intuitive awareness, and Wednesday was named after Woden, a Germanic god credited with inventing divination.

To try cleromancy yourself, place three dice in a cup and shake them with your stronger hand while thinking of a question. Roll them out on a velvet surface with a twelve-inch circle drawn on it. Add together the number of dots facing up on the dice that land inside the circle. If one die lands outside the circle, plans may go astray, and if two land on the floor, there may be trouble ahead. If the dots on the die or dice within the circle total less than three, no answer is possible right now. The remaining numerical significances are:

3: A happy surprise or event

4: Troubles, unpleasant encounters, and obstacles

5: Fulfillment of a hope or wish; a friendly stranger

6: Some type of loss or setback

7: Business or financial difficulty; undeserved slander

8: Criticism or misunderstandings

9: Unity, partnership, successful relationship; the end to a quarrel

10: New beginnings, fertility, and birth

11: Separation, moving away, or distancing

12: Important news forthcoming

13: Sadness, depression, foreboding

14: The blossoming of a friendship or partnership

15: The need to hold off on your current plans for a while and watch for ill-motivated people

16: Travel of some sort, usually pleasant or successful

17: The need to change your strategy or methods

18: Good luck, success, overcoming the odds, and victory

Dice Casting Circle

To improve the interpretive value of the three-dice system, divide your casting circle into twelve sections, each of which represents a different matter in your life:

1. The future or the coming year
2. Finances
3. Travel or adventure
4. Home and family
5. Present circumstances
6. Physical health
7. Relationships
8. Legal matters
9. Mental health
10. Jobs or career
11. Obstacles
12. Spiritual health

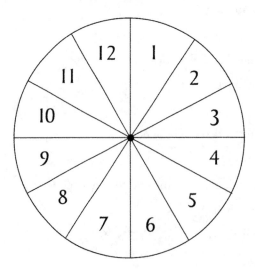

The value of the number in any one section can be used separately or in conjunction with the total of all three dice.

For this particular casting, the number one landing at any position is basically favorable, depending on the rest of the reading. Two shows you will need help to obtain a goal. Three indicates a victory, four, difficulties and possible losses. Five is a fairly good omen with some uncertainty, and six is dubious. If, for example, a four lands in position eight, one might expect problems in resolving a court case. Take care not to cast this system more than once a week. It is said more than that will tempt the fates.

If you have only two dice available, they will suffice. Perform the ritual as first described, not counting a die that falls outside the circle, and read the values as follows:

1: A positive omen or "yes."

2: A negative omen or "no."

3: Things are not as bad as they seem, so be careful.

4: Options must be considered before making a move or finalizing any decision.

5: Improved fortune is on the way, so don't lose hope.

6: A good sign for new projects, the proverbial "green light."

7: Faith will guide you, if you let it.

8: Patience is needed now, so don't rush or be hasty.

9: A definite "yes", there's no need to wait.

10: Good grounds for doubt here, so reconsider your line of reasoning.

11: This question is silly, because you already know the answer in your heart.

12: This is unlikely to take place, so don't get your hopes up.

Related Systems: Bones, Dominoes, Numerology

Adaptations: Dice divination is very easy and marvelously portable. Find a special pair (perhaps carved from wood or a semiprecious metal) and keep them in a pouch. Try using traditional numerological associations as portents for your dice. If employing three dice, you can either use the total of the dice, or each one as its own separate omen, revealing the past, present, and future (or possibly the situation, action, and outcome).

The *Mo* system from Tibet has been adapted into a thirty-six card deck by Jay Goldberg and Lobsang Dakpa. The kit includes a book of explanation and a Tibetan styled die. This was originally produced by Snow Lion in NY (1990), but is somewhat difficult to find.

• DICTIONARY

(see Bibliomancy, Books)

• DILOGUN

(see Shell)

• DIRECT REVELATION

Direct revelation was common among the Hebrew prophets, to whom Jehovah appeared in various forms (as a burning bush, a bright light, etc.) when delivering messages. This was often true in other cultures as well. For example, a Babylonian text recounts a similar experience by Gudea, an important ruler, who received instructions on matters of state this way. The diviner or prophet who receives such a revelation is rarely using a tool, and quite frequently doesn't even expect a vision.

Related Systems: Clear Sight; Dreams; Oracles, Mediums, Prophets

• DOLLS

Women among the Khanti and Mansi tribes of Eurasia make birchwood dolls with ribbons at the waist to divine the health of their unborn children. To determine how the baby fares, the woman holds the doll's ribbon between her fingers. As long as the movements are steady and uniform, the prognostication for both baby and mother is favorable.

Adaptation: This is a type of sympathetic magic that has some connections with poppets. Something like this specially made for an expectant mother might be a good gift idea.

• DOMINOES (CLEROMANCY)

Dominoes are used in a type of cleromancy that originated in China around the twelfth century B.C. Originally there were thirty-two in a set (versus the modern twenty-eight), decorated with red spots instead of black and white. Versions of dominoes also existed in Alaska, where 148 pieces were used.

Practitioners of cleromancy suggest not consulting this oracle more than once a week (as with dice) and to abstain from readings on Monday or Friday. The reason for this has been lost to antiquity.

To try this yourself, lay the faces of the dominoes downward on a table and shuffle them. Draw one and look to see what configuration you get. Or draw three, using the first to represent the past, the second, the present, and the third, the outcome of the question. The interpretive values are:

Double-Six: A very auspicious omen of luck, joy, and prosperity.

Six-Five: Good for relationships and friendships; social occasions.

Six-Four: Arguments; negative outcomes in legal matters.

Six-Three: Enjoyable travel, leisure time, and improved relationships.

Six-Two: Overall improvement; an unexpected gift.

Six-One: A problem ends, often due to your kindness.

Six-Blank: Caution, someone is gossiping.

Double-Five: Movement and change, sometimes to a new residence or job.

Five-Four: A windfall, lady luck favors you.

Five-Three: Meetings with authority figures that will go well.

Five-Two: Difficulties in long-term relationships.

Five-One: Being busy, often in social settings.

Five-Blank: An ending, sometimes a funeral; a friend needs aid; time to watch your money.

Double-Four: Reason for celebration; work progressing smoothly.

Four-Three: Worrying needlessly.

Four-Two: Career movement or financial change; time to read the fine print on all documents.

Four-One: Firm relationships but shaky finances.

Four-Blank: News of a heated nature; disappointment.

Double-Three: Abundance; a sudden partnership.

Three-Two: Taking risks brings losses.

Three-One: An important discovery; need to beware of those who slander you.

Three-Blank: Arguments at home.

Double-Two: Jealousy plays a role in this question.

Two-One: Bad time for financial dealings.

Double-One: Good luck comes in an odd place.

One-Blank: Unexpected visitors.

Double-Blank: Trouble for which you are unprepared.

Related Systems: Cartomancy, Dice, Numerology

Adaptations: Since these are all the same size, you may use them in drawings and castings too. For example, to get an overall feeling for your day, draw out one domino and read the associated fortune. Or, shake the dominoes in a bag and cast them on a flat surface. Read only those that face upward, from left to right, like a sentence.

• DONKEYS (CEPHALOMANCY)

Cephalomancy was a zoological foretune-telling technique that involved boiling a donkey or goat head and examining the skull afterward. In thirteenth century Europe, a variation on this called for soaking the skull in wine, drying it, and then inspecting the remains. While this seems rather gruesome by modern standards, it likely grew out of the same tradition as divination by bones and entrails.

Related Systems: Animal Omens, Bones, Entrails, Offerings

Adaptation: The next time you make homemade soup from leftover turkey or chicken bones, think of a question. Review any unusual markings on the bones after they're boiled. Consider some of the interpretations listed under Bones and Shells as a starting point for your own interpretation.

• DOWSING (RHABDOMANCY)

> *"I will pay you out of the treasures which you enable me to find."*
>
> —Ennius

The ancient use of wands, rods, or twigs is suggested by myths of gods and goddesses like Minerva, Circe, and Hermes, who wielded rods for magical purposes. The ancient Chinese, Turks, and Etruscans all dowsed for water, the latter often adding incantations. The Scythians detected perjurers with dousing rods.

By the 1400s, people in Germany and England had adapted earlier methods for themselves. Applications for dowsing include finding ore deposits, uncovering lost landmarks or property lines, detecting criminals, analyzing character, curing disease, finding lost domestic animals, tracing underground streams, and finding the cardinal points. The rod has also been carried as a fetish for good health. After the advent of Christianity, the earlier dowsing invocations were replaced with prayers, which allowed the church to use dowsing to help with problems periodically. For example, in 1568 Friar Antonio used dowsing to find water for St. Teresa of Spain who wished to build a convent.

Dowsing (also known as Water Witching) uses a forked branch held in the hands. Some of the favored woods for dowsing include dogwood, peach, hazel, mulberry, juniper, maple, willow, and apple. In Tuscany, dowsers preferred almond branches. When these could not be found, a sprig of goldenrod or a pomegranate branch were both considered suitable substitutes, especially for locating treasure.

The suggested length of the forks in the Y-shaped stick range from fourteen inches to eighteen inches, with a neck of four to eleven inches. As a dowser walks an area, he or she watches for the branch to dip downward when the desired item is located. At the turn of the century, this art was held in high enough regard that the U.S. Department of the Interior published a report on it, and oil companies hired dowsers to help them find where to drill.

The theories about how dowsing works vary, but the most popular one seems to be that the dowser becomes like a sonograph, using the forked wood like a needle. Other theories range from the speculation that there is a magnetic field between the rod and the ground, to the idea that the perceptive powers of the individual, like clairvoyance, are responsible. Only about one-tenth of the population shows a gift for dowsing, and in more recent years it has been used chiefly for discerning lay lines and, among holisticians, for helping define health problems.

Related Systems: Pendulum, Rods, Wands

Adaptation: Many New Age stores sell dowsing kits, one of which includes two thin, metal, L-shaped rods. The small leg of the rod is held in each hand while walking an area. When the two rods cross at a center point, this is considered a "hit." Most people double check these results several times before marking a lay line, building a sacred structure, or whatever.

•DREAMS (ONEIROMANCY)

> *"Dream vision is an awareness in the part of the rational soul in its spiritual essence; a glimpse of the forms of events."*
>
> —Ibn Khaldun

In ancient Sumeria, the ruler Ennatum wrote of a personal prophetic dream as early as 2540 B.C. The Mesopotamians collected dream omens and signs on eleven tablets for their seers to use. Among the Hebrews is the story of Joseph, who served Egypt by correctly interpreting portents of famine that appeared in the Pharaoh's dreams.

The oldest surviving instructional text of dream interpretation is the Leden Papyrus of 1350 B.C., in which words like those used in modern psychoanalysis are employed. Later, some of these correspondences traveled into Europe with merchants and explorers, allowing for cultural adaptations and expansions.

Dream books circulated readily in Greece around 400 B.C., and the Romans developed special rituals to invoke prophetic dreams. The most influential of all the early dream books appeared in A.D. 140, written by Artemidorus of Asia Minor. He traveled the known world collecting information on dreams and their interpretations from Greek, Egyptian, and Assyrian sources to write his *Oneirocritica*. This text has been used ever since by those studying dream analysis.

Accounts of dream signs and their related interpretive values existed all over the ancient world and were often written down by notable figures. Plato, for example, wrote that the sleeping mind shared warnings and perspectives through a dream's symbols. Other Greek philosophers wrote of the soul's freedom during sleep, which allowed it to gather prophetic information. In Greece, experts in receiving and interpreting prophetic dreams were called *oneiropoli*.

In Iceland, people took dream visions very seriously. Those gifted with the art of "dreaming true" were highly honored. The writings of both Caesar and Tacitus indicate that the Germans and Celts held dream prophesy in similar high regard.

In Arabia, Mohammed became known as a prophet due to his insightful dreams. Early in the first century A.D., Ibrv Sirin collected dream interpretation data and developed the divination system known as *Ta'bur al-ru'ya*. This method included a complete background interview with the dreamer before attempting an interpretation, sometimes followed by incantations or mantralike prayers.

Some of the most detailed rituals for invoking prophetic dreams come to us from Japan. Around the fourth or fifth century A.D., the Japanese Emperor communed with the supernatural world to be the dreamer for his people. This required certain periods of seclusion in a specially built Hall of Dreams. The ritual evolved, and later Dream Oracles dotted the countryside. These were popular until around the fifteenth century.

To receive visionary dreams at one of these oracles, querents would make a pilgrimage, abstaining from meat and strong vegetables during their travels. Once they arrived, they committed themselves to stay a specific number of days, praying and making offerings. The questions posed at the oracle were frequently about how to cure sickness, relieve misfortune, or gain insight into the future. With the last type of question, reports of a lone figure appearing in the querent's dream with a cryptic poetic message were common. The classically styled poetry helped the dreamer remember the message clearly.

The common thread binding ancient belief systems regarding prognosticative dreams is the idea that somehow the human spirit frees itself during sleep, that it communes with gods or other powerful beings, collecting insights. Today, according to the psychological view of dreams, most reflect a person's hopes, fears, and desires, though some may activate a subconscious skill for foresight. The predictive value of the dream, however, is subject to the individual's experiences.

Two different people dreaming of an accident at sea could have vastly different perspectives on that dream's futuristic meaning. One might interpret it as a warning against taking a planned trip, while another might avoid fishing. Additionally, all precognitive dreams are reflections of what may happen, not necessarily what will happen.

The number of dream harbingers and the diversity of interpretations for each are astounding. Consequently, only a few are listed here with some common associations. Please realize that this list only scratches the surface of possible interpretations for the signs revealed in a prophetic dream. Additionally, exactly if and when the prophesies in the dream will manifest cannot be known or conjectured, except vaguely, perhaps, by its setting. Nostradamus saw hundreds of years forward into time, while you may dream of future hours, days, or months.

Abbey: Liberation from present anxiety, or safety offered

Abyss: Unavoidable trouble

Ache: Sickness; take care with your health

Acorn: Prosperity and love soon to follow (see *Nuts*)

Adventure: Change is forthcoming; break free from constraints

Alligator: A crafty enemy against whom all caution should be taken

Almond: Joy, possibly engendered by traveling

Ants: Frustration or hard work ahead (see *Insects*)

Apple: A long happy life with success in business (see *Apple*)

Armor, wearing: A warning against coming sickness (Tibet)

Battle: Upcoming disagreement with family or friends

Bear: Injury, mishaps, and hardships preceding success (see *Animals*)

Bells: Good news coming (see *Bells*)

Bread: If plentiful, you will never want for worldly possessions (see *Bread*)

Butter: Festivities follow success in a dispute

Cage: Marrying early and happily in life

Cake: Sweet cakes portend joy

Camel: A heavy burden will soon be yours (see *Animals*)

Carpet: Watch for advancement and opportunity

Chicken: A coming streak of bad luck, especially in relationships

Children: A large task or crisis will come out positively

Combat: Rivalry can be avoided with planning

Comet: Calamity, war, or sickness; a very bad omen (see *Comet*)

Crab: Reversals or the need to withdraw (see *Fish*)

Crops, vast amounts of: The symbol of coming wealth (Tibet)

Crown: Favor with an authority figure will reveal itself

Death: Literal or figurative losses on the horizon

Deer: Quarrels or dissension (see *Animals*)

Dice: Changes in business; unnecessary risk taking (see *Dice*)

Dock: News arriving from abroad (see *Herbs*)

Drum: General disorder and confusion (see *Drums*)

Dust: Dispersing people or business trouble

Echo: Favorable response to a question or request

Elderberry: Uncertainty in relationships

Evergreen: Lasting efforts that bring honor (see *Trees*)

Explosion: Violence or intense transition

Fable: A good associate will be coming into your life

Fair: Neglecting situations or false friends

Falling: A temporary or permanent loss of personal status (see *Falling*)

Fever: Ups and downs, especially financial

Fire: Renewed hope, good fortune, and joy; alternatively a quarrel (see *Fire*)

Flood: Negative legal outcome or dissolving health

Flying: Escape from present difficulties

Frog: A prosperous season (usually three months)

Fruit out of season: A sign of conception and fertility

Gardens: General abundance or improvement (see *Flowers*)

Giant: If it was faced boldly, you will overcome an enemy

Hail: A hope or wish will go unfulfilled

Handcuff: Temptation will entice you

Hermit: Temporary failure or setbacks

Horse, White: Riches (see *Horse*)

Hounds: Unproductive pursuits (see *Animals—dogs*)

Hurricane: Dangerous travel

Imp: Annoyances or falseness

Instruction: Advice of good friends needed before making a move

Itch: Restless feelings; apprehensions (see *Itching*)

Judge: A dispute is imminent

Jumping: Obstacles and trials that are overcome through perseverance

Kite: Personal elevation; setting your sights higher (see *Kite*)

Ladder: Reaching a long-awaited goal

Lion: Greatness and honor await you (see *Animals*)

Locks: A hindrance to your success will become evident

Lute: News from a friend is on its way

Magnet: An alluring idea captivates you

Maypole: Joyous occasions

Medicine: Temporary unpleasantness

Mice: Meddlers will try to undermine you (see *Animals*)

Money: Losses; take care and be frugal (see *Coins*)

Moth: A problem leads to separation (see *Insects*)

Muddy water: Troubles, sickness, or confusion

Musical instrument, playing: Coming notoriety (Tibet)

Nightingale: Victory (see *Birds*)

Oak: Growing steadiness and foundations (see *Trees*)

Onion: The discovery of a treasure (see *Onion*)

Pancake: A hope is fulfilled (see *Food, Pancake*)

Peacock: Deceit or doubts about a person or situation (see *Birds*)

Pineapple: Invitation to an event

Poison: Treachery afoot (see *Poison*)

Quicksand: Temptation of which you are unaware

Uprooted tree: A harbinger of death or devastation (England)

Race: Defeating a competitor

Rainbow: Change for the better (see *Rainbow*)

Shop: Moderate comfort throughout your life

Snow: Safety, despite how things seem

Thieves: A lost cause

Violin: Social occasions

Volcano: Your anger will rebound against you

War: Rivalry and competition result in a great loss

Yeast: Your next undertaking will prove successful

Related Systems: Any technique with symbolic results, like Scrying

Adaptation: Always bear in mind that your perception of a dream is more important than "book values." Personalize and update your dream dictionary so that it better reflects your experiences and perspectives on what symbols mean.

For more information on dream interpretation, read *The Language of Dreams* (The Crossing Press, 1997).

•DRESSING (STOLISOMANCY)

Omens that derive from odd happenings related to dressing, like putting something on inside out or buttoning a shirt incorrectly, fall into the category of stolisomancy. For example:

Apron: Accidentally putting an apron on backwards brings luck throughout the day (see *Apron*).

Buttons: If you misbutton your shirt, stop and name each button (except the one misbuttoned) in order: "rich, poor, beggar, thief, doctor, lawyer, chief." Continue the sequence until you run out of buttons. The last word indicates your future mate's or child's career. An even number of buttons on a new item of clothing portends good fortune for the wearer.

Coat: Putting on a coat and discovering it is torn indicates someone will soon speak ill of you (Suffolk, England).

Cotton: Finding a piece of cotton stuck to your garment means that an important letter will soon arrive.

Hems: If a hem turns up while dressing, this indicates a forthcoming gift.

Shoes: Putting one's shoes on the wrong feet predicts an accident, usually on the same day, so be extra cautious.

Shoe Laces: If shoe laces repeatedly come untied, the arrival of a letter is foretold.

Related Systems: Apron, Clothes, Shoes

•DRUMS (TYMPANA)

The art of ritual drumming has strong roots in tribal and shamanic traditions. In Lapland and Siberia, shamans placed a ring or antler horn on a drum while a querent posed a question. The drum was struck regularly throughout the ritual, and the final resting place of the ring or antler determined the interpretive value. Similarly,

Hungarian Gypsies placed colored kidney beans on a drum's head, then interpreted the beans' movements during play and final resting places afterward.

The Celts fashioned a flat divining drum from wood harvested on Whitsunday. The creator painted the skin of the drum to indicate nine directions. The diviner placed the drum on an even surface or held it in one hand while a querent posed a question. Twenty-one thorn apple seeds were then dropped on the surface, and a ritual hammer tapped the skin causing vibrations that put the seeds in patterns. The final patterns were interpreted. Three or more seeds inside the four main indicators was a positive sign. Two seeds between the north and center points meant good luck for a woman. Two seeds between the center and south points meant good luck for a man. If most seeds were outside the directional lines, it was a negative omen.

To increase the interpretive value of this system, consider the quarter in which seeds land, and their number. For example, four seeds in the east might be interpreted as a good portent for financial matters, especially those just starting. Two seeds in the southern quarter may mean a passionate relationship or an energized partnership (see *Numerology*).

Related Techniques: Dance or Movement, Lots, Tambourine

Adaptations: Paint the drum head with personal emblems that increase the interpretive values. For example, create twelve points instead of four, representing the twelve coming months or the astrological houses. Note that any type of seed works for this, but slightly heavier ones like pumpkin seeds are nice because they don't fall off so easily.

• EARS

All five senses are used in divination efforts. Some of the omens and characteristics associated with ears include:

Ringing in the ear: Misfortune will befall a friend.

Right ear warm: You will soon receive praise.

Left ear warm: People are gossiping about you.

Large ears: Intelligence, sincerity, friendliness, and prudence.

Small ears: Kindness, refinement, frugality, modesty, and charity.

Pointed ears: Self-esteem and a tendency toward jealousy.

Projecting ears: Affection, egocentricity, and shrewdness.

• EARTH (GEOMANCY)

Geomancy includes everything from the observations of the earth's movements, noises, and physical configurations, to the interpretation of patterns in dirt scattered on the ground. Some people call it "the astrology of the earth."

Scandinavians brought geomantic techniques to Iceland in the ninth century. Specifically, they looked to waterfalls, mountains, and other natural features for guidance in daily affairs. In rural England, a person might go to a crossroad, make a hole in the ground, and listen for the earth to give them counsel and whisper their fortunes. *Raml*, a geomantic system from the Middle East, called for the examination of cracks in the soil made by long-term exposure to heat and sunlight. In India, Burma, Africa, and Arabia, a diviner or querent pierced the ground with a stick to create patterns, and subsequently interpreted them. West Africans would sometimes leave these patterns overnight and incorporate into the interpretation any animal tracks found in them the next day.

Another interesting form of divination using geomantic designs is the Dream Oracle. In it, you create a pattern from the numbers associated with the age of a querent and the day of the week, day of the month, and month of the year of a dream occurrence. For example, Tuesday equals 3 (counting starts with Sunday), which as an odd number becomes a single dot in the pattern. April equates to 4, an even number, which becomes two dots, and so on. Once the pattern is complete, the diviner looks it up on a detailed chart having sixteen main patterns for overall themes and more patterns for specific details. *Napoleon's Book of Fate* works similarly, except that the querent randomly draws dots in four sets of lines, each of which is reduced to one or two dots to create a pattern.

The easiest method of geomancy involves making a line of random holes in dirt or sand while thinking about a question. Repeat this sixteen times, always keeping your question in mind. An even number of holes in a line becomes two dots, while an odd number becomes a single dot. The table on page 122 gives an example with equivalencies.

Each pattern and interpretive value is exactly the same as that used for the Druid Rods (see *Rods*).

Related Systems: Clouds, Feng Shui, Plants, Trees, Water (sounds)

Adaptation: Once you finish making your line of holes in the dirt, stop for a moment before counting them and look at them from all angles. If you see any images or symbols with interpretive value (see Appendix B), add these to the geomantic interpretation for more details.

ORIGINAL PATTERN	GEOMANTIC EQUIVALENT	PATTERN CREATED
o o o o	2	
o o o o	2	
o o o o o	1	
o o o	1	

Fortuna Major

o o o o o o o	1	
o o o o o	1	
o o o o o	1	
o o o o o o o	1	

Via

o o o o o o	2	
o o o o o	1	
o o o o	2	
o o o	1	

Acquisitio

o o o	1	
o o o o	2	
o o o o o o	2	
o o o o	2	

Laetitia

• ECLIPSES

Numerous myths exist about the origins of eclipses. In the East, it was believed that a great dragon flew in front of the sun or moon, hiding it from view. In the *Edda*, a thirteenth century collection of Norse poetry, and among original native Brazilians, an eclipse represented the possibility of the world's end. To the Chinese it symbolized decay, and in Mexico it meant that evil had temporarily gotten the upper hand. At one time or another, most cultures thought solar eclipses indicated forthcoming bad luck, war, or famine, and doomed children born during them to misfortune and poverty (see *Birth Omens*).

No matter the culture, most ancient people regarded an eclipse as a negative omen, since it "took away" welcome light. Many earlier civilizations had special rituals to chase away the darkness or, conversely, to bring back the light. These included throwing things (like spears) toward the sky, shouting, and building a fire to give the sun or moon the strength with which to win back the sky.

Related Systems: Astrology, Celestial Omens, Meteors, Moon, Stars, Sun

• EGGS (OVOMANCY, OVOSCOPY, OOMANTIA)

Divination with eggs was popularized in Europe in the 1600s.

One method of ovomancy entails taking a raw egg and poking a hole in the small end. Holding the egg over a glass of water while pondering your question, you interpret the patterns formed as the egg white drips onto the surface of the water.

A second method might be best undertaken around Easter when there is an abundance of colored eggs. Take seven eggs of different colors, place them in a bowl, and blindly choose one. The colors of the eggs have the following associations:

Red: Activity; a warning; arguments

Orange: Unavoidable change; reaping rewards from your actions

Yellow: The need to think before you act; untrustworthy emotions

Green: Creativity and the muse; growth

Blue: Good relationships of all kinds; renewed peace of mind

Pink: Improved prospects; friendship

Undyed: Fate's hand at work; the unknowable

Mixed: Confusion or multiple options

Many other beliefs have been associated with eggs. Mexicans rolled eggs against a sick person's body, then cracked them open to see if a negative spirit or magic was the cause of the sickness. Dreaming of several eggs is a prediction of wealth (see *Dreams*). Finding a double-yoked egg is an omen of coming good fortune (see *Findings*). And the first egg laid by a white hen is believed to bring prophetic dreams if placed under your pillow. (Warning: hard boil it first!)

Related Systems: Cloth, Color, Food, Lots, Oil, Water, Wax

Adaptations: For the first technique, instead of wasting the egg, let the white drip into a hot frying pan and see what pattern it makes. Then consume the results! In the second method, consider adding emblems to the eggs (see Appendix B) to make them more visually meaningful.

•ELAEMOMANCY

(see Water)

•ENLIGHTENED MANIFESTATION

Known in Ireland as *Imbas Forosna*, enlightened manifestation was common throughout the British regions. To begin, a seer stayed in a totally dark place for up to three days. Afterwards, he or she was brought into sun or fire light, which somehow inspired prophetic or helpful insights. I suspect this technique creates a sort of sensual deprivation, like a mock death, followed by sensual overload, a "new life," likely resulting in mysterious utterances such as those obtained in other ecstatic states.

Related Systems: Clear Sight, Direct Revelation

•ENTRAILS (HARUSPICY, HEPATOMANCY, EXTISPICY)

In Mesopotamia, those who divined omens from sacrificial animals were known as *baru*, or seers. The first documentation of this practice dates back to the late Babylonian period (1900 B.C.). Long lists of haruspicy omens were compiled, so that by 7 B.C. the *baru* had fifty-five detailed tablets to consult when making an interpretation.

During this time, sacrifice of sheep and subsequent examination of their parts was very popular. This particular job was left to a subclass of the *baru* called *mas-su-gid*, "one who stretches his hand into sacrificial animals." It is actually a listed profession of this era! Usually the body parts were interpreted in a counterclockwise fashion, then summed up at the end. For example, a lung exhibiting red coloration on both sides indicated a positive answer, which might be reconfirmed by a liver with "two roads" in it. These types of inquiries were sometimes considered important enough to take the *baru* into military campaigns for examinations after each battle.

The Hittites embellished this technique with further details and methods. And because of the number of examinations required for a efficient reading, the cost in sacrificial animals became terribly high. Thus in both Mesopotamia and among the Hittites, this type of divination was usually reserved for the wealthy or for major undertakings of the state.

The Greeks favored a lamb for extispicy, while the Romans used an ox. In both cases, as related by Plato and Plutarch both, respectively, the liver and intestines were focal points of the examination. The fifty-five predictive zones marked out by Babylonian diviners were still in use, often combined with Etruscan concepts that regarded inflamed or diseased areas as inauspicious omens. Effectively, this laid the foundation for what would become the science of autopsy.

Haruspicy is specifically the observation of the sacrificial creature for omens both before and after death. The idea was that any gods who accepted such a valuable offering would provide the worshippers with signs before, during, and after the ritual. As distasteful as this practice may seem to us today, it was popular until 650 B.C., and it was considered to be one of the few reliable forms of divination in ancient Mesopotamia.

Inspection of the internal organs of pigs, goats, and chickens for omens still exists today in remote regions of Burma, Thailand, Nepal, Ethiopia, and Borneo. These organs are sometimes thrown to the ground, and other times carefully removed. In all cases, however, the practice is considered a sacred art and treated accordingly.

Related Systems: Animal Omens and Signs, Anthropomancy, Offerings

Adaptations: If you call upon a Divine Being to aid and bless your divinatory efforts, a small burnt offering other than that of an animal may be considered. In this case, I recommend fruits, vegetables, or other nonliving matter that is meaningful to both you and the god or goddess invoked. As you burn the offering, watch the movements of the flames for omens and signs, using the guidelines given under *Pyromancy* or *Botanomancy*.

• EYES (OCULOMANCY)

Eyes are the proverbial "windows to the soul." Here is a list of associations with eye color and sensations of the eyes:

Gray eyes: Prudence, practicality, and moral strength

Hazel eyes: Intelligence, firmness, sincerity, ambition, and friendliness

Green eyes: Pride, impetuousness, but also considerable passion

Blue eyes: Forthrightness, gentleness, generosity, loyalty, modesty, and forgiveness

Brown eyes: Consistency, hope, nobility, nervousness, and truthfulness

Black eyes: Goal orientation, self-assurance, extravagance, devotion, and passion

Right eye itching: Humorous circumstances and laughter in store

Left eye itching: Impending sorrow

Eyes set closely: Intelligence

Large eyes: Sincerity, industry, loyalty, affection, and intelligence

Small eyes: Honesty, with a tendency toward a heated temper and recklessness

Related Systems: Ears, Facial Features, Feet, Fingernails, Fingers, Hands, Itching, Physiognomy

• FACIAL FEATURES

Joseph Addison aptly summed up the idea behind divining a person's characteristics by their facial features when he said, "A good face is a letter of introduction." Here are some common associations:

Dimple in cheek: Someone who is always looking for love.

Dimple in chin: A person who will always know success in romance.

Chin: A child with a protruding chin will grow up aggressive and curious. One with a small chin will tend toward cowardice. A thin chin foretells intelligence; a pointed chin, aptitude and cunning; and a square chin, the need to learn self-control.

Eyebrows: If eyebrows meet across the nose, it indicates a person with a brooding nature. In Iceland, Greece, and Germany, the same characteristic reveals a shape-shifter. In Scotland, a person with closely knit eyebrows is regarded as very fortunate.

Forehead: Divination by observing the shape and lines on a person's forehead is known as metopomancy. People with high foreheads tend toward ill fortune, especially if there are moles on them (see *Moles*). High foreheads also reveal intelligence, and wrinkled ones are the sign of an anxious person. A wavy line running across the head portends a life of sea travel, while three S-shaped lines over the right eye indicate generosity.

Jaw: A jutting jaw indicates an aggressive personality.

Lips: When your lips itch, you will either receive a kiss, or someone has been telling lies about you. Thin lips are the sign of a stingy or harsh nature.

Mouth: A wide mouth reveals a person who communicates effectively.

Nose: When your nose itches early in the morning it predicts good news or visitors coming later that day. Itching at other times reveals anger or that you will be kissed by a fool. Long, pointy noses reveal predatory people.

Teeth: Someone with wide gaps in their teeth will experience a lifetime of prosperity and joy. Those with the gap specifically in the front of the mouth will have a wandering spirit but exhibit strong communication skills.

Temples: Itching temples precede weeping (see *Itching*).

Related Systems: Ears, Eyes, Feet, Fingers, Fingernails, Hands, Moles, Palmistry, Physiognomy

•FANS

Among Surinam tribes, handheld fans are sometimes used for binary fortune-telling. The diviner, called a *Lukuman*, asks questions in the presence of a closed fan. If the fan falls open after any query, the indicated answer is "yes."

•FEATHERS

The use of feathers in divination was a natural outgrowth of the Greek tradition of bird augury. The Greeks based their system on the type of bird a feather came from, the position in which the feather was found, and its color. A peacock feather, for example, foretold bad luck. Some of the color correspondences included:

Red: Good fortune

Orange: Promise of delight

Yellow: False friends; the need to be wary

Green: Adventure

Blue: Love

Gray: Peace

Brown: Good health

Black: Death or bad news

Black and white: Trouble averted

Green and black: Fame and fortune

Brown and white: Joy

Gray and white: A wish coming true

Blue, white, and black: New love

Purple: An exciting trip

Related Systems: Birds, Findings, Random Divination, Spontaneous Divination

Adaptations: If the bird's feather is pointing away from you, this may indicate that the forecast associated with that omen is also moving away. For example, if a green and black feather points in an opposite direction from where you approached it, perhaps a temporary fall from the limelight is on the horizon.

•FEET (PODOMANCY)

Signs related to the feet have the following associations:

An extra toe: A lucky life (Europe)

Flat geet: Very bad luck

Being born feet first: The ability to heal (Celtic tradition)

Second toe longer than the first: An ill disposition

Itching feet: An imminent journey (see *Itching*)

Scraping the left foot: Disappointment on the horizon (Victorian Era)

Scraping the right foot: An upcoming meeting with a friend (Britain)

•FELIDOMANCY

(see Cats)

•FENG SHUI (GEOMANCY)

The Chinese system of geomancy known as *Feng Shui* predominated during the Sung Dynasty, A.D. 960–1279. Since that time, it has become interrelated with cosmology and other sciences. In Asia, people associate geomancy with nature's patterns, specifically those unaffected by human affairs.

Feng Shui holds that nature is the best unbiased oracle, even if its interpreters are not. The *Feng Shui* expert assesses a parcel of land for its appropriateness to a planned building or event. The diviner's job is to find a place for a burial, wedding, new home, or whatever, that has beneficial spiritual energies for the people or spirits involved. He or she considers the visual flow of the land and its positive or negative energies, known as *ch'i* and *sha*. "Sacred geometry" recognizes these forces as ley lines, sometimes called Dragon Lines by the Chinese. For example, a north-south line in a home promotes joy and security. The *Feng Shui* diviner must be attuned to both the obvious and the unseen elements (such as underground streams) that may affect the overall serenity of the location. Many Chinese believe to this day that Hong Kong has prospered because of the nine dragons, or mountains, to the north whose energy protects the city.

Over time, the intuitive processes involved in *Feng Shui* were explained in books, with suggestions for specific astrological timing and the use of geomantic devices. The earliest known geomantic tool was found in a tomb dating from 165 B.C. This was a fairly simple board representing the heavens, the earth, and the reader. Later, detailed geomantic compasses were devised with *I Ching* hexagrams, eight tetragrams for universal rhythms, symbols of the five phases, and topographical and astrological information.

A common modern geomantic device is an octagonal mirror. On the frame of this mirror the eight trigrams of *I Ching* are depicted as talismans. The mirror is considered most effective if concave or convex. When hung on the proper wall, it helps dissipate harmful energies. *Feng Shui* experts do not, however, recommend hanging this device in one's bedroom as it may interrupt sleep.

Related Systems: Earth, Geomancy

Adaptation: Combine geomancy with dowsing to determine positive energy lines in or around your home. Sit near these for improved results when attempting any type of divination.

•FIG LEAVES (SYCOMANCY)

Sycomancy is a type of botanomancy in which a drying fig leaf is observed. The longer the leaf holds its shape and moisture, the better the portent. Sycomancy may owe its origins to the Far East, where legend says that Buddha gained enlightenment beneath the shade of a fig tree.

Related Systems: Burning, Flowers, Herbs, Plants, Rose, Trees

•FINDINGS

Throughout Europe and early America, finding certain objects was thought to indicate certain fates. Here are some examples:

Half pennies, buttons, and snippets of wire: Good luck

Holey stones found by the water: A gift of the sea that may be carried to improve your future fortunes

Horseshoe: A positive omen, especially for one's luck

Iron nail: A windfall

Needles: Company arriving

Pin with its head facing toward you: Improved luck

Hair pin: A new friendship, good luck

In some Native American traditions, a querent posed a question to the spirit of nature. The first stone found afterwards was picked up and interpreted for any obvious patterns on the surface. Examples include:

A straight line: The power of one's spirit to overcome a problem

An "X": Respect and friendship as the key to resolving the question

A square: The need for foundations and organization

A triangle: Freeing oneself from fear; quality efforts yield quality results

A diamond: Protection from the four winds; no need to worry

Related Systems: Random Divination, Spontaneous Divination, Stones

Adaptations: Consider expanding this list to include other small objects. For example, a gum wrapper might be a sign to watch one's words, a tack could portend a difficult or dangerous path ahead, and so forth.

• FINGER ENDS

A Celtic divination system called *Dichetel Do Chennaib* used finger ends like some type of Ogham. Though information about it is very sketchy, historians believe this was a counted system, possibly repeated like the *I Ching*, where each finger represented (or was possibly painted with) an emblem. When the diviner stopped the count at a particular finger, that became the first symbolic portion of a reading.

• FINGERNAILS (ONYCHOMANCY, ONIMANCY)

Onychomancy is a very ancient form of divination similar to the art of scrying. It uses the reflective surface of polished fingernails in lieu of other reflective mediums, like mirrors or stones. Palm readers also examine fingernails in practicing their art. Some associations are:

Short square fingernails: A temper

Short fingernails: Criticalness

Large fingernails curved at the bottom: Good business sense

Broad, long, and round at tip: Good judgment

Long, almond-shaped: An easy going dreamer

Wedge-shaped: Too much sensitivity

Pink or red-edged fingernails: Irate anger that occasionally flares up

All pink: Outgoing, friendly personality

Rigid or yellow fingernails: Health problems

White fingernails: Imminent travel; potential for selfishness

Large half moons: Long life expectancy

White spots toward the bottom: Good news

Blue spots: Misfortune or sickness

Flecks: The ability to foretell the future

Related Systems: Ears, Eyes, Feet, Fingers, Hands, Palmistry, Physiognomy, Scrying, Wax *(The-bon)*

Adaptation: It might be fun to scry fingernails using glittery fingernail polish in a candle-lit room.

• FINGERS

The shape, size, and general appearance of a person's fingers may reveal much about his or her personality and potential for the future. Some traditional associations:

Pointy fingers: A tremendous potential for imagination

Short, knotty fingers: A good grasp of the large picture and sound reasoning skills

Small, coarse fingers: Lack of imagination; brutally harsh personality

Fingers longer than palm: An active mind that loves debate

Fragile, long fingers: Idealism, vision, and tenderness

Subtle fingers: Versatility

Stiff fingers: Rigidity; practicality

Fingers curved toward palm: Prudence and aggressiveness

Supple fingers: Unconventionality

Fingers curved away from palm: Rebelliousness; talkativeness

Backcurved, supple fingers: Open-mindedness and curiosity

Short fingers: Hastiness

Large fingers: Painstaking methodology

Slender fingers: Introversion

Thick and short fingers: Selfishness

Crooked fingers: Ire; malicious personality

Puffy fingers: Hedonism

Smooth joints: A quick mind

Knotty joints: Dignified, deep thinker

Large joints: Deliberateness

First finger pointy: Intuitiveness and a love of reading

First finger square: Honesty

First finger spatulate: An overly dramatic personality

First finger set low: Shyness

Second finger pointy: A tendency toward carelessness

Second finger square: Frugality and prudence

Second finger spatulate: Love of the outdoors and gardening

Third finger pointy: The sign of an artist

Third finger square: A logical mind

Third finger spatulate: A theatrical flair; love of art

Third finger set low: Frustration, especially with work

Fourth finger pointy: A talent for diplomacy and eloquent speech

Fourth finger square: A talent for scientific thought

Fourth finger spatulate: Tendency towards melancholy

Fourth finger set low: Struggles

Index finger same length as middle finger: Stern, cruel nature

Additionally, if a person holds his or her fingers stiffly together while being examined, this reveals a cautious personality. Evenly spaced fingers indicate balance. Well-separated fingers disclose independence, and wide gaps are a sign of frankness. If the largest space between fingers occurs at the juncture of the thumb and first finger, this indicates generosity; between the second and third finger, light-heartedness; and between the third and fourth finger, originality. If the fourth finger is inordinately far away from the rest, this indicates difficulty in relationships.

The pricking of one's thumb is thought to be an ill omen, as with the saying, "By the pricking of my thumb, something wicked this way comes." And itchy knuckles portend a fight.

Related Systems: Ears, Eyes, Feet, Fingernails, Hands, Palmistry

• FIRE (PYROMANCY)

"Secrets are revealed by the subtle spirit of fire."

—Nostradamus

Legends from around the world portray fire as a sacred element stolen from gods. Numerous peoples worshipped the sun and honored the hearth-fire as the figurative heart of their homes. This veneration of fire encouraged the development and practice of pyromancy, the attempt to discern divinatory information from coals or fires. In some traditions salt or sugar is added into the flames to create images. Devic spirits known as Salamanders are believed to move within and communicate from divinatory fires.

One version of pyromancy is called causimomancy. In it, a flammable object is placed on a fire source to burn. A slowness or refusal to burn is either a positive or negative omen depending on diviner's tradition. Most often, however, it is interpreted badly (see *Botanomancy*).

Another method prescribes that you take a burning brand and twirl it before your face while repeating your question. As the brand starts to go out, observe the last few sparks to jump from it. Many round sparks say there's money in your future. Small sparks that go out quickly indicate a loss. This tradition comes from Northern England.

Fire scrying entails observing a fire for specific behavior in the sparks and flames. To try this yourself, sit comfortably in front of the fire and look deep within the embers. Try not to focus on anything specific, but stay mindful of your question. Watch until you feel as if the fire is dancing just for you, and note its movements. Here is a brief list of potential interpretations:

• Bright dancing flames indicate a positive answer or the well-being of loved ones.

• Pale flames indicate bad weather or sickness on the horizon.

• Sudden blazing of a fire portends a stranger coming or trouble soon to follow.

• A coal leaping out of the fire and landing at your feet presages twelve months of good luck and joy.

• Blue flames talk of storms (natural or emotional) and/or the presence of spirits.

• Sparks reveal anger or forthcoming news.

• Fires that will not light are a negative omen, indicating that a lot of hard work or difficult times await you.

• Sputtering fires foretell of snow in the forecast, crackling ones warn of frost, and a roaring fire presages a tempest (see *Weather Omens*).

• Smoldering fires are a sign of bitterness and trouble.

• Circles or rings in the fire portend happy relationships.

Related Systems: Ashes, Burning, Butter Lamps, Candles, Scrying, Smoke, Torches

Adaptations: This is a fun type of divination to do around a camp fire when you're really relaxed and away from the mundane world. If this is not possible, try using oil lamps, enclosed candles, a tiki torch (outdoors only), or even the fire from your stove as a source.

• FIRE TONGS

St. Augustus once said that all things should be treated like the implements of a sacred altar. Along these lines, it seems that many household items found their way into divination, often in the form of signs and omens. Two associated with fire tongs: If they fall into the ashes of a fire, a stranger is coming; and if someone accidentally walks on them, it is a bad day for fishing.

Related Systems: Random Divination, Spontaneous Divination

• FISH AND SHELLFISH (ICHTHYOMANCY)

Ichthyomancy is a form of divination that bases its interpretations on the examination of live or dead fish, their appearance and movements. For example:

Crab: Place a crab in a bowl of water and observe its movement. If it escapes, your efforts portend to be likewise successful. In Africa, this system varied a little. The shaman put a crab in a bowl of damp sand, then read the patterns made before the creature escaped the bowl.

Fish: Watch fish in a tank while thinking about a yes-or-no question. Movement by all the fish to the right indicate a positive answer, and to the left, negative. Happening to see a lone fish in water is an omen of a happy, prosperous life.

Herring: The membranes (the inner skin) from herring were once used in Scottish and Irish regions to determine the characteristics of future mates. The querent tossed the membrane against a nearby wall. If it stuck to the wall evenly, it meant the person would have a straightforward personality. If it stuck unevenly, the omen was one of dishonesty. If it didn't stick at all, but landed in a small heap on the ground, this revealed the person would be small in stature.

Salmon: In Celtic tradition eating a salmon caught in the Well of Segais was thought to bring illumination and prophetic insights.

Salted herring: Eating salted herring is said to provoke prophetic dreams.

Shark: In New Zealand, a white shark spotted at sea portends the presence of unwanted persons in the water.

Related Systems: Animal Omens and Signs, Insects

•FLOATING

In a type of hydromancy with Greek origins, various objects such as a piece of bread, a leaf, or a feather were floated on the surface of water then observed for movements. The querent placed the object on the water while asking a question. If the object floated the answer was "no"; if it sank, "yes".

Two other versions of this method were used for divining information on relationships. In one, the querent put a note from a beloved into a can and placed it in running water. If the love was true, the can would float downstream without sinking until out of sight. This tradition originates in the southern United States. The other involved placing two acorns in a bowl full of water. If they came together it meant your mate loved you truly. If they floated apart, things were perhaps not what they seemed.

Related Systems: Bread, Flower, Paper, Scarf, Water, Well

Adaptation: To broaden the interpretive value, also watch to see how long the object floats before it sinks and if it moves at all. For example, a leaf that remains afloat for a while, going in a circle, then sinks could indicate that you have been going in circles on an issue, and that you won't be successful until that cycle is broken.

•FLOUR (ALEUROMANCY)

Aleuromancy originated in Greece at Apollonian temples where a female priestess sprinkled flour on water and scried the patterns it created. Alternatively, small pieces of paper with "fortunes" written on them were placed in flour dough balls. These were placed in a bowl of water, then randomly drawn out to answer questions.

Related Systems: Floating, Food, Paper, Water

Adaptations: Fortune cookies work well, especially since you don't prepare them yourself. Alternatively, bake little heat-resistant tokens into a cake, carefully cutting a piece while thinking of your question. Whichever token you find first reveals the answer. Please eat carefully!

•FLOWERS (FLORIMANCY)

Hawaiians and ancient Greeks both used flowers in a form of hydromancy. A flower petal that symbolically corresponded to a question was placed in the bottom of a bowl. The querent posed a question while slowly pouring water into the bowl. If the petal rose to the surface and stayed there, the answer was "yes." If not, or if it rose and sank quickly, the answer was "no." An alternative approach would be to place differently colored rose petals in a dish, each of which represents a different course of action. The one that floats the longest suggests the best course to take (see *Roses*).

Other forms of florimancy focus on specific blossoms. Some traditional associations include:

Aloe: Blossoming aloe is an omen of very good fortune.

Bachelor's button: Put a bachelor's button in your pocket. If it stays fresh for longer than normal, the relationships in your life are true and trustworthy.

Carnation: In Korea, children wear a carnation in their hair to see what the future holds. If the top dries first, old age will be harsh. If the bottom dries first, they will experience a difficult youth.

Clover: If a clover blossom is attached to a four-leafed stem, it brings the best of luck, especially when carried as a charm.

Daffodil: Finding the first daffodil of spring foretells improved finances. At other times of the year, finding a daffodil facing toward you warns of bad luck for the rest of the year.

Daisy: Traditional in love-related divination, the binary method of picking daisy petals off while alternating between saying "loves me" and "loves me not" can accommodate any yes-or-no query. To vary this approach further, dye some daisies in symbolic colors, then pluck the petals in succession, seeing which color remains to answer your question. For example, receiving a red "no" might indicate that your temper has become a stumbling block to achieving your goal.

Dandelion: In the traditional language of flowers, dandelion represents ancient oracles. Take one gone to seed and think of your question. Blow on it once. If all the seeds fly free, your wish will manifest, or the answer to your question is "yes." Or meditate on the question of how many children you will have. The number of remaining seeds is your answer.

First flower of spring: If you see the first flower of spring on a Monday, it brings luck; on a Tuesday, the future will be filled with success; on Wednesday, a marriage or partnership offer is forthcoming; on Thursday, you will receive a small profit; on Friday, it is a sign of prosperity; on Saturday, it warns of misfortune; and on Sunday, the future looks wonderful, so be happy!

Geranium: Planted by your doorstep, geraniums predict the arrival of guests by the manner in which the blossom turns.

Lilac: Finding a five-petaled lilac brings as much luck as a four-leafed clover.

Myrtle: Myrtle in bloom indicates serendipity.

Pairs of flowers growing together: Name a pair of flowers growing together after two people in a relationship (or yourself and a situation). If the flowers have entwined after ten days, this means a close-knit relationship. If they both grow well but stay apart, it foretells harmonious co-existence. If one wilts or dies, this indicates an unhealthy situation. Pairs that blossom early reveal children (in literal or figurative terms).

Pansy: In 1847, Thomas Miller detailed a method of prediction based on the number of lines found in a randomly plucked pansy petal. Four lines meant hope. Five branching off a central line meant aspiration with some fears. Thick lines to the right were a sign of abundance. Thick lines to the left portended trouble ahead. Seven lines indicated constant love; eight lines, fickleness; and nine lines, changeability. Ten lines warned of a death for either a person, an ideal, or a project.

Roses: Roses predict love and romance. There is also an old form of divination called phyllorhodomancy in which the sound made by a rose petal when struck indicates the future.

Shepherd's purse: Open the seed vessel of the shepherd's purse. If the seed is yellow, there is money in your future; if green, financial losses.

Wisteria: Wisteria portends faithfulness in relationships or foretells the arrival of a message from someone you love.

During the Victorian Era, people sometimes went into their gardens and randomly picked flowers while thinking of a question. These were taken inside where the querent consulted a floral language guide to interpret the blossoms' meaning.

Related Systems: Botanomancy, Floating, Herbs, Plants, Victorian Flower Oracle, Water

Adaptations: Choose a flower that reflects the theme of your question and gently pull its petals free. Toss these into a body of water and watch the patterns they make on the surface. Also observe movements, clockwise being most favorable. A scattering of the petals without any pattern or specific movement means no answer is available right now. When this happens, make a wish and allow the flowers to carry your desire to the water, which will convey it to all of creation.

• FOOD (CRITOMANCY)

Divination by food, especially those used in offerings is called Critomancy. In Medieval and Elizabethan times, people baked small symbolic items in cakes, such as brambrack in Scotland. The token that one received in his or her piece of cake foretold their future. For example, a ring represented marriage, and a coin, prosperity (see *Bread*). Other foods that held symbolic charms to foretell a recipient's fate included syllabub on May Day, pancakes on Shrove Tuesday, and Christmas pudding (see *Holiday Omens and Signs*).

Other types of food have had traditional, specific meanings and uses in a variety of divination systems. Examples include:

Alphabet soup: Think of a question while consuming alphabet soup. When there are only a few spoonfuls left, see what words are formed by the remaining letters. These letters can also relate to initials of persons involved in your question, or you may relate them to numerological correspondences instead (see *Numerology*).

Apricots: Some Chinese believe eating apricots aids prophesy, since this was a favorite food of Confucius.

Beltane cakes: In Scotland, Beltane cakes are rolled down a hill on May Day. If they arrive at the bottom without breaking, they portend living well for the next year.

Carrots: Finding a forked carrot on the Sunday before Michaelmas is considered an omen for a lucky year in Scotland.

Christening cake: Eating a christening cake before bed will bring dreams of future mates.

Coffee: Finding bubbles in coffee means that money will soon arrive.

Corn: Finding a red ear of corn foretells exceptional luck for a full year, as long as the finder keeps the corn and does not eat it (see *Corn*).

Goose: If you are served goose on Michaelmas, you are insured of a prosperous year.

Gooseberries: When eaten on Whitsunday, gooseberries improve your future fortune.

Grapes: Eat grapes before bed to encourage prophetic dreams (see *Raisins, Onions*).

Last portion of food or beverage: If you receive the last bit of food or drink without trying, it will bring you blessings and luck, especially if you hope to marry.

Meat: Observe meat when cooking it on a Sunday. If the meat shrinks, that is an unfortunate sign. If it swells, it portends prosperity.

Milk: In Native American tradition, seeing milk immediately upon waking in the morning is a good omen for the entire day.

Mince pies: When a child opens a mince pie, the number of currants stuck to the lid predict the number of girlfriends or boyfriends he or she will have. If one piece is eaten on each of the twelve days of Christmas, your next twelve months will be filled with joy.

Olive oil: In Greece, spilling olive oil while preparing dinner is an omen of improved finances (see *Spilling*).

Pancakes: If you stir pancake batter after it's been poured onto a cooking surface, while thinking of a question, a pattern to answer the question will appear on the bottom side.

Peas: If you find a pea pod with nine peas in it, you may sleep with it under your pillow to dream of future loves.

Tea: Finding bubbles in your tea portends the arrival of guests later in the day.

Wedding cake: Placing a piece of wedding cake under your pillow allows you to dream of the one you will someday marry. When eaten, it brings luck in relationships (see *Ring* and *Marriage Omens*).

Related Systems: Beans, Bread, Cheese, Flour, Wine

Adaptation: Watch different types of food for images as they cook. Thick soups work particularly well for this type of scrying. Alternatively, look to see how foods are arranged on your plate for symbols.

•FORTUNE COOKIES

Because of the fortune cookie's name, this sweet edible deserves brief mention in this book. While not regarded seriously as a divination method, there is no reason why specially prepared fortune cookies could not be part of one. Fortune cookies originated in ancient China, where essay topics were baked into tea cakes to amuse aristocrats. The Greeks and Europeans added a slight twist to this practice, baking fortunes in balls of flour dough and tokens into cake.

Related Systems: Flour, Food

Adaptation: Find a good recipe for wafer-style cookies and prepare several, each with a slip of paper inside, upon which is written a possible outcome to a situation you're currently experiencing. The first one you eat provides your answer.

• FRITH

Frith was a traditional Scottish hereditary augury. In it, the diviner fasted on the first Monday of a quarter and stood bareheaded, barefooted, and blindfolded on his or her threshold before the following sunrise. Speaking an invocation and taking off the blindfold, the diviner made a prediction based on the first person or object seen. Frith was part of an oral tradition that has unfortunately died out.

Related Systems: Clear Sight, Direct Revelation, Enlightened Manifestation

• GALGAL

A Cabalistic form of prophesy that originated around A.D. 1200, galgal was based on the twenty-two paths of the Tree of Life and the twenty-two letters of the Hebrew alphabet. A complete set of galgal cards numbers fifty-six, each of which has a series of patterns. The reader lays out fourteen cards on a rectangular red board, the twelve along the edges corresponding to the external triads of the Tree of Life and the zodiac houses. The two center cards focus on the matter inquired about. Each galgal card may be interpreted differently depending on the house in which it lands, but instructions for this system are minimal to encourage the querent to discern and discover their own answers.

Related Systems: Cartomancy, Hebrew Letters, Tarot

Adaptation: Use the Hebrew letters combined with any personal emblems you choose and lay twelve out in a clockwise manner. Each of these symbols may be interpreted according to the house in which it lands (see *Astrology*), numerically, or by the corresponding month/season of its position (one being January, and so on). Use the two center cards as significators.

• GELOMANCY

(see Laughter)

• GEMS

Our ancestors often used valuable items like gems for magical purposes, believing that the precious character of the gem, and its indwelling spirit, somehow aided the effort. One version of gem divination related to lecanomancy entailed dropping a stone into water and asking questions. If the stone made a whistling sound in the water, it announced a positive answer.

Luminescent gems, in particular, had many superstitions associated with them. For example, someone receiving an opal, who did not have it as a birthstone, often gave it away for fear of incurring bad fortune. Likewise, some jewels are said to warn their wearers of forthcoming troubles by turning dull in color (rubies and coral) or shattering (turquoise). To this day people wear birthstones to encourage continuing luck. Other gems and their divinatory associations include:

Agate: High quality agate was used in Asia for scrying (see *Crystal Scrying*).

Amethyst: Receiving or finding an amethyst portends good hunting.

Aquamarine: Placed under your pillow, aquamarine brings visionary dreams.

Azurite: Put under your pillow, azurite brings prophetic and psychic dreams.

Bloodstone: Wearing or sleeping with a bloodstone improves psychic ability, especially foretelling the future.

Emerald: Carrying an emerald will improve your ability to prophesy, and it is so sensitive to the truth that it will shatter in the presence of lies.

Jet: Jet was used in scrying because people believed it absorbed part of the users soul, making it more potent. Jet in powdered form may be tossed on a scrying fire to improve the effect (see *Burning, Fire*).

Moonstone: Carrying or wearing a moonstone increases divinatory talents.

Obsidian: Obsidian was used in Aztec mirror divination (see *Mirrors*).

Pyrite: Pyrite was used in Mexican mirror divination.

Star Ruby: Staring at the "star" of the star ruby summons futuristic visions.

Related Systems: Crystals, Pebbles, Stones

Adaptations: In the eighteenth century, a language based on stones developed and became a popular form of expressing sentiments in Europe. This language could provide basic interpretive values for those of you wishing to create a gem casting kit. Correspondences include:

Faith or trust: Fire opal, tourmaline, or amethyst

Hope: Pearl, hematite, olivine, or hyacinth

Charity or kindness: Cat's eye, aquamarine, carbuncle, or rose quartz

Luck or destiny: Garnet, obsidian, or two-toned onyx

Honor: Quartz

Friendship or partnership: Feldspar, pyrite, or moldavite

Good timing (or "yes"): Beryl, opal, hematite, or rhodonite

Peace or truce: Alexandrite, moonstone, or topaz

Love and devotion: Lapis, labradorite, or white onyx

The Aquarian Press produces *The Crystal Oracle* by Leroy Montana, Linda Waldron, and Kathleen Jonah. This system uses five semiprecious stones, a casting cloth that allows for 140 possible readings, and a book of interpretive instructions.

Blue Pearl (1-800-822-4810) produces *The Sacred Stone Oracle* with fifteen semiprecious stones, a casting cloth, bag, and interpretive book.

Both of these systems are cast, basing the interpretations on the myths, legends, and lore of stones.

•GENETHLIALOGY

(see Birth Omens)

•GEOMANCY

(see Earth)

•GO

Some historians believe that the ancient Chinese game of Go may have had some early links with divination. For example, the historian Ban Gu (A.D. 32–92) wrote in *The Essence of Go* that the square board represented the laws of earth, the lines symbolized divine virtues, and the stones signified the yin and yang energy in all things. In a twelfth century Go manual, the author discusses there being 366 points in the game, one for each day of the year, and one for the point of origin. There is also mention of the Go board being divided into four quarters to reflect the four seasons. This configuration becomes a geomantic model for the heavens and the future, akin to magic squares, in which the numbers are replaced with black and white Go stones.

Related Systems: Earth, Mah Jongg, Stones

Adaptation: Unfortunately, I could not find instructions on how the divination system actually worked. If you wish to adapt it, you can use it like casting lots or interpret the patterns formed while playing.

•GOLD

As a precious metal, gold was used in numerous mystical applications, including those of healing and magic, so it's not surprising that gold found its way into divination as well. One fortune-telling technique instructs the querent to place a gold ring into a glass of water before a mirror. The center of the ring's reflection is scried for images, much as with a crystal (see *Rings*, *Cups*).

Alternatively, tossing a piece of gold into a well is said to clear the water for scrying purposes. More than likely this tradition originated as a propitiation to the spirit of the well, who would accept the offering, then provide answers.

Related Systems: Mirrors, Scrying, Water, Well

•GRAINS

The ancient Romans used grain to predict the sex of an unborn child. A grain of wheat and a grain of spelt were soaked with the urine of a pregnant woman. If the wheat sprouted first, it revealed the baby was a boy.

The Romans and Greeks also used grain as an indicator to forecast the outcome of battles in a divination method involving both chickens and roosters (see *Rooster, Bird Augery—Chicken*).

Related Systems: Flowers, Seeds

Adaptation: Choose several types of seed, each of which can represent a different outcome to the question at hand. Plant them at the same time, in the same area of soil. The first to grow represents your answer.

•GRASS

Plant a small area of soil with fresh grass seed while thinking of a question. Wait for seven days, then count the sprouts. An even number is a positive response. Two other divinatory techniques using grass were borrowed from late nineteenth century England and America. First, place two pieces of knot grass crosswise on a chair and sit on them. If they stay that way when you stand up, your love is true. Second, tie four knots in a long piece of grass. If they stay tied, it is a good sign. If they break, the omen is very negative. Should the knots come untied, your chances are "iffy" (see *Knots*).

Related Systems: Grains, Flowers, Seeds

•GYROMANCY

Gyromancy is a form of divination in which a person spins around inside a circle of letters or symbols laid out on the floor until overcome by dizziness. A querent poses a question and watches to see what letter/symbol the spinner touches before falling down. Some people have oracular visions while chanting and spinning, which are interpreted after they fall to the ground.

Related Systems: Dance or Movement, Laughter

Adaptation: Instead of using a person, spin a top or a coin in the center of a circle of emblems. Note the order in which symbols are touched, and then read them like a sentence for your answer.

•HAIR

Numerous ancient stories center around the power of hair, such as the one of Samson and Delilah. Modern magicians still sometimes use hair in spells to increase the spell's potency. Hair-related character divination developed alongside physiognomy and featured the following associations:

Blonds: Tendency toward intellect, creativity, and artistry.

Sudden graying: Sickness or possible imminent death.

Good hair: Good health.

Cow's lick: In a child, vitality and intelligence.

Red heads: Intense passions. It is considered unlucky for fishermen to meet a red-haired woman before sailing.

Wavy hair: Intelligence, ambition, generosity, and strength.

Curly hair: Sincerity, high energy, indiscretion, and artistry.

Straight hair: Firmness and a strong work ethic. Among the Hebrews, when combined with silkiness, straightness is also a sign of a good companion and business person.

Thin hair: Confidence, frugal outlooks, and willfulness.

Premature baldness: Among the Hebrews, a sign of craftiness that leads to success in business.

Dry, frizzy hair: In Cabalistic tradition, the sign of a choleric temper.

Dark brown hair: Morality, ambition, loyalty, and love.

Black hair: Resoluteness and devotion with lots of nervous energy.

Auburn hair: Inconsistency, friendliness, action, and confidence.

White hair: Candor, consistency, gentility, bravery, grace, and methodicalness.

Hairy chest: Longevity, vitality, and luck.

Hairy hands: A destiny of prosperity.

Dropping a comb while doing your hair: Disappointment.

Related Systems: Color, Ears, Eyes, Facial Features, Fingernails, Fingers, Hands, Physiognomy

• HALOMANCY

(see Salt)

• HANDS (PALMISTRY, CHIROMANCY)

The art of palmistry is covered separately in this book. This entry specifically focuses on divining personality types and one's futures from the shape, size, and appearance of one's hands and/or fingers. Palmistry does take these characteristics into account but focuses more on the lines and configurations in the palm of the hand.

The earliest accounts of hand divination came from India nearly 5,000 years ago, where legend has it that this art was given to humankind by the ocean god Samudra. Asians and Mesopotamians adapted the Indian concepts, and the Greeks began to use it around 2,500 years ago. Aristotle was a notable advocate. By A.D. 1000, the clergy in Europe were speaking out against chiromancy, leading to a gradual decline in its use until it was revived during the Victorian Era. Some traditional associations include:

Short hands: A quickness to judge

Square hands: Industriousness and honesty

Broad based, tapering palm: Wit and artistry

Thick, broad, with short fingers: Physical nature

Square palm, broad fingers: Practicality and convention

Spatulate: Ambitiousness, energy, and independence

Broad palm, heavy joints: Logical thought and introversion

Long, flexible palm with tapering fingers: Sensitivity and creativity

Long, delicate hand: Dreaminess and mysticism

Fan-shaped: Daring and abundant energy

Bony, irregular hands: Adeptness in philosophy and problem solving

Long hands: A detailed personality

Equal-sized palms: Good instincts

Hard hands: Tenaciousness and perseverance

Soft hands: Laziness or procrastination

Thick hands: Selfishness or egotism

Scratch on back of hand near thumb: A portent of a journey

Itching hands: Money, a letter, or guests coming

Hands crossing while reaching for food: A sign of forthcoming arguments

I find it interesting that many people continue to judge another's character by their handshake, and I cannot help wondering if this is related to palmistry or chiromancy.

Related Systems: Ears, Eyes, Facial Features, Fingernails, Fingers, Moles, Palmistry, Phrenology, Physiognomy

• HANDWRITING ANALYSIS (GRAPHOLOGY)

The Romans studied people's characteristics as reflected in their handwriting, as did the scholars and monks of the Middle Ages. The Chinese analyzed an individual's calligraphy as early as 1,000 years ago. In 1622, the first known treatise on this topic appeared in Bologna.

By the nineteenth and twentieth centuries, the subject became more scientific in its approaches. In 1906, Alfred Benet studied the relationship between graphology and personality. Noted psychologist Carl Jung felt that handwriting held important clues to personality. Handwriting analysis is included in some American, French, German, and Israeli college-level criminology courses. Additionally, experts believe that drastic changes in a person's life can result in drastic changes in handwriting.

For analysis, each person's script is divided into three parts. The uppermost portion is related to spiritual aspirations, the middle portion represents practical attitudes, and the lower portion reveals physical conditions and interests. Each portion is examined and interpreted as follows:

Loops: Long, round loops in letters indicate romanticism, while triangular ones indicate a tyrannical nature or someone who is disappointed by life.

Margins: Wide upper margins show formality, while wide lower ones reveal a fear of physicality. Narrow lower margins appear with people who hoard things out of fear. Wide left margins appear in cultured individuals, and narrow left margins indicate an overly friendly personality. Wide right margins show apprehensiveness, and narrow right margins reflect the lack of discrimination.

Slant: A right slant is that of an extrovert, a left slant that of an introvert, and varying slant reveals a changeable, versatile person.

Thickness: Heavy-handed writing shows passion and sensuality. Lightness is the mark of sensitivity. Very light handwriting indicates an individual who lacks vitality, and medium thickness, an average person.

Size: Very large script is common among active, social, and outgoing individuals, as well as those who are abrasive. Medium-sized script reveals the proverbial "middle-of-the-road" person. Small handwriting occurs most often with academic types, and tiny handwriting is the sign of an inferiority complex. Variations in size reveal inconsistency, and small letters at the end of words indicate maturity.

Slope: Straight slope occurs in steadfast, unwavering people. Uphill slopes suggest optimism and ambition, while downhill sloping insinuates pessimism or depression.

Spacing: Narrow spaces between words reveal the need to socialize. Wide spaces occur with people who are very choosy about their acquaintances. Narrow spaces between lines is the sign of poor organization, while wide ones show someone with good outlooks and a sense of structure.

Connected writing: Connected handwriting belongs to a logical, systematic thinker who is cooperative and reasonable.

Disconnected writing: Handwriting that is not connected is the product of a stubborn, moody person with strong ego and creative ability.

Ink colors: Conventional people choose blue ink, sensual people choose red, assertive people like black, and "gypsy spirits" like green.

Numbers: People who write their numbers clearly tend to have practical attitudes regarding money. Small, thin numbers are often associated with calculative minds (like in accountants). Heavily written numbers indicate materialism.

Adaptation: Some on-line services and computer programs offer handwriting analysis now via the use of scanners.

• HATS

There is a contemporary variation on divination by lots in which options are placed into a hat and one is drawn out to determine the right course of action. Hat divination may have arisen out of fashion, hats being readily available containers for lots, but there is also the ancient symbolism of the head being the seat of god.

Related Systems: Lots, Omens, Signs

Adaptation: Inscribe words, phrases, or symbols on sturdy art paper or card stock and treat them with protective spray. Create a good diversity of these, perhaps twenty-five in number like with runes. Designate a special hat for use with these tokens, and you'll have a tool that you can use again and again. You can draw several of them from the hat during the reading to indicate different facets of a situation, such as past or future influences.

• HEAD BUMPS/STRUCTURE (PHRENOLOGY)

In 1796, Dr. Franz Joseph Gall, a Viennese physician, formulated the theories of phrenology. Dr. Gall believed that a person's character could be determined by the shape of the skull and its anomalies. In the 1800s, Orson Fowler in the United States took up phrenological study and established a phrenological publishing house, and later a school, dedicated to this "science."

Phrenology begins with an examination of the overall shape of the head. Round heads reveal an outgoing, brave person. Square heads reflect good foundations and practicality. Narrow-headed people are thought to be shy, and those with oval-shaped head, scholarly.

Next the phrenologist examines each part of the head, looking for bumps or indentations. The entirety of this information, combined with the shape, determines the personality "diagnosis." The illustration on page 150 shows the areas that are examined, and the following list, their general correspondences. A bump in a particular region means the associated characteristic is overcultivated, while an indentation is a sign of underdevelopment.

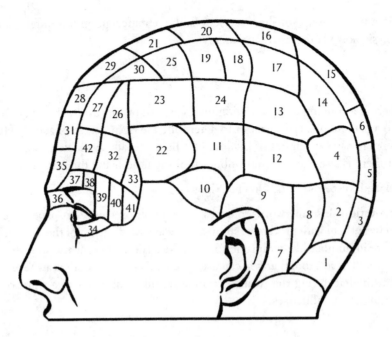

Phrenological Regions of the Head

1. Interest in sex; overall sex appeal

2. Faithfulness; ability to commit

3. Ability for filial love; charitableness

4. Sociability; the ability to give and receive love or friendship

5. Love of home or country

6. Focus and reasoning

7. Zeal; enjoyment of life; heartiness

8. Aggressiveness; resistance to change; bravery

9. Leadership skills; tenacity

10. Appetite

11. Materialism

12. Discretion; the ability to keep secrets

13. Caution

14. The need for approval and acceptance from others

15. Assurance; the need for (or desire for) an authority figure

16. Will; fortitude

17. Honesty; principles

18. Optimism

19. Beliefs; potential psychic or spiritual interests

20. Respect for the law

21. Kindness; empathy

22. Hands-on abilities; serviceability

23. Idealism

24. Ability to see the larger picture; perspective

25. Dramatic and social ability

26. Happiness; humor

27. Reason, logic, and analytical skills

28. Judgment; discernment

29. Communication

30. Memory

31. Awareness of time; promptness

32. Musical inclinations

33. Foreign language skills; writing skills

34. Curiosity; ability to integrate what one learns

35. Visual acuity

36. Proportional perspective (judging size, weight, etc.)

37. Physical balance

38. Ability to use color effectively

39. Organization and cleanliness

40. Math skills

41. Sense of direction; wanderlust

Related Systems: Ears, Eyes, Facial Features, Fingernails, Fingers, Hands, Moles, Palmistry

• HEBREW ALPHABET

In the esoteric tradition of Cabalism, each letter of the Hebrew alphabet had a specific significance and numeric correspondence. This interpretive value was often used to discern the deeper meaning of scriptures, but it also appears in the Higher Arcana of Tarot cards.

Below is a list of the letters and their meanings. These may be added to the interpretations you presently have for your Tarot deck.

LETTER	NAME	MEANING
א	Aleph	Self-mastery; control of one's fate; esoterically, oneness and stability. Aleph increases the significance of any emblem that follows it.
ב	Beth	Matters of home, fertility, and communication; the need to act or move. In combination with aleph, beth is an emblem of progressive ideas and motivation.
ג	Gimel	Opportunity; an opening, but one that may still have some type of impediment.
ד	Daleth	Motherly energy; divine sustenance; a change for the better in a material sense; in a negative position, a sign of division.
ה	Hal	Energy in abundance; the element of air; new, vitalizing projects or people.
ו	Waw	Vision and insight; the element of water; a warning to watch your desires and know that there are some things that you cannot comprehend just now; a temporary holding pattern.
ז	Zain	Hurry and noise abounds; natural progressions; a sign to watch for unusual connections between yourself and situations or people.
ח	Cheth	Work and effort; reaching a balance between jobs and home or between leisure and responsibility; potential need for solitude.
ט	Teth	Safety and retreat; a warning not to hide from the inevitable or resist change.

LETTER	NAME	MEANING
י	Yod	Manifestation and power; long-lasting effects.
כ	Kaaw	A transition or halfway point; possible indifference in communications.
ל	Lames	Growth and maturity; finding your proverbial wings; elevation that comes partially from coincidence.
מ	Mem	Fruitfulness and unity that comes from celebrating diversity.
ם	MM	The self; self-awareness, individuality, and self-expression.
ס	Samech	An unrealistic goal; recognizing limits; karmic justice.
ע	Aim	The need to listen carefully to messages from those around you, to separate yourself from dissension; in a negative position, the feeling of emptiness and loneliness.
פ	Pei	The need for effective and honest expression.
צ	Tzaddl	Accomplishment that comes from caring for one's health and balancing yin-yang energies; possible tempting situations that look too good to be true.
ק	Q-Oph	Hidden matters and the subconscious self; also our primal nature.
ר	Reisch	Tenacity and determination; depending on yourself for achievement.
ש	Shein	Light and goodness; a positive sign of progress.
ת	Taw	Reciprocity with the world and the universe; an awareness of life's network working in harmony; sympathetic connections.

Related Systems: Arithmancy, Galgal, Names, Tarot

Adaptation: Use the letters as part of a cast or drawn system by painting the letters on stone, wood, or paper surfaces of similar size and shape.

• HEPATOSCOPY

Hepatoscopy is a system of divination that uses the liver of a sacrificial animal as the basis for interpretation.

Related Systems: Animal Omens and Signs, Entrails, Offerings

• HERBS (BOTANOMANCY)

Herbs have been used in divination in numerous ways. Some people placed them under pillows to invoke prophetic dreams. Others burned them and observed the flames, used them in pendulums, and planted them and watched their growth. No matter the approach, however, herb divination is supposed to be most successful on Halloween and Midsummer's Night. Midsummer is also when magical herbs are harvested for potency, so there may be some connection here. In matters of love, Valentine's Day is considered advantageous.

Here are some traditional methods and interpretations associated with specific herbs:

Basil: Place two basil leaves in a fire. If they burn slowly, this indicates strong positive energies that support your efforts. If they snap and pop, trouble or arguments will come up with regard to your question.

Lovers in Italy exchange pots of basil on Midsummer's eve. If the basil grows thick and well, it is a positive augury for the relationship.

Holly: Nine holly leaves tied with nine knots in a scarf under your pillow helps to inspire dreams of the future, or may answer a specific question through your night visions.

Heliotrope: Place heliotrope under the pillow of someone who was robbed to evoke dreams of the identity of the thief.

Mullein: In the Ozarks, mullein is used for love divination. Bend the stalk to point toward your beloved's home. If it springs back up and lives, your love is reciprocated.

Sage: Finding a sprig of sage is an omen of good health.

Vervain: Medieval European healers placed vervain on the heads of the sick to foresee their fate.

Yarrow: Cut yarrow during the new moon and place it under your pillow to receive dreams of the future. Note that the yarrow stalk was used in the *I Ching* system of divination (see *I Ching*).

Related Systems: Bay, Flowers, Leaves, Plants, Rose, Trees

• HIPPOMANCY

(see Horse Divination)

• HOLIDAY OMENS AND SIGNS

Different holidays throughout the year have had specific omens and signs associated with them, Christmas, Easter, and New Year's being the most popular.

New Year's Day: On New Year's, Babylonians observed snake holes. If a snake emerged from its resting spot, it predicted a death by the end of the year. The only way to avert this fate was to shave your head.

In England, it was custom to open a Bible to the book of Proverbs on New Year's day and randomly choose one of the thirty-one verses in the last chapter. This would indicate your fortune for the coming year, or perhaps your best choice for a career. For example, if the word "linen" appeared in the text, it indicated working as a seamstress or cloth merchant.

On New Year's, if a horse looks at you, or if you find a horseshoe facing toward you or a pin pointing toward you, it is a good omen for the year.

Count the buttons that appear on the clothes of the first person you see on New Year's. If they have only one button, it's a lucky omen. Two buttons portend joy; three, a new vehicle; four, some type of travel; five, new clothing; six, accessories; seven, a dog coming into your life; eight, a new cat; nine, an important letter; and ten, a pleasurable year. This is from an old Victorian tradition.

Ground Hog's Day: One of the most famous days for prognosticating weather is Ground Hog's Day. A sunny day allows the ground hog to see its shadow, thereby dooming humankind to six more weeks of winter (see *Animal Omens and Signs, Weather Omens*).

Valentine's Day: The most propitious day to enact any type of love divination is Valentine's Day.

April Fool's Day: If you are fooled by a young girl on April Fool's Day, you will befriend or marry her. If a couple marries on this day, the wife will rule the roost.

Easter: Finding a two-yoked egg on Easter indicates money in your future.

In Belgium, when Easter falls on Annunciation Day, it is considered an omen of terrible mishaps in the country, so much so that the celebration for Annunciation is often moved to another date.

May Day: In Northumberland, it is customary to prepare a syllabub with a wedding ring in the bowl on May Day. The person who fishes out the ring with the ladle will be lucky for a year and the first to wed (see *Rings*).

Saint Agnes' Day: Fasting on St. Agnes' Day, then placing a pin on your sleeve and a sprig of rosemary in your shoe will allow you to dream of your future love.

Saint John's Eve: St. John's Eve is a good time for necromancy.

Saint Luke's Day: Rub your hands and lips with a mixture of marjoram, thyme, honey, and vinegar on St. Luke's Day to dream of future loves. This tradition comes from England.

Saint Paul's Day: If it rains on St. Paul's Day, it will be a good year for corn.

Saint Swithun's Day: Rain on St. Swithun's Day means that forty more days of rain will follow (see *Weather Omens*).

Winter's Eve: Winter's Eve is considered an excellent night for divination.

Christmas: The sun shining through apple trees on Christmas day foretells a good crop of fruit and luck in the coming year (see *Sun*).

In Germany, people believe that if Christmas falls on Tuesday, winter will be cold, spring will be windy, summer will be wet, and fall will arrive early (see *Days*).

•HORSE DIVINATION (HIPPOMANCY)

Germanic peoples once kept white horses in sacred groves for divinatory observations. The Roman historian Tacitus (A.D. 55) says this was because of a prevalent belief that horses had the confidence of the gods. Observing this creature's behavior when yoked to a special chariot would yield information conveyed directly from a god's mouth to the horse's ear.

A different version of hippomancy was practiced south of the Baltic Sea, in which there was a sacred horse that only a priest could ride. In book XIV of Danish historian Saxo's *Histories* (A.D. 1150), a black horse and another horse of uncertain color are also mentioned. When information was desired, spears would be laid on the ground in patterns, either crossed, in three pairs, or nine in a row. The horse would be ridden over them, and interpretations made based on whether it touched any of the spears, and if so, with which hoof.

Related System: Animal Omens and Signs

Adaptation: The Romans simplified the latter system and interpreted patterns made by a horse's hoofprints, as with some forms of geomancy. This approach could be adapted to the footprints of any beloved pet.

• HYDROMANCY

(see Water)

• HYPNOTISM (METAGNOMY)

Hypnotism is a relatively modern way of inducing a trancelike state from which past or future information may be obtained.

Related System: Meditation

• I CHING

(see Pa Kua)

The *I Ching* originated in China, where the hardy yarrow plant grows well under a variety of conditions. Because it exhibits both fertility and longevity, the Chinese credited it with supernatural powers and used the yarrow stalk in divination. King Wen began formalizing the forerunner to the *I Ching* about 3,000 years ago. The work was completed by his son, the Duke of Chou, and called *Chou I*, or the Changes of Chou. Confucius (Kung-Fu Tse) made significant revisions to it, and in 136 B.C., an imperial authority arranged for a special study of the *Chou I*. It became the fundamental study of this divinatory practice.

By the first century A.D., the Changes of Chou became collectively known as the *I Ching*. It was considered both a philosophical and divinatory system. Through a detailed ritual of repeated casting, reduction, and counting, fifty yarrow stalks yielded a hexagram, one of sixty-four binary-based symbols that represent the various stages of material creation and phases of existence. This process was not thought to be an exercise in mere change. Direct interaction between the seen and unseen worlds was believed to be a regularly occurring fact.

The Japanese began using the *I Ching* sometime around A.D. 600. Marco Polo described it upon his return from China, and people in Europe began using it around A.D. 1300. Western translations were available in the late 1800s, and during the 1960s, its use among Americans experienced a tremendous upsurge, which continues today with the New Age movement.

There are two approaches to *I Ching* divination. The first uses the traditional bundle of fifty yarrow stalks, or a reasonable substitute like equal-sized sticks. A detailed explanation of this complex ritual can be found in the Bollingen Series edition of the *I Ching*. A second more common method involves tossing a set of three coins six consecutive times. Traditionally, these were old Chinese bronze coins with a hole in the middle and an inscription on one side. Any three coins will work fine, as long as you predetermine which side will correspond to the inscribed or yin side, having a numerical value of two. The opposite side is then the yang side, having a numerical value of three.

With either method, you create a structure of six horizontal lines, each line of which will take one of four forms, depending on the numerical tools you derive: 6 results in a changing yin (or broken) line, 7 results in a resting yang (or solid) line, 8 results in a resting yin line, and 9 results in a changing yang line. These lines are arranged in order, from bottom to top, to make one of sixty-four possible hexagrams. Each hexagram represents a different aspect or situation in life, which is summarized in a short poem or "judgment." The hexagram's component trigrams also contribute to the interpretive value. The trigrams are three-line substructures that make up the hexagram, the top three making the upper or outer trigram, the bottom three making the lower or inner trigram, and the four middle lines making two possible nuclear trigrams (see *Pa Kua* for list of trigrams). And with each hexagram there is additional text that explores the subtleties of interpretation and offers advice.

If all the lines are resting lines, you take the meaning of the hexagram as a whole in answer to your query. If, however, any are changing lines, they will provide additional meaning to the answer. Also, these changing lines become their opposites (i.e., yang to yin, or yin to yang), creating a new hexagram. This second hexagram adds a final dimension to your answer.

The complexity and subtlety of the interpretive values in the *I Ching* make them difficult to capture in a brief overview. The hexagram may have an overall positive connotation, like number eleven, *T'ai* or *Peace*, but the added judgment of an individual line may suggest "humiliation" or "remorse." And with just one changing line, it can turn into a second hexagram with a more adverse judgment, like number thirty-six, *Ming I* or *Darkening of the Light*. Fortunately, there are a number of good books that explore the *I Ching* from different perspectives, traditional, New Age, and feminist, to name a few.

Related Systems: Coins, Herbs, Rods, Wands

Adaptations: *I Ching* readings are now available through some on-line services. US Games Systems also presently offers *I Ching* cards with accompanying coins for ease of reference and use.

If you choose to use *I Ching* coins, consider choosing special ones that have meaning to you. Examples include coins bearing the year of your birth, silver coins to accentuate your intuitive nature, or old coins from a country that represents your personal spiritual path.

•ICHTHYOMANCY

(see Fish)

•IFA

Part of the African Yoruba tradition, Ifa is a religious and fortune-telling system that includes special chants and songs recited during a divinatory rite. Each verse identifies the correct sacrifice to make in order to solve the querent's problem or answer her or his question. There are approximately 1,000 verses for the Ifa diviner to memorize, many of which incorporate myths, folktales, proverbs, and riddles. But because this is part of an oral tradition, the exact verses often vary slightly between tribes.

The central tools for Ifa are a divinatory tray (*Opon Ifa*), water, powdered wood, an ivory wand, and sixteen palm nuts. The tray represents creation, the nuts symbolize wisdom, the powder equates to transformation, and the wand represents manifestation. The ritual begins with the priest sitting on a mat in front of the divinatory tools, facing east. He or she sprinkles wood dust on the tray and divides the dust into four equal sections by drawing a cross in it. These four quarters represent four different stages necessary to the resolution of the question. Then the priest recites an invocation, tapping the tray with the ivory wand to awaken and honor the spirits.

Next the diviner sprinkles water over the palm nuts, each of which is held up to the sky while a primary god is invoked. One of these nuts is touched to the querent's forehead while the priest prays, and is then returned to the others. From here the priest places all the nuts in the left hand and randomly grabs several with the right hand. If all nuts are gathered, no mark is made on the board. If the diviner grabs one nut, he or she draws two lines on the board, and if two nuts, one line is drawn.

This process continues until eight indicators are completed, two per section. This allows for 256 possible octograms that bear a strong similarity to geomantic patterns, and 256 instructional verses. In the end, the querent must accept the total message of the Ifa verse, giving thanks through an offering of food or cloth, and then act on the message, or be considered disobedient and ungrateful to the gods.

Another means of divination in the Ifa tradition is direct consultation with elemental spirits for omens and signs. A priest might go to a mountain top, for example, to commune with air spirits regarding questions of growth, or to obtain futuristic visions. Water spirits are consulted in questions of sexuality and stability, earth spirits for finding ways to clear obstacles, and fire spirits for queries regarding spiritual maturation. To obtain this information, the priest makes offerings on behalf of the querent, meditates, and recites prayers. They may also refer to the *Opon Ifa* if signs are slow in coming.

Related Systems: Dafa, Earth, Geomancy, Nuts, Rods (Druid Sticks), Shells

•INCENSE (LIBRANOMANCY)

Any divinatory method that requires incense as part of its ritual or interpretive process can be considered libranomancy, and in most cases, it is all but indistinguishable from divination by smoke. One exception originates in Mexico. Balls of coapal incense are put into water to see if they sink or float in response to a question, sinking being interpreted negatively.

Related Systems: Fire, Offerings, Ritual, Smoke

Adaptation: If using the smoke from incense to accentuate your divinatory efforts, consider making your own. To do this, start with one cup of powdered sandalwood (or other aromatic wood) as a base. Add two to three other herbs that correspond to your question. Prepare this mixture during the time of a waxing or full moon to increase insightful energies, then burn it while performing your reading.

•INK (ATRAMENTAMANCY)

The ancient Persians and Arabs used dark ink for scrying. For this, the ink was either mixed with water in a bowl or cupped in the diviner's right hand. On the surface (or just below), images would appear as in crystal scrying. According to a Victorian tradition, spilling ink while writing a letter presages a streak of improved luck, even if it requires rewriting the letter. In Greece and other areas of the world, people dropped ink into water or onto a piece of paper and scried the shapes it made.

Related Systems: Lead, Scrying, Tin, Wax

Adaptation: Food coloring or water-soluble paints can be substituted for ink.

•INSECTS

As with animals, the appearance of insects in odd formations or locations have been indicators of many things, from weather to matters of love. Many of these beliefs originated in Europe or rural America:

Ants: If nesting near your door, ants indicate providence will soon find you. In Africa, shamans sometimes insert two tall leaves into an ant hill, one representing a negative answer and the other positive. Whichever is eaten first indicates the answer.

Bees: Swarming bees presage death. One stinging you warns of betrayal. Bees flying around you tell of news on the way. Dreaming of bees indicates forthcoming honors (see *Dreams*).

Beetle: A beetle walking over your shoe brings bad luck for the day (Scotland).

Butterfly: A butterfly winging into the house is a harbinger of a wedding or another positive partnership.

Cricket: A cricket entering your home is most fortunate. It means that friends are coming your way, and that you will experience domestic bliss.

Grasshoppers: Grasshoppers appearing near you bring luck and presage an enjoyable journey, according to Eastern traditions.

Katydid: Expect a frost six weeks after you hear the first katydid (see *Weather Omens*).

Lady Bug: Most often the lady bug was consulted in questions of love. In Britain, an even number of spots on "her" wings meant one's love was true. Additionally, if asked nicely, she would fly in the direction of a future lover after resting on your arm or hand.

Lightning Bug: The Penobscot Indians say that seeing a lightning bug late in spring predicts a plethora of salmon in the streams.

Moth: Among tribes in New Zealand, moths are a welcome sign. They indicate that an upcoming fishing trip will be successful. The moth's appearance also marks a good time to collect shoreline foods. A moth flying toward you presages the arrival of an important letter.

Praying Mantis: If a praying mantis lands on your hand, you will soon meet a distinguished person or gain some type of personal honor.

Termite: In Africa, some creative diviners cut two sticks from two different trees and placed them on a termite mound. One stick indicated an affirmative answer, the other a negative answer. They posed the querent's question to the termites, then returned the next day to see which stick was consumed in response.

Wasp: A wasp acts as a warning to guard against deceit or jealousy in the near future.

•INTOXICANTS

While generally not recommended in modern divinatory practices, the use of herbs and/or alcohol was part of some ecstatic rituals. The herb or beverage was considered a "spirit" that could possess the body of the diviner and aid in making interpretations. For example, some historians believe that the Pythia at Delphi inhaled mind-altering smoke before making predictions, and many shamanic rituals use natural substances to encourage an altered state of awareness and improved communion with the divine. No matter the setting, however, the substance was always considered sacred, and anyone abusing it would be liable to severe punishments.

Related Systems: Dance or Movement, Laughter, Ritual

•ITCHING

Itching means different things depending on where it occurs. In symbolic terms, the itch is like a notice from the Universe that gets our attention through the annoyance. Here is a list of locations and common meanings:

Crown of head: A sign of advance.

Right eyebrow: You will meet an old friend.

Left eyebrow: Trouble lies ahead.

Right eye: Pleasure (see *Eyes*).

Left eye: Depression

Right cheek: Others approve of your actions.

Left cheek: Your actions are suspect.

Mouth: A secret meeting.

Neck: Sickness in the home.

Right shoulder: A windfall, often financial.

Left shoulder: Dissatisfaction

Right elbow: Exciting news is coming your way, possibly a new lover.

Stomach: An opening awaits you.

Thumb: A threat to your security.

Genitalia: A quarrel will be reconciled.

Thigh: You may soon move or travel.

Left knee: A journey will be difficult.

Ankle: Increased income or a positive partnership is forthcoming.

Left ankle: You will soon be paying out money.

Both feet: Difficult travel lies ahead; be careful with your plans.

Related Systems: Ears, Eyes, Facial Features, Fingernails, Fingers, Hands, Palmistry, Twitching

• KEYS (CLERDOMANCY)

Clerdomancy was a type of pendulum divination in which a key was suspended by a string and placed into a glass. As the key moved via automatism, it answered questions by rapping. One rap was a positive response, two raps were negative. Alternatively, the key was observed for the direction of motion, clockwise revolutions being positive. Some instructions for this technique recommended that the string be held by a virgin and that psalms be recited during the reading.

Related Systems: Automatism, Ouija, Pendulum

Helpful Hint: Look for interesting old keys at yard sales and flea markets.

• KEYHOLE

If you wish to know the future of your relationships, both intimate and social, look through a keyhole on Valentine's morning. If you see more than one object, things bode well for friends, lovers, and partners in the coming year (see *Holiday Omens and Signs*).

Related System: Enlightened Manifestation

Adaptation: Change the date on which you try this method to one that better represents your question. For example, peek through a keyhole on New Year's to see what the next year has in store. The first object you spy is the symbol you should interpret.

•KIN

(see Ouija)

•KITES

It is quite plausible that kite divination owes its origins to Eastern mysticism and symbology because of its prevalence in cultural celebrations. Moroccans still believe that a kite flying well is a good omen. One that breaks free predicts that misfortune is on the horizon. A kite that gets tangled indicates forthcoming delays and difficulties.

Adaptation: Any wind-sensitive item can be used for this technique. For example, try freeing some flower petals to the wind. If they fly away easily, the sign is positive; if most of the petals fall, it is negative (see *Flowers*).

•KNIFES/DAGGERS/SWORDS (MACHAROMANCY)

People often used the shiny surface of a blade for scrying when other, more expensive tools (like mirrors) were not available. In another approach, a knife is laid on a table and spun around to determine the direction of a lost item or an area from which trouble originates. Alternatively, the knife may be encircled by letters of the alphabet and spun thirteen times to reveal a message. If the knife point stops at "Y" or "N" on the first spin, make no further efforts. These indicate a simple "yes" or "no" answer, respectively. Gypsies and North American Indians sometimes used twelve words or symbols at the clock face hour points around the knife instead.

Related Methods: Crystal Scrying, Mirrors, Ouija, Scrying, Wheel

Modern Alternatives: For households in which a sharp knife is not a good idea, try any item with a point, like a pen or pencil. Replace the alphabetical letters with twelve personally chosen symbols that relate more directly to your question. Spin three times to reveal how the past, present, and future relate to your question. Or, the three spins may also represent the situation, action called for, and outcome.

•KNOTS

People have used knots in a variety of occult practices because they lend themselves to the symbolism of binding and releasing energy. A rural English tradition instructs that one should tie nine knots in a garter and place this around your bed post to have dreams of the future.

Related Systems: Clothing, Dressing, Grass

Adaptation: Have the number of knots correspond to your question (see *Numerology* for correspondences).

•LAMPS (LYCHNOMANCY)

In lychnomancy a new oil lamp, from a temple and with a clean wick, was taken to a dark building with an opening to the east or south and no cellar beneath it. The oil lamp was then set on a new, clean brick. Next the diviner placed fresh oil in the lamp, lit it, and stood a young boy between his or her feet while reciting chants. Myrrh or a willow leaf were common offerings to enhance this rite. Finally a spell was cast on the boy, who was asked, "What do you see?" The boy became an oracle. This particular method was found in the London/Leiden magical papyrus text.

Related Systems: Burning, Butter Lamps, Candles, Fire, Torches

•LAMPADOMANCY

(see Torch)

•LAUGHTER (GELOMANCY)

Closely related to gyromancy and other ecstatic forms of divination like dance, gelomancy interprets the omens in hysterical laughter. One rather sedate version of this occurs during the Zurich Spring Festival on April 16, which is celebrated with feasts, toasting, and a joke-telling competition. If the jokes cause uproarious laughter, they augur a good spring.

•LEAD (MOLYBDOMANCY)

Molybdomancy is a type of scrying in which molten lead is dropped into cold water and observed for symbolic shapes. Sometimes the lead was instead poured on the ground and allowed to harden into a pattern (see Appendix B for possible shapes and meanings). Molybdomancy was most frequently employed to determine the outcome of a sickness or the occupation of a future mate.

Related Systems: Ink, Tin, Wax

•LEAVES (SYCOMANCY)

There are numerous traditional methods and interpretations with sycomancy.

- Write your question on a green leaf and put it away. If it withers quickly, this indicates "not now."

- Listen to the sound of rustling leaves or watch the patterns they or their shadows create while they move. This method comes from Greece.

- For every autumn leaf you catch before it touches the earth, you will have one happy week to follow. This also protects against winter colds.

- If you find an ash leaf with an even number of divisions, keep it as a charm. This is a sign of very good luck soon to come your way.

- Gather nine holly leaves on a Friday and put them in a handkerchief tied with nine knots under your pillow (see *Knots*). This is a charm for prophetic dreams.

- Scratch a word or symbol onto a leaf that somehow represents the essence of your heart's desire. Wear this near your heart for twenty-four hours. If the scratching is more visible afterward, your wish should be fulfilled.

- Write three different outcomes to a question, or three different potential futures, onto three leaves and place them in the sunlight. The first leaf to dry reveals your answer. This method comes from Greece.

Related Systems: Apple Blossoms, Bay, Botanomancy, Flowers, Herbs, Plantain, Plants, Rose, Trees

Adaptation: Gather different-colored leaves from various trees and wax or laminate them. Use the symbolism of the tree itself, or the leaf's hue, as the foundation for interpretive value. These are best used for a cast system on a large piece of cloth that allows for gentle drifting.

•LECANOMANCY

(see Gems, Oil)

•LEMON JUICE

Gather together a short stick, a candle, a cup of fresh lemon juice, and several evenly sized slips of paper. While thinking of a question, use the juice as ink and the stick as a pen to write potential answers or outcomes on the slips. Let these dry. Light the candle. Place the slips in a bowl and mix them. Randomly pick one with your left hand. Hold it over near the flame to darken the lettering and reveal your answer.

Carry lemon peel with you an entire day while you concentrate on a question. Rub this on your bed posts before retiring. Pay attention to your dreams for answers (see *Food, Dreams*).

Related Systems: Hats, Lots (for the first method discussed)

•LIBRANOMANCY

(see Incense, Smoke)

•LIGHTNING

The ancient Greeks associated lightning with male sun gods. In other words, lightning was sacred fire falling from the sky, often exacting divine judgment. Consequently, the Greeks took lightning observation very seriously. They divided the sky into sixteen sections. They interpreted each streak based on where it appeared.

The Romans also developed a method of divination by lightning observations. Their system took into account the proximity of the strike, its location, and its intensity. These three factors, figured together, portended the success or failure of endeavors, especially a household's overall fortune for a coming decade. Put simply, if the first flash in a storm was seen on the left, it warned of trouble and heartache. If on the right, it was a propitious omen to proceed unhesitantly. Lightning overhead indicated a mixture of success with some losses. Lightning without thunder warned of war and uprisings.

Related Systems: All forms of Aeromancy, Thunder, Weather Omens

Adaptation: Think of a question upon seeing lightning, then count the seconds until the thunderclap follows. An even number of seconds is a positive response.

•LITHOMANCY

(see Crystal Scrying, Stones)

•LOTS (SORTILEGE)

Lots were very popular for divination, appearing in Mesopotamia, Babylonia, Greece, Rome, Germany, China, Africa, and Oceania, just to name a few. In ancient Mesopotamia, lots were used to determine inheritances, elect officials, resolve the fate of accused prisoners, and foretell the future.

The tools for lot casting varied from culture to culture. While Sumerians favored wooden sticks, Assyrians used clay dice, and Babylonians preferred bone dice. In the Finnish epic, the *Kalevala*, diviners cast alder branches to discern cures and rowan branches to determine if the year would be peaceful. In modern times, flipping coins, drawing straws, and playing the lottery remain as examples of this enduring tradition.

In the tenth chapter of *Germania*, Tacitus described German lots in great detail. One version from the late Viking era was quite simple, using black and white pieces of wood to determine a yes-or-no answer. These were cast three times over three days to confirm the results. Older women often performed this ritual for the community and received an honorable title that Tacitus translated as *matres familiae*.

Like the Mesopotamians, the Germans used lots to determine many things. Among certain Saxon pirates, the system determined the life and death of prisoners. Lots were also employed to make important military decisions. If the lot turned out negative, leaders would hold off on going to war no matter how favorable their chances appeared otherwise. Writings indicate this practice still existed as late as the ninth century A.D., when lots determined not only if war should be undertaken but also tactical moves.

Depending on the culture and the urgency of the situation, lots were sometimes combined with other methods, chiefly animal sacrifice, in order to gain favor with the gods. In Germany, this combination may have resulted from an ancient practice of sprinkling runes with blood to improve their accuracy in obtaining secret knowledge.

Related Systems: Bamboo Sticks, Beans, Blocks, Castings, Coconut, Coins, Dice, Sortilege

Alternatives: Hundreds of everyday items can be used for lot casting, including bracelet charms, pieces of colored string, and colored toothpicks.

•LUCK BALL

The luck ball is a hoodoo charm or fetish made from chicken bone, ash, and a white silk thread tied with sixteen knots. As the charmer makes the luck ball, they spit on it regularly to emphasize magical sympathy. It is then worn against skin.

This fetish must be "fed" whiskey once a week to rejuvenate its powers. If made and maintained properly, the wearer may ask it questions of any sort and "feel" the answers. Additionally, this charm, as its name implies, is said to improve one's fortune.

•LYCHNOMANCY
(see Candles)

•MACHAROMANCY
(see Knife/Dagger/Sword)

•MAH JONGG

"Truth and sincerity generate the gift of prediction."

—Confucius

A game from China, Mah Jongg may be a direct descendant of an ancient oracular method. When Chinese astronomers first recorded the movement of celestial objects, they used a board to calculate their future positions. The astronomers moved counters around the board to indicate motion into different parts of the heavens. Over many hundreds of years, this developed into a game, ludo, later called dominoes. Later still, domino-like emblems were put onto tiles or playing cards for Mah Jongg. Mah Jongg celebrated this heritage with distinctive rituals, some of which are still used to prepare for playing the game.

Tradition dictates laying out the tiles/cards on a table oriented north to south, with the reader in the east and querent in the west. Next, the reader spreads out the tiles/cards face down before the querent. The querent focuses on a question and draws thirteen possible symbols, leaving them face down. The number thirteen corresponds to the number of lunar months in a year. The querent then chooses three of these for the westerly position, three for the east, three for the north, and three for the south, leaving one card for the center point of the layout. All symbols remain face down until read. The center point represents the question at hand. The western area represents objectives, the south, the future, the north, the outcome, and the east, the querent.

This system is quite complex and detailed, and instructions are often difficult to find. So I've given it a little more attention than most other systems in this book (see illustration on page 170).

The center card is read first, being the focal point around which all other cards/tiles will be related. Moving to the east, the reader reveals the two outer cards (1 and 3 in the diagram), which show either the querent's observable personality traits or the dominant factors in the question. The middle card/tile (2) marks hidden wishes, unspoken desires, and similar matters. Next, to the south, the cards are read left to right indicating events that are taking place (4), about to occur (5), or under consideration (6). Moving to the west, the first external card shows obstacles (7) and other hindering factors (9). The center card/tile reveals how to overcome these hindrances (8). Finally the reader reveals the tiles/cards in the north. These show outcomes and future developments. Reading left to right, the first two warn of where trouble lies (10 and 11), while the final represents the result of all actions and events (12).

TRADITIONAL MAH JONGG SPREAD

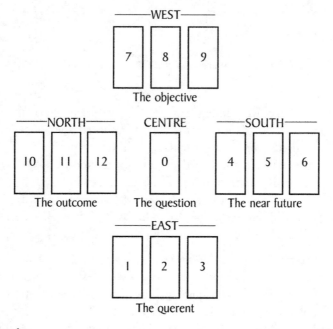

Suit of Bamboo

The suit of bamboo illustrate the themes of utility, flexibility, strength, honesty, refinement, careful decision making, steadfastness, inner peace, and service to others or the community. A large number of bamboo cards in a reading indicate favorable health, paced progress, and an opportunity for travel.

1 **Bamboo (the Peacock):** Success, however, that which must be tempered so that one's ego does not bloat. The Peacock may also represent a mature woman. If this card lands in the center position, it portends new events in which prudence plays an important role. At the third eastern position, this equates to self-esteem. At the second eastern position it represents fidelity, especially in relationships. In the eighth position of the west, the Peacock speaks of good advice from an elderly woman, while in the seventh and ninth positions, it warns of change and the need for realistic outlooks. The worst position for the Peacock is the first, which symbolizes arrogance that may lead to a downfall.

2 Bamboo (the Duck): The longevity of partnerships or relationships. At center, it is the emblem of beneficial unions. In the east, it is always positive, representing a caring person, or anxiousness about being able to serve others. In the south, this is a happy portent of warm feelings. In the north, it represents desires still pending. In the west, specifically the seventh and ninth positions, the Duck warns of problems with one's partner.

3 Bamboo (the Toad): Matters of health. In the center, it is symbolic of well-being or ambition. News is forthcoming as long as one does not overextend oneself. At west 8 and north 12, the Toad happily tells of recovery. In west 7 and 9 it warns of delays resulting from one's own actions or inactions.

4 Bamboo (the Carp): Peace, wisdom, thoughtfulness, effectively managed finances over the long haul, and relief from pressures. At center, your hopes will have a good outcome, but with delays. Nothing can be rushed now, especially if the Carp lands at west 7 or 9.

5 Bamboo (the Lotus): Beginnings, enlightenment, fertility, intense transformation, and the potential to fulfill goals that previously seemed impossible. At center, the Lotus indicates a birth or an opportunity. In almost all positions, the Lotus speaks of awareness that leads to peace, except west 7 and 9, which symbolize the potential for financial fraud. Read the fine print on any contractual obligations.

6 Bamboo (Water): Communication or travel. At center, it is a favorable sign for health, career moves, and journeys. It's most positive when Water appears adjacent to any wood card, whereas neighboring fire cards counsel caution.

7 Bamboo (Tortoise): Situations that need resolution, and the knowledge that comes through experience. Tortoise is most fortunate when it lands in the north or when combined with Water. At center, it indicates slow progress that eventually yields results. Have patience. Develop tenacity and forbearance.

8 Bamboo (the Mushroom): Generally, a strange turn of events, independent decision making, or behavioral transformations. At center, the least expected outcome will come to pass. At west 8, you will find help from an unanticipated source. In the south, the Mushroom represents a happy change, and in the east, intense creativity and personal style exhibit themselves. The positions of west 7 and 9 indicate possible danger from a trusted or unforeseen source.

9 Bamboo (the Willow): Temporary reversals, matters of health, and the need for flexibility and tact. In the center, it's a positive sign for the querent's well-being, but it cautions against abrupt decision making, as current problems will pass. In the east, your receptive nature will help with adjustments. At west 8, be ready to accept modifications, while at west 7 or 9, the Willow advises confronting problems and showing backbone. In the south, it may warn of overlooking or ignoring important details with regard to the question.

Suit of Circles

The suit of circles was the first one devised for Mah Jongg, patterned after the heavens, the sun, and the moon. Like the suit of coins in a Tarot deck, most of the circles tiles/cards equate to matters of finances and business, although they sometimes indicate a girl or young woman who figures into the question. Numerous circles in a reading reveal a monetary focus that is not going to change for a while.

1 Circles (the Pearl): Wealth and abundance, sometimes honor or respect. At the center, the Pearl indicates that improvement is on the horizon, sometimes aided by an unexpected or undervalued source. In the south, it predicts victory, rewards, and advancement. When in the north, success is forthcoming, but not necessarily quickly. In the east, the Pearl counsels against frivolity and misplaced priorities, and at west 8 it warns that more money will soon be spent.

2 Circles (the Pine): Firmness, writing or drawing skills, and diplomacy. The Pine can also symbolize a young man. At the center, it predicts that tenacity is the key to your victory. Pine in any spread is almost always positive, as it reveals courage, endurance, and the ability to overcome. When in the west, at either 7 or 9, it portends potential rivalry or trouble from an outsider.

3 Circles (the Phoenix): Joyful gatherings or events. At the center, the Phoenix represents oneness, accord, and smooth sailing. In the south, it is especially favorable, indicating great luck. At west 7 and 9, however, it warns of pleasure that cannot last and may actually deter success.

4 Circles (the Jade): Hard work that has lasting results; justice. At the center, the Jade is a sign that your efforts are about to see reward despite all the difficulties endured. In the east, Jade reveals good morals and characteristics.

5 Circles (the Dragon): Generally, luck and fortune of an unexpected nature. At the center, Dragon foretells winnings and gain that bring joy and advancement. At east 2, it represents the need to temper rashness or explore creativity. At south 4 and 5, it indicates good outcomes. A Dragon at west 8 reveals the need to expend money to overcome difficulty. In north 12, it is a sign of change, possibly travel, and at east 7 and 9, wastefulness caused by anger or spite.

6 Circles (the Peach): Beauty and influence that may lead to extravagance. Alternatively, Peach may symbolize a young woman. At the center, it means that either a young woman is the focal point of the question or that the querent needs to watch for extravagance. In east 1 or north 12, Peach reveals successful relationships, while at west 8 it portends a problem's solution in which a young girl is a key. When it lands in any of the southern positions, the querent should be warned not to overextend finances. At west 7 and 9, Peach is a sign of jealousy or unfaithfulness, and at north 10 or 12, it reveals unscrupulous business dealings.

7 Circles (the Insect): Industry that brings rewards and happiness. Alternatively, the Insect may symbolize a transient problem or situation. At center, it indicates activity with small gain or possibly a marriage. Insect is most propitious when it lands in the south, revealing tenacious team efforts. At west 7 or 9, it is a sign that one's finances are at risk. In the eastern positions, it represents a job only halfway completed.

8 Circles (the Tiger): Leadership, courage, and aggression. Alternatively, Tiger may symbolize a father figure. At the center, it represents a suitor or someone of authority who plays an important role in the question. At west 8, Tiger is an especially strong card, one offering aid. At east 2, it warns that the querent has strong personal morals, sometimes to excess. When revealed at west 7 or 9, or any northern position, problems with authority or authority figures are foretold.

9 Circles (the Unicorn): Foresight, prognostication, and good judgment. At the center, the Unicorn is a sign of good news or information gained. In the south, it suggests that the positive conclusion of a situation is at hand and that the querent should watch for opportunity's door to open. At east 2, the Unicorn indicates latent or underused clairvoyant talents. When the Unicorn appears in the west or north, the querent should be looking and planning ahead more.

Suit of Wan

A suit focused on ideals, theories, and the mystical or otherwise "nonconcrete" world as opposed to practicality. Layouts exhibiting many of these cards signify intricate situations, sometimes technological or scientific.

1 Wan (the Entering): Opportunity that can open the way to new life and a barrier being lifted. At the center, this indicates a second chance. At west 7 or 9 and north 10 or 11, the Entering portends failure, an insurmountable obstacle, and loss of trust. In the east, it represents innovative ideas that bring refreshment. When combined with the Toad (3 Bamboo), the Entering indicates wellness, while with the House (5 Wan), it literally portends a new residence.

2 Wan (the Sword): A two-edged situation, a stalemate, or sometimes separation and endings. At the center, the Sword indicates a need to make a decision, one option of which requires sacrifice. The Sword can break restricting bonds, especially those in which sincerity is a question. In the east, it represents fairness in judgments and endings.

3 Wan (the Earth): Foundations and stability. At the center, the Earth is a very good omen. Your boundaries are well marked, and a land acquisition may also be forthcoming. In combination with Wan 2, it is a sign of wealth, whereas with Wan 6, it is a warning of drained resources.

4 Wan (the Lute): Rest, leisure, or pleasure that is well earned. At the center, the Lute predicts good health obtained by proper rest or a time of relaxation. In the south, it symbolizes a holiday for happy occasion; at north 12, possibly a vacation as reward for hard work. In the west and at north 7 and 9, the Lute is unfavorable, indicating impractical behavior or distraction.

5 Wan (the House): Any building, tangible or figurative, as with a well-founded association of people. At the center, the House signifies durability or the desire for a stable residence. In the south, the adjacent cards tell the querent what to pay attention to. At west 7 or 9, it shows the need to break free from this structure.

6 Wan (the Fire): The mind, but in this case one that is not being exercised. Alternatively, it can symbolize a waste of valuable resources. At the center, Fire warns that danger or a neglected problem is at hand. East 1 or 3 reveal knowledge, whereas east 2 indicates this intelligence is not being used effectively. In the south, it is an indication of tension leading to exhaustion. In the north, Fire predicts legal problems.

7 Wan (the Seven Stars): Dreams and whimsy, or a person who can take either and make them a reality. At the center, the Seven Stars symbolize that the querent's wishes or ambitions must be tempered with practicality. At west 8, it suggests acting on a good idea, whereas at west 7 or 9, it represents unrealistic goals.

8 Wan (the Knot): Both ties and freedom. At the center, the Knot indicates a heavy responsibility for which one may not be prepared or an impasse. In the east 1 or 3, it represents the querent's inability to make a decision, whereas in east 2, it reveals serious doubts. Coupled with the Duck (2 Bamboo), the Commence, or the Jade (4 Circles), the Knot suggests a favorable partnership is at hand.

9 Wan (Heaven): Completion and order, and the ending and beginning of cycles. At the center, Heaven indicates a new stage of life. Depending on adjacent cards, it may signify that a birth (the Pine, 2 Circles) or marriage (2 Bamboo) is on the horizon. When it is next to the Seven Stars (7 Wan), the Dragon (5 Circles), the Phoenix (3 Circles), the Tiger (8 Circles), or the Tortoise (7 Bamboo), fortune favors the querent and heaven will give aid.

The Honours Suit

Interpretations for the directional cards of the Honours suit are intimately linked with the seasons they represent. South generally means victory and abundance, symbolizing summer. North indicates hardships like winter, East, beginnings like spring, and West, endings and rebirth like fall. These also correspond to the four winds, and the center position, the pivotal point. When any of the seasonal cards land in their quarter of the layout, it is a harmonious sign. When they land opposite to their quarter, the omen is negative. The Commence card is the proverbial motivator.

East: An important, possibly life-changing, incident. At the center, East reveals a matter of personal relevance that needs the querent's full attention. When next to other favorable cards, it foretells of some financial reward. In the south, it is an omen of happiness. At east 1 or 3, the querent is hindered by too much self-importance.

South: A favorable outcome. At the center, South symbolizes smooth sailing and success. At east 1 or 3, it means a cheerful outlook is a good ally. In the south, joy and luck come out of present events. At west 8, renew your hope, for eventual victory is in sight. At west 7 and 9, however, it warns not to be egotistical.

West: Facing an objective or overcoming an obstacle. At the center, West represents a partner or opposition, depending on the question. Overall, this card is a good omen for marriages and partnerships. At west 7 and 9, however, it indicates some hindrance to your plans.

North: Difficulty, discomfort; a period of conflict or sadness. At the center, it means that the answer to this question is "no." When appearing in the north, it suggests that foresight will aid your problem. In the west, trouble with authority figures or financial losses will prevail.

Commence: A blessing, or an individual intent on achievement. At the center, this indicates the proverbial green light for your plans. Commence is very favorable when preceded by Heaven (9 Wan) or Entering (1 Wan), both of which open doors. At west 7 or 9, Commence reveals that some type of fear or anxiety exists over your planned actions.

Center: Realizing goals. Center is a good sign of both luck and success, especially in the center position. It is doubly fortunate if it lands next to Earth (3 Wan) in any reading. In the east, the Center card shows a quiet, possibly overly fundamental, personality. At west 7 or 9, it is a warning against being too aspiring or rigid.

White: The unknown, mysterious, or secret. At the center, White indicates mystical interest or contemplation, especially with regard to the afterlife. At north 12, it is some type of blessing that brings improvement and more happiness. In the east,

White indicates interest in occult arts, at west 7 or 9, an overwhelming fear of the unknown.

The Guardian Suit

When one of the Guardian suit appears, the querent chooses another card to place just above it. It is then interpreted with the added association of the newly drawn card, sometimes indicating a time period in which the situation will come to light. As the name of this suit suggests, the guardians are advisors, shedding light on troubled times.

Plum Blossom: Romance, awakening of love, revitalized life, innocence, and youthful, sometimes immature, outlooks. When in the east, Plum Blossom represents the querent's situation, warning them to guard against stress caused by unacknowledged problems and difficult obligations. At center, it indicates a positive outcome even with difficulties.

Orchid: Personal improvements, honor, reward for hard work, and striving toward perfection; high moral standards and the safety of valued things or people. In the south, Orchid is an omen of prosperity. At the center, it is a favorable sign indicating recovery or profit and solutions to problems that may not be immediately obvious.

Chrysanthemum: Charm, kindness, and other similar endearing qualities especially in a woman; maturity, contentedness, and leisure. At the center, Chrysanthemum represents social occasions. The additional card here will determine if these times are beneficial or not. Furthermore, in matters of health, rest is called for.

Bamboo: Writing, education, communication, and scholarship; possibly successful exam results. In a young man, Bamboo is a sign of virtue. When placed in the north, it indicates help during difficult times. At the center, it advises to look for a specific document to clear up matters.

Fisherman: Common sense and the ability to manage things using tact, patience, and practicality. In the east, the Fisherman indicates that situations can be eased through tolerance and understanding. When placed with an unfavorable card, it advises waiting for better timing. At the center, it portends an event will come about happily but not always quickly.

Woodcutter: Vitality, ambition, and tenacious enterprise; leadership and teamwork bring success. In the south, Woodcutter foretells a very prosperous outcome. It is also an advisor who reminds us that the more diligent our efforts, the greater the rewards. At the center, it is an excellent omen for new ventures, especially those based on mental knowledge.

Farmer: The harvest that comes from honest physical effort (as opposed to mental). In the west, Farmer advises that difficult objectives can be overcome through diligence and boldness. When combined with Earth (3 Wan), it brings a message pertaining to land acquisitions. At the center, it predicts favorable outcomes if the querent doesn't stop trying.

Scholar: Wisdom developing through studies and practice. In the north, the Scholar represents the culturing of the mind, creativity, and attention to detail. It is an excellent card for teachers, counselors, and anyone who must communicate effectively. The only warning is to remember that theory and practice are two very different things. At the center, the Scholar indicates that studious individuals will discover great hope that motivates success.

There are three alternative ways of interpreting this oracle. The first is to consider each of the four directions as seasons and use their traditional correspondences as the foundation for interpretation. With the second method, you assign each of the twelve cards to one month of the year. Either use the month's symbolism for interpreting the card/tile or view the card/tile pulled as a portent for one month of the coming year. In this case, the first card/tile always represents the next month after the one you are currently in. Third, you can use the numerical significance of each position as part of the interpretive value. For example, the tile/card in the second position can equate to important partnerships or relationships, while the twelfth position may represent the outcome.

Related Systems: Dice (loosely related), Dominoes, any laid-out system like cartomancy and the Tarot.

Adaptations: You can use three-by-five cards marked with suitable words or emblems. If you are not comfortable with Eastern symbolism, I suggest finding Western equivalents for the emblems noted to improve the interpretive value. If, on the other hand, these symbols work well for you, and you can find an actual Mah Jongg set, I highly recommend them as they are very lovely and fairly portable.

• MARGARITOMANCY

(see Pearls)

• MARRIAGE OMENS

As one of the most important decisions in a person's life, marriages have been observed very carefully for positive and negative signs. Some traditional associations are:

- Marrying on a Monday or Friday bodes poorly for a marriage. It will be filled with bad luck.

- Rain, broken cups, or dropped rings at or during a ceremony is a bad omen for the relationship.

- Rubbing shoulders with the bride or groom augurs an early marriage in Yorkshire, England.

- Finding a coin or being greeted by a stranger during a wedding is a good sign for the marriage (see *Coins; Random Divination*).

- Hearing a bird sing on the day of the wedding predicts that the couple will never argue (see *Birds*).

- Finding a spider on the bride's veil is an omen of plenty.

- A stray cat rubbing against the bride predicts good luck and fertility (see *Cats*).

- Falling in a wedding procession means it will be a long wait before the person has a successful relationship. Falling upstairs is a good sign for those wishing to marry; a proposal is forthcoming.

Related Systems: Days, Months, Omens, Signs

• MASKS

In Mayan and several other shamanistic traditions, a fortune-teller would often wear a mask as part of the divinatory ritual. The mask served two functions. First, it helped the diviner contact and commune with a specific spirit through mimicry. Second, it represented the power of that spirit as the source of any predictions to the querent.

Related Systems: Dance, Gyromancy, Ritual

Adaptation: It might be fun to make your own divinatory mask out of cardboard, scrap fabric, and miscellaneous craft items.

• MEDITATION

Meditation may be used in preparation for, and a means of, divining the future. This is a quiet time when the diviner stills the external world and seeks the internal or higher worlds for insight. In many ways meditation resembles sleep, a time when we are far more open to impressions from the Higher Self, the collective unconscious, or the Divine.

Most meditations begin with a singular focus, that of a candle flame or a symbolic emblem like a mandala. Additionally, deep breathing and gradual relaxation are also part of the process. People who need an additional focus might turn to chanting, which has the unique side effect of blocking out distractions through sound.

Once reaching a deeper level of awareness, the individual is free to let go and begin tapping into the universal well of inspiration from which not only creative ideas can flow, but also insights about the future. It does take time and practice to meditate effectively, especially as a means of prognostication. But once a person learns how, meditation helps with divination and many other areas of life, too, including stress reduction.

Related Systems: Clear Sight; Oracles, Mediums, Prophets; Ritual; Shamanism

• METAGNOMY

(see Hypnotism)

• METEORS (METEOROMANCY)

The lore surrounding the use of meteors for divinatory efforts includes:

- In England, a woman seeing a meteor shower could be assured of fertility or marriage in her future.

- To receive the answer to a simple question, pose it to the sky. If a shooting star is seen within fifteen minutes, consider the response positive.

- In China, seeing a falling star on the Birthday of the Moon (around September 15) predicted children for women and prosperity for men.

Related Systems: Astrology, Celestial Omens, Comets, Stars

• MIRRORS (CATOPTROMANCY)

> *"Then from his secret art the Sage Vizyr a magic mirror made…reflecting in its mystic compass all within the sev'nfold volume of the world."*
>
> —Jami (Persian poet)

The art of divining the future with a mirrored surface probably originated in Persia or China. Later it appeared in Greece, Rome, India, and Tibet. In Tibet, for example, *Tra* was a system in which the diviner chanted and focused their attention on a shiny, mirror-like surface for a vision. If no such surface was available, suitable alternatives were a still lake or a clear sky. The Roman experts in this form of divination, called *specularii*, often used the shiny surface of the fountain water at Ceres' temples for scrying. The Aztecs used polished obsidian, a natural glass. In Europe, polished metal anointed with oil or shiny stone surfaces often took the place of costly mirrors, even after they were introduced in fourteenth century Italy.

The ancient Cabalists prepared mirrors for divination at special times with specific materials to increase their effectiveness. Mages made gold mirrors on Sunday for obtaining information on authority figures and silver mirrors on Monday for questions about dreams or wishes. They fashioned iron mirrors on Tuesday to determine legal outcomes, mercury mirrors on Wednesday for business and finance questions, copper mirrors on Friday for divining information on relationships, and lead mirrors on Saturday to find lost items or uncover secret matters. Square mirrors were considered best for predicting physical conditions, and round mirrors for matters of spirit.

In the sixteenth century, the Swiss physician Paracelsus recommended using a specific formula for making magical scrying mirrors. Lead, mercury, gold, silver, and copper were all melted together, mixed with iron filings and bark, and poured into a mold. This was polished during an auspicious astrological phase. Around the same time, obsidian was favored for scrying in both Mexico and England.

To try mirror scrying yourself, ensure your privacy, get comfortable, and face a northerly direction. Try not to expect anything specific. Empty your mind of random thoughts. Watch the mirror, allowing your eyes to look past the surface. After about ten to fifteen minutes most people can begin to make out vague images, like veils or clouds forming. This is an excellent sign. With practice the images will become more and more detailed to the point of forming discernible objects. If you find you don't succeed at first, wait a few days before trying again. This helps to rest your eye muscles, which you use in a new and unique way for this art.

In considering the images that appear in the mirror, here are some common interpretive values:

Red clouds or veils: Danger; care needed

Yellow clouds or veils: Frolicsome times filled with energy and creativity

Purple clouds or veils: Thoughtfulness, especially on spiritual matters

Green clouds or veils: Growth and maturity coming to the seeker

Blue clouds or veils: Solitude and relaxation needed

Movement to the left: No

Movement to the right: Yes

Movement downward: Decline or negative energies

Movement upward: Improvement or advance

Related Systems: Crystal Scrying, Fire, Ink, Sky Scrying, Water, Wax

Adaptation: People sometimes smeared the surface of their scrying mirrors with olive oil. This oil can be enhanced by steeping "insightful" herbs in it over the three nights of the full moon. Good choices include sandalwood chips and dandelion flowers.

•MOLES (PHYSIOGNOMY)

Physiognomy is a form of body reading that considers moles, their shapes, and locations as indications of personality traits and potential futures. It was highly favored in Ancient Greece. During the Victorian Era it became almost a game to see how closely one's moles reflected reality.

Some associations and indications with moles are:

High on forehead: Bad luck

On center of forehead: Active, hard working disposition

On bridge of nose: Extravagance

On nose: A traveler

On chin: Wealth to come; sign of good character

On shoulder: Restless nature

On arm: A country life

On throat: A fortunate person

On hand: The sign of wealth, fertility, and industry

On wrist: Ingenuity

On finger: Potential for thievery or exaggeration

On back: A challenging life ahead

On buttocks: The sign of a lazy person

On chest: Quarrelsome disposition

On side: Excessive fear or cowardice

On hip: A contented life

On back: Hidden matters undermining plans

On stomach: Lack of common sense

On thigh: On the right side, a good temperament

On knee: On the left, a sign of haste; on the right, sign of a good friend

On leg: A tendency toward extravagance

On foot: A melancholy disposition

On ankle: Courage

On heel: Spitefulness

On toe: Wealthiness accompanied by unhappiness

Round-shaped: A generally good sign; kindly nature

Oblong-shaped: Moderate fortune

Angular-shaped: Mixed luck

Light-colored: Good luck

Black: Trouble before success

Related Systems: Ears, Eyes, Facial Features, Fingers, Hands, Palmistry

•MOLYBDOMANCY

(see Lead)

•MONTHS

Just as certain months have specific predictable weather patterns, which then fore-tell other climatic conditions, so some seem to bode better than others for specific activities, especially marriages (see *Marriage Omens*). For example:

January: Marrying during January means that one partner will have an early death.

February: Marriages during February will experience smooth sailing.

March: If you begin building a new structure during March, the effort is destined to be most successful and enduring. If you marry in March, expect to move away from your home town.

April: People who marry in April will experience up and down relationships.

May: During the first week of May, it bodes well for a man to start a new endeavor; during the second, for a woman. Marrying during May ensures a couple of many acquaintances.

June: June is, by far, the best month in which to marry for a joyous future. This originated in Rome.

July: Marriages performed in July will be bittersweet.

August: The couple that marries in August will be both friends and lovers to each other.

September: Marriages in September bring serene relationships.

October: Marrying in October effects hardship.

November: November is the second most auspicious month for marrying.

December: December marriages will foster growing love.

Related System: Days

• MOON (SELENOMANCY)

There is an enormous amount of material written about the moon and its effect on the future. The moon apparently not only influences destiny, crops, and the weather, but it can also affect the accuracy of one's dreams and the success or failure of projects. Here are a few examples of prognostications based on the moon:

- Watch to see where you first notice the moon after its new phase. If on your right, it portends good luck. Over your left shoulder, behind you, or viewed through glass, it is a bad omen for the entire month.

- Hold a silver coin up to the full moon and ask a question. Put this under your pillow to dream of the answer. Alternatively, when the moon is new, make a wish for prophetic dreams. Go to bed silently each night, and they will come before the next phase of the moon.

- The first moon in May helps bring dreams of the future. Stare at it for nine nights in silence. On the last night, think of your question, and the dream will come.

- A pale moon precedes rain. A red moon foretells of a windy, sometimes rainy, day. An upright crescent warns of a wet month ahead, and a small moon with fog precedes easterly winds (see *Weather Omens*).

- Thunder during the new moon means that both crops and markets will prosper (see *Thunder*).

Related Techniques: Birth Omens, Days, Months, Moon Scrying, Moon Signs, Numerology

Adaptation: Many diviners like to work by moonlight because it emphasizes the intuitive nature.

• MOON SCRYING

In ancient times, maidens would go out on a moonlit night and view the moon's reflection off a body of water through a silk scarf. They would then pose a question concerning how long it would be before love or marriage came. The number of reflections seen through the scarf revealed the number of days, months, or years.

Related Techniques: Crystal Scrying, Sky Scrying, Water Scrying

Adaptation: Take a cauldron and paint the inside black. Fill it with water and drop a silver-colored coin in it to represent the moon. Hold a silk scarf over the water and think of a time-related question. The number of reflections seen through the scarf indicates the number of hours, days, weeks, months, or years before manifestation occurs.

• MOON SIGNS

As the moon makes its transit from one astrological sign and enters another, its influence on human affairs changes. These changes can enhance or deter your activities. Some general advice for the lunar positions include:

In Aries: Things will move very quickly over the next two days, but don't take any unnecessary risks or be too impulsive.

In Taurus: Don't make any changes until after this transit.

In Gemini: Take care in your communication. Anything that happens during these two days is transitory.

In Cancer: Emotions are high, so consider your words and actions accordingly.

In Leo: Watch for opportunity's knock during these two days and act on it! The results will be favorable.

In Virgo: Great days for bargain hunting, increasing knowledge, and paying close attention to details.

In Libra: Any artistic effort undertaken during these two days should prove quite successful.

In Scorpio: Be suspicious of any financial deals and watch out for a possible argument, especially over money.

In Sagittarius: Take a break from your routine for the best possible outcomes. Also, be totally honest with people or a "white lie" will haunt you.

In Capricorn: Stick like glue to the rules or you will regret your haste. Obstacles can be overcome during these days through hard work.

In Aquarius: Avoid thinking too hard or too long for the next couple of days, as the energy will be wasted. Socialize instead.

In Pisces: Look within yourself for the answers to questions that have been heavy on your heart, or consult an oracle.

Note that in the highly detailed art of astrology, these associations can vary depending on the zodiac sign you were born under and other constantly changing aspects.

Related Systems: Astrology, Celestial Omens, Days, Moon, Stars, Sun

• MYOMANCY

(see Animal Omens and Signs—Mice)

• NAMES (ONOMANCY)

Names have power. In ancient times it was widely believed that if you knew the true name of an entity, you could command it. Similarly, people who believe in onomancy feel that giving a child an auspicious name will positively affect that child's personality and future. In Scotland, tradition has it that a child will take the character of the person after whom he or she is named. In Ohio and Massachusetts, local superstition has it that if a person's initials spell a word, they will be wealthy!

It is always interesting to look up a person's name in a book of names to see how closely the traits match. Here is a sampling of names, characteristics, and derivations:

Adam: From the Hebrew meaning "red earth." Not always a lucky name. A tendency for frailty.

Alan: Anglo-Saxon for "cheerful." A courageous energetic man with a love of adventure.

Alexander: Greek for "helper of men." Commercially successful, bright, and alert.

Alexandra: A derivative of Alexander. A passionate, charitable woman.

Amy: Latin for "beloved." A gracious, faithful woman.

Ann: Hebrew for "grace." A very giving, pragmatic woman.

Anthony: Latin for "inestimable." A deeply introspective loner.

Aurora: Latin for "dawn." A quiet, emotional woman with good manners. A devoted friend.

Barbara: Greek for "stranger." A woman of ideals, but one who keeps an emotional distance.

Benjamin: Hebrew for "son of my right hand." A homebody with a gentle spirit.

Brian: Celtic for "strong." A pleasure seeker with good humor.

Bridget: Celtic for "strength." A homebody with great willpower.

Charles: Teutonic for "man." Outgoing, passionate, and happy man.

Christopher: Greek for "Christ bearer." A kind, honorable person who motivates good in others.

Claudia: Latin for "lame." A very impulsive, brash woman with a good heart.

Colin: Latin for "dove." An anxious, emotional, and melodramatic man.

Cynthia: Greek for "from Cynthus." An impish woman.

Daniel: Hebrew for "god the judge." A level-headed person, but with tendencies for brief flashes of anger.

Diana: Latin for "goddess." A romantic, vital woman who loves nature.

Dominic: Latin for "Sunday child." A strict, truthful man.

Doreen: Origin uncertain. An introspective, creative woman.

Douglas: Celtic for "dark gray." A friendly man of many abilities.

Edward: Teutonic for "rich guard." A loving, sensitive man with very traditional views.

Elizabeth: From Hebrew, "oath of god." A smart, determined, and artistic woman.

Emily: Teutonic for "work." A tenacious, independent sort with an upbeat personality.

Eric: Teutonic for "ever king." A moody dreamer with high ideals.

Francis: Teutonic for "free." A talented, brave, fiercely independent person who verbalizes opinions readily.

Grace: Latin for "thanksgiving." A creative, reciprocal personality.

Gregory: Greek for "watchman." An effective, patient man with little tolerance for deceit.

Gwendolen: Celtic for "white-browed." A mysterious loner who is very faithful to the people she lets into her life.

Helen: Greek for "light." A refined, kindly person of sentiment.

Henry: Teutonic for "home ruler." A man with a strong work ethic for monetary rather than religious reasons. A committed mate.

Isaac: Hebrew for "laughter." A happy, charitable man with strong opinions.

Ivy: Teutonic for "clinging." A steadfast, charming woman.

Jennifer: Celtic for "white wave." A brave, forthright, independent soul.

Jesse: Hebrew for "the Lord is." An even-keeled person who is polite and work-oriented to a fault.

Jonathan: Hebrew for "the Lord's gift." A dutiful, stern man with high expectations.

Julia: Latin for "downy cheeked." A woman with a sparkling facade that hides shallowness.

Justin: Latin for "just." An honest, sports-minded person.

Katherine: Greek for "pure." A fulfilled, affectionate pragmatist.

Kenneth: Celtic for "comely." A very intelligent, serious, well-spoken man.

Laurence: Latin for "laurel." A committed, brave man devoted to his family and worthy causes.

Lewis: Teutonic for "famous war." A heroic, humorous spirit.

Lilian: From a Latin word for "lily." An anxious idealist with lots of imagination.

Luke: Latin for "light." A man of changeability who ranges from being very meticulous to impractical.

Margaret: Persian for "pearl." A free spirit with intelligence and good communication skills.

Mary: Hebrew for "bitterness." A cool demeanor that hides deep feelings.

Matthew: Hebrew for "gift of the Lord." A forthright, pragmatic, kindly person.

Michael: Hebrew for "he who is like unto God." A sagacious, caring man with a love of travel.

Monica: Latin for "advisor." A flighty person who rarely puts foundations under her dreams.

Nadine: Slavonic for "hope." A somewhat gauche, energetic woman.

Neal: Celtic for "champion." A communicative, thoughtful, leader.

Nicholas: Greek for "victory of the people." A diligent, effective worker.

Patricia: Latin meaning "noble." A quiet, honorable woman of deep affections but little passion.

Paul: Latin for "small." A very nostalgic, romantic, argumentative man.

Peter: Greek for "rock." A strong, firm man who commands respect.

Rebecca: Hebrew for "noose cord." A passive but loving woman with a quiet personality.

Richard: Teutonic for "strong king." A humorous, outgoing, forthright man with lots of energy.

Robert: Teutonic for "bright fame." A successful man with great oratory skills but little patience.

Rosemary: Latin for "sea dew." An attractive, insightful woman.

Steven: Greek for "crown." A friendly, courageous, and cultured man with a tendency for quick decision making.

Stephanie: A version of Steven. A woman who is very determined and social but often imprudent.

Susan: Hebrew for "lily." A woman of good intentions and simple approaches to life.

Theresa: Greek for "reap." A successful woman with distinct goals.

Timothy: Latin for "fear god." A prankster and gypsy at heart.

Victor: Latin for "conqueror." A vital, impassioned person with little tolerance.

Victoria: Feminine of Victor. A woman who is brave, willful, smart, and insightful.

William: Teutonic for "helmet of resolution." A welcoming, energetic man who prefers entertaining at home to social affairs.

Related Systems: Arithmancy, Numerology

•NECROMANTIC DIVINATION

The Babylonians and Hittites both consulted the spirits of the dead for blessings and insights, despite the general disapproval of the government. As described in I Samuel, Chapter 28, of the Bible, Saul uses a necromancer to call up the spirit of Samuel to act as counsel in war.

In Southern Arabia, Muhammad's servants known as *sayyids* believe in consorting with "familiar spirits" for aid in many matters. By popular belief, these people can even summon the jinns. In this region of the world, it is also believed that anyone wearing a ring inscribed with the secret name of God will be visited by jinns who will subsequently offer their assistance on any question.

Germanic sagas also tell about a means of gaining knowledge from the dead. A seer sat next to a burial mound for many days, employing different meditative methods like fire gazing to heighten awareness. These meditations also aroused the attention of a spirit, which was then consulted for responses.

In Medieval Europe, necromancers commonly used a mirror, a crystal, the blade of a sword, the surface of a shiny fingernail, or a young person's visage. The necromancer summoned a spirit to provide symbolic images in these media for interpretation. These divining efforts were often confined to a magic circle drawn on the ground or inscribed in fabric, and they included evocations, special incense, and other elaborate preparations. The magic circles contained sacred sigils of great complexity, sometimes including saints' names for protection and a place in the center for the diviner and tools. These procedures safeguarded the necromancer from the ire of any spirit who didn't take kindly to having their after-life disturbed!

In more recent history, the table-tipping sessions of the Victorian Era and use of the *Ouija* are both considered mild forms of necromancy. Around the same time, some early forms of what became known as mesmerism used hypnosis to encourage a semislumbering state. From this trance, people could consult with various spirits to gain prophetic insights.

Related Systems: Automatism, Crystal Scrying; *Ouija*; Oracles, Mediums, Prophets; Shamanism; Table Tipping

•NEEDLES

Some divination methods using needles include:

- Float a handful of twenty-one needles in water. According to Gypsy lore, if they cross, it is a bad omen, meaning forces are working against you.

- Cherokee medicine men used needles to determine a patient's welfare. The healer put two needles on water. If they stayed equally spaced or floated away from each other, they foretold the patient's recovery.

- To determine the sex of a baby, suspend a needle from a linen thread over the mother's wrist or stomach. The needle acts like a pendulum. Clockwise movement indicates the child will be a boy (see *Pendulums*).

•NEPHELOMANCY

(see Clouds)

•NUMBERS (NUMEROLOGY)

> *"Were it not for Number and its nature, nothing that exists would be clear to anyone, either in itself or in relation to other things."*
>
> —Pythagoras

In 529 B.C, Pythagoreans formed a secret society about which only traces of information remain today. Through this information, historians theorize that Pythagoreans believed in reincarnation and the mystical nature of numbers. Not only did the Pythagoreans teach that each number had its own vibration and influence, but they felt that numbers held clues to the structure of the Universe.

The best known instance of someone using the Pythagorean system of numerology for a prophesy was that of Cagliostro in predicting Louis XIV's death during the French revolution. Cagliostro translated both the King's name and that of Marie Antoinette into ancient Persian, then worked out the numerical value for his reading. This prediction came true in 1793. Unfortunately, because of Cagliostro's reputation for black magic, few believed this happening was by chance, but that somehow through his magic Cagliostro helped bring about the King's demise.

Today most numerological systems base their values on primary numbers. To make any date or name into a primary number, a form of addition is used. For example, to determine your birth number, which reveals personal attributes, you add the month, day, and year of your birth together. So February 21, 1960, becomes $2 + 2 + 1 + 1 + 9 + 6 + 0 = 21 = 2 + 1 = 3$. The number of your birth name, indicating traits and habits, is derived similarly by giving each letter a numeric value as shown in the chart below. Note that the earlier Cabalistic system only used eight numbers, leaving the ninth to symbolize the sacred name of god. There are similarities between the two:

VALUE	MODERN SYSTEM	CABALISTIC SYSTEM
1	A, J, S	A, I, Q, J, Y
2	B, K, T	B, R, K
3	C, L, U	C, G, L, S
4	D, M, V	D, M, T
5	E, N, W	E, H, N
6	F, O, X	U, V, W, X
7	G, P, Y	O, Z
8	H, Q, Z	F, P
9	I, R	

The vowels in your name, added together, reveal the inner self. Beyond this, any number that repeats itself in these calculations, or regularly in your life, can be taken into account as an overshadowing influence. These numbers, and others similarly derived, can then be used to reveal hidden potentials and dangers in many situations. For example, if considering a new job, numerologically analyze the company name (or the job title) and compare it with your own to see how well you will "fit" into that setting. Some interesting bits of insight might be gained by comparing one's nickname to one's given name, or one's single name to one's married name. Or, before buying or renting a new residence, review the numerical value of the address compared with your birth year.

The numerological associations with personality traits are:

1: A fiery person with pioneering energy. A creative leader who dislikes restraint. An ambitious, stubborn, aggressive, and self-dependent type who commits themselves wholly without fully evaluating things first.

2: Sensitive, peace-loving types who make great diplomats. A magnetic personality, a socializer, and a good communicator, with the capacity to motivate others, while feeling less than self-confident.

3: Inventive, versatile people with restless spirits. Appearance is important, as is diversification. Threes are often very busy, independent, and contentious to a fault.

4: Logical and practical, these people are committed to working in an orderly, dutiful manner. They have trouble making friends, but are very charitable and loyal once a relationship is established. Good researchers.

5: Impulsive adventurers. These people live intensely, seeking pleasure wherever it can be found. Fives take risks, have intense relationships, know how to adapt to change, and sometimes make good leaders.

6: Loving beauty and the arts, having high ideals, and caring about human affairs, sixes are trustworthy, romantic, and fairly good judges of character. They need regular approval and support from others.

7: Philosophical, intuitive people who always seek the answers to mysteries, often by retreating from the world. Sevens are very disciplined, intelligent, and a little bit lucky.

8: People of great dichotomy who can go from tremendous success to great failure very quickly, and then back again. Eights have a well-developed sense of self, strong emotions, and tend to be the "odd ones out."

9: A warrior spirit with the will and ability to succeed through hard work. Sometimes people of harsh tempers, nines can also be brave and helpful when someone most needs them.

A few numerological systems also choose to include the values of 0, 11, 12, 13, 22, and 40. If you decide to use these, any birth name that adds up to one of these secondary numbers is not broken down further, but all other secondary numbers are broken down as shown before.

0: To any number preceding the 0 (such as the 1 in 10, the 2 in 20, and so forth), 0 adds latent power and potential. It represents the creative expression of Spirit. So, for example, 10 might be indicative of an explorer whose work uncovers new information.

11: Mystical people who try to maintain the balance between good and evil in all things. Inventive, active, influential folk who live intensely.

12: A very complete person; fulfilled and self-aware.

13: Someone with recurring bad luck. Personality here tends toward negativity and depression.

22: Enlightened people with an ability to build. A large scale "doer" with a knack for manifesting a vision.

40: People capable of single-minded completion, often by one's own hand or resulting from a time of seclusion.

To know what to expect in the current year, first take the numbers in the year itself and add them together. 1997 = 1 + 9 + 9 + 7 = 26 = 2 + 6 = 8. Next, add together only the month of your birth and date (e.g., February 21 = 2 + 2 + 1 = 5). Add this figure to the year figure (8 + 5 = 13 = 1 + 3 = 4). The correspondences below indicate major trends for the given years:

1: A fresh start. This year sets the pace of all that will come in the next nine. Accept change and move with it; lay the foundations for new projects and trust your instincts. Self-development is a key here, as is self-assurance. You may find yourself somewhat the loner, but this actually will help things along.

2: Harmonious collaboration will help everything this year as will effective communication. Focus on your talents, especially in an art, and also take time to tie up any loose ends. After a time of solitude, love and friendship find you.

3: Busy, busy, busy! Lots of opportunities begin to open, as do social occasions. The problem here could be in scattering your focus between too many things. Be careful with decision making, travel often, and develop personal skills while finances are on the upswing.

4: Paced and quiet, this year provides the opportunity to reinforce well-loved projects and complete other responsibilities. A good year for house hunting, sticking with an exercise program, and just generally completing what you've begun. If there are problems at home, heal the wounds.

5: Transformation and unexpected surprises await you. New and often unique people enter your life, each of which offers fresh insights to ponder. Opportunity will knock, but only briefly, so don't dawdle. Liberate yourself from old habits and learn the value of flexible adaptation.

6: Hearth and home are central issues this year, so take the opportunity to improve and strengthen those connections. Don't rush any decisions, and whatever happens don't speak before you think. Patience is a good friend now. Continue the work begun last year and finish things, especially in business.

7: Introspection and personal development allow a change in perspectives. Expand your mind and spirit rather than your social circle. Good planning and balance are two keys to making this year successful. Take some time to be alone and learn to trust yourself.

8: Prosperity and abundance set the tone for this energetic year. Much of this is thanks to hard work, so watch for the openings that come through diligence. Focus energy on outcomes. Progress is coming, as are the answers you seek.

9: An ending with some type of completion. Emotions are at an all-time high, so watch for proverbial "knee-jerk" reactions. A time to release the responsibilities that are not really yours, and develop resoluteness. Purge, clean, organize, and prepare, so that the next nine-year cycle can be even better than the last.

Related Systems: Any that use counting, odd/even as an indicator, Days, Dice, Dominoes, Tablets

Adaptation: Think of your question and then check your VCR counter, a car odometer, a clock, or a passing license plate for a random numerological response.

•NUTS

In old England, young women placed nuts in the hearth fire and spoke their beloved's name. If the nut jumped, they knew this love would last and that their young man was devoted. This tradition continued in Victorian Era America.

The betel nut, harvested from Asian palm trees, is also used for lot divination in West Africa. Here, the diviner prays to the goddess Fa, then tosses the nuts on the ground. Their patterns and movements determine the significance of the casting. The cola nut is used in this region in a system closely resembling that which uses cowrie shells (see *Seashells*). An alternative to both these approaches is used by the Dogon tribe, in which nuts are scattered at night, then the paw prints of the animals that consumed them are interpreted the following day.

Related Systems: For the second method, Lots, Seeds, Shells

Adaptation: Assemble an assortment of nuts for a cast system, using the magical attributes and/or correspondences of the nuts as their base interpretive value. Also, the tops of acorns make a wonderful base for a set of runes.

•OCULOMANCY

(see *Eyes*)

•OENOMANCY

(see *Wine*)

•OFFERINGS

The tradition of making a gift to the gods is so old, its origins are lost in the prehistory of oral tradition. By offering an animal, grains, beverages, gems, or other valuables, people hoped to gain a spirit's favor in aiding their goal. This was also true of divination, with the belief that the power necessary to peek into the future was costly, requiring more than a mere supplication on the part of a querent. In fact, the fees collected for oracular efforts in places like Delphi were probably solicited as an offering, whether or not the coins or objects ever made it to the altar.

Related Systems: Animal Omens and Signs, Entrails, Ritual

Adaptations: If you wish to give a token of appreciation to a god or goddess in thanks for his or her help with your divination efforts, leave out seeds or grains that animals can enjoy. This way your gift serves both the Creator and the Creation.

•OGHAMS

The ogham is a Celtic alphabet dating back to the fifth century A.D. Mythically, the ogham was thought to be invented by *Ogma* or *Ogmios*, and is strongly identified with the *Tuatha de Danaan*, which are the primal gods of poetry and speech in Irish/Gaelic traditions. The letters of this alphabet consisted of lines or notches cut into stone or wood, each symbolizing a tree or other natural object. Learning this alphabet was part of a student's mastery of the Druidic arts, and it eventually developed into a divinatory method.

There is some discrepancy as to how many letters the divinatory system actually used. There are over 300 oghams, only eighteen to thirty of which have ever been associated with this art. Bear this in mind if you use oghams for divination.

Beyond the symbols themselves, you will also need a cloth with three concentric circles drawn on it, each of which represents a truth and an aspect of the greater Divinity (see illustration on page 196). From an esoteric standpoint these may also symbolize body, mind, and spirit, or the threefold character of both the Sacred and humankind.

To perform a reading, you may follow any layout used for runes and potentially any of the smaller Tarot layouts. Richard Webster (see Bibliography), recommends placing the first ogham at the point along the outer circle nearest to you. Place the second ogham at the centerpoint of all three circles, and the third at the point on the outer circle directly opposite you. Next, place oghams at positions 4, 5, 6, 7, 8, and 9 as shown below. The line on the left Mr. Webster calls the Pillar of the Goddess, and the one on the right, the Pillar of the God.

OGHAMS

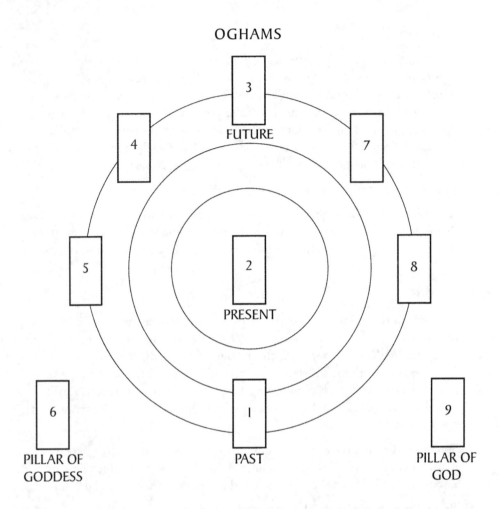

To read the layout, the Pillar of the Goddess equates to the intuitive or emotional aspects of a question, the Pillar of the God to the logical/rational aspects, and the center line to the self in the past (bottom), present (middle), and future (top). Alternatively, the Pillar of the Goddess may represent underlying or hidden energies in a situation, while the Pillar of the God, the active and obvious energies. If you are using an alternative layout, the interpretive value of placement will be dictated by that layout. One interesting method entails drawing twelve oghams on New Year's, which reveal the overall energies for each successive month of the coming year.

Here is an overview of the ogham's interpretive values:

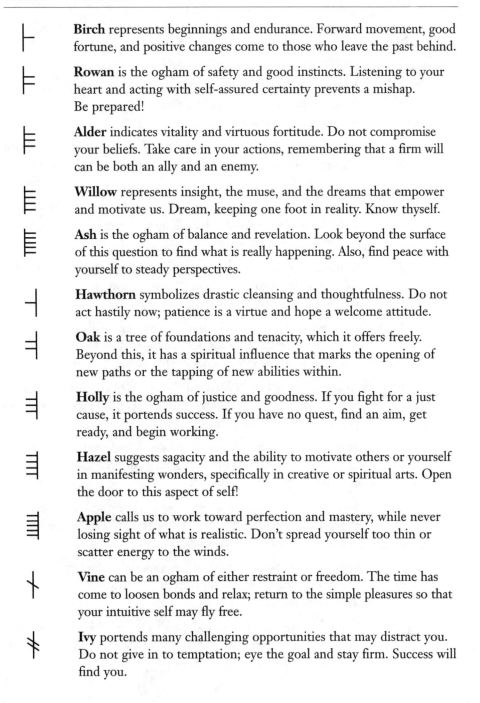

Birch represents beginnings and endurance. Forward movement, good fortune, and positive changes come to those who leave the past behind.

Rowan is the ogham of safety and good instincts. Listening to your heart and acting with self-assured certainty prevents a mishap. Be prepared!

Alder indicates vitality and virtuous fortitude. Do not compromise your beliefs. Take care in your actions, remembering that a firm will can be both an ally and an enemy.

Willow represents insight, the muse, and the dreams that empower and motivate us. Dream, keeping one foot in reality. Know thyself.

Ash is the ogham of balance and revelation. Look beyond the surface of this question to find what is really happening. Also, find peace with yourself to steady perspectives.

Hawthorn symbolizes drastic cleansing and thoughtfulness. Do not act hastily now; patience is a virtue and hope a welcome attitude.

Oak is a tree of foundations and tenacity, which it offers freely. Beyond this, it has a spiritual influence that marks the opening of new paths or the tapping of new abilities within.

Holly is the ogham of justice and goodness. If you fight for a just cause, it portends success. If you have no quest, find an aim, get ready, and begin working.

Hazel suggests sagacity and the ability to motivate others or yourself in manifesting wonders, specifically in creative or spiritual arts. Open the door to this aspect of self!

Apple calls us to work toward perfection and mastery, while never losing sight of what is realistic. Don't spread yourself too thin or scatter energy to the winds.

Vine can be an ogham of either restraint or freedom. The time has come to loosen bonds and relax; return to the simple pleasures so that your intuitive self may fly free.

Ivy portends many challenging opportunities that may distract you. Do not give in to temptation; eye the goal and stay firm. Success will find you.

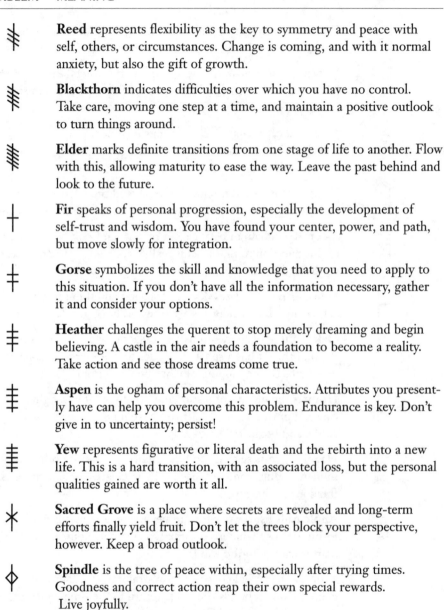

Reed represents flexibility as the key to symmetry and peace with self, others, or circumstances. Change is coming, and with it normal anxiety, but also the gift of growth.

Blackthorn indicates difficulties over which you have no control. Take care, moving one step at a time, and maintain a positive outlook to turn things around.

Elder marks definite transitions from one stage of life to another. Flow with this, allowing maturity to ease the way. Leave the past behind and look to the future.

Fir speaks of personal progression, especially the development of self-trust and wisdom. You have found your center, power, and path, but move slowly for integration.

Gorse symbolizes the skill and knowledge that you need to apply to this situation. If you don't have all the information necessary, gather it and consider your options.

Heather challenges the querent to stop merely dreaming and begin believing. A castle in the air needs a foundation to become a reality. Take action and see those dreams come true.

Aspen is the ogham of personal characteristics. Attributes you presently have can help you overcome this problem. Endurance is key. Don't give in to uncertainty; persist!

Yew represents figurative or literal death and the rebirth into a new life. This is a hard transition, with an associated loss, but the personal qualities gained are worth it all.

Sacred Grove is a place where secrets are revealed and long-term efforts finally yield fruit. Don't let the trees block your perspective, however. Keep a broad outlook.

Spindle is the tree of peace within, especially after trying times. Goodness and correct action reap their own special rewards. Live joyfully.

Honeysuckle indicates an insight into the true motivations and causes behind your situation. Trust your instincts without vacillating. Build self-esteem, then move forward.

Beech entreats us to understand how our past effects the "now." Learn from mistakes and move on. Also realize that "old" does not mean outmoded. Let history be a teacher and guide.

 Pine relates to growth in the spiritual self, especially in your intuitive nature. Walk strongly and peacefully along your path, with light as a guide.

Related Techniques: Runes, Trees

Modern Adaptations: While traditionally the oghams were carved into wood, many other options exist. You can draw them on stiff cards, paint them on stones, or engrave them on metal, for example. A beautiful option is to decoupage cards with leaves from the appropriate trees. Also, try carving each ogham into a piece of wood from the tree that bears its name to increase the overall symbolism and power. For purchasing a system, the Celtic Tree Oracle (see Bibliography) is an excellent choice.

•OIL (LECANOMANCY)

A tradition that originated in the Middle East, specifically Babylon, lecanomancy was often a family practice, handed down through generations. To begin, the diviner sits cross-legged in front of a bowl of water and floats oil on the top. The oil's movement creates the portent. Most often this system was used to predict the outcome of a sickness or an endeavor. The basis for interpretation in this system include:

Oil dividing: A negative sign; separation, or argument

A ring: Profits, recovery, or protection

Droplets: Fertility or prosperity

Thin covering of oil: Trouble ahead or a clouded perspective

Crescent or star: Very good luck

One large drop and one small: Recovery for a patient, or an omen of the birth of a baby boy

Related Systems: Bowl, Floating, Flour, Oil, Water, Wax

Adaptations: Perhaps try using colored water as a backdrop. Clockwise movement is positive, counterclockwise is negative. Also scry the surface for shapes and patterns.

• OINOMANCY

(see Wine)

• OLOLYGMANCY

(see Animal Omens and Signs, Dogs)

• OMEN OBSERVATION

> *"Whether a nation or a family, if it is about to flourish there will be fortunate signs, and when about to perish, there will be evil omens."*

—Confucius

In humankind's earliest history, the most prevalent type of divination was watching for omens and signs. Since animistic faiths believed that the wind, animals, and many other living things had spirits, it was natural to look to these powers for helpful harbingers. Individuals who became adept at reading these signs became the first shaman-priests, using their abilities for the good of the tribe. A shaman's or medicine person's caliber was judged according to how well he or she interpreted the signs.

Omen observation entails the careful scrutiny of specific occurrences or objects, watching for prescribed trends. Omens can be found in nearly every aspect of life. Birds are one excellent example, having carried omens and signs on their wings to many cultures, including those of Greece and Tibet. If the omen observation had to do with movement specifically, movement to the left was usually interpreted negatively, to the right, positively. Likewise, upward movement was a good sign, downward, a bad one.

Related Systems: Animal Omens and Signs, Birth Omens, Death Omens, Marriage Omens, Signs, Weather Omens

• ONEIROMANCY

(see Dreams)

• ONIMANCY

(see Fingernails)

• ONIONS (CROMNIOMANCY)

Exactly why people started using onions in divination is uncertain. It may have originated with the Egyptian's veneration of this plant. They considered it a symbol of the Universe. Some examples of divining with onions include:

- Plant several onions at the same time in separate pots, using the same potting soil. Each onion represents one possible outcome. The first to sprout indicates the most possible future.

- Onions are used in Germany for weather prognostication. Three onions are cut in half, and the six halves placed in a row in the attic on New Year's Eve (see *Holiday Omens and Signs*). They represent, in sequence, the months of January through June. The next morning, the halves that are damp reveal a rainy month, and those that stay dry indicate fair weather (see *Weather Omens*).

- Eating onions before bed is said to inspire prophetic dreams, especially with regard to matters of love. In Welsh custom, this is often done on Christmas or St. Thomas' Day.

Related Systems: Botanomancy, Flowers, Foods, Herbs, Plants, Roses

• OMOMANCY

(see Names)

• ONYCHOMANCY

(see Fingernails)

• OOMANTIA; OOSCOPY; OVOMANCY

(see Eggs)

• OPHIOMANCY

(see Serpents)

• ORACLES, MEDIUMS, PROPHETS

A seer or prophet is someone whose mental ability is beyond "normal" levels of awareness. Such a person has a knack for unraveling, understanding, and following universal patterns to their most probable outcome. Some ancient prophets gained favor or employment in high places, furnishing leaders with counsel on important matters of state. In Islamic regions, for example, a poet often acted as the oracle of the Divine for the ruler. The Arabic word for oracle, *Hajis*, literally translates as "muse" or "inspiration." Other seers, such as Nostradamus (A.D. 1500) and Edgar Cayce (Victorian Era), left behind their unnervingly accurate predictions for us to ponder.

In Babylon, a medium was called an *aplio*, literally meaning "answer." The *aplio* were usually associated with a temple and often gave their information to none but the king himself. Another version of the prophet in this region was the *raggimu* or shouter, who, as the name implies, would cry their utterance loudly, often beginning with the phrase "Be not afraid."

The Hebrew tradition had several oracles, most of which resided at the temples of Yaweh. In fact, prophesy was considered one of the major priestly functions for Jewish rabbis. The prophet would employ all manner of divinatory techniques to achieve an answer, including actual possession by Yaweh during an ecstatic state often aided by drink or music.

Of all the world's prophetic centers, however, the most famous were those of Greece. One was Dodona, believed to be the first with an associated cult, dating back to the eighth century B.C. Homer's *Odyssey* suggests that an oak may have been Dodona's original oracle, which was mediated by an interpreter called a *hopophetai*. According to this account, the oak was said to speak, sometimes through its leaves and indwelling birds. Sophocles tells us of a prophetic priestess at Dodona, leading historians to conjecture that divination methods there evolved from omen interpretation to the spiritual possession of women, who imparted the will of Zeus. This is supported by the writings of Plato from fourth or fifth century B.C. There is also evidence suggesting that the women of this oracle prophesied by lots.

A second important oracle in Greece was that of Delphi. The first ministers at Delphi were Cretans. There was an oak tree here, too, and other similarities to Dodona, except that the tripod in the inner sanctum where the oracle sat, was unique to this location. The original oracle seat was built from woven laurel branches, the symbol of Apollo.

In Delphi, a woman past her child-bearing years, called the Pythia, went to the tripod seat in a shrine believed to be occupied by Apollo's spirit. The querent remained in an outer chamber and sacrificed a goat. The question was likely put in written form, and the response returned in hexameter verse or riddle, as provided by an interpreter. Generally, God visited himself on the Pythia once a month except in winter. This day was the only time queries were accepted.

A vase dating from 440 B.C. depicts the Pythia gazing into a flat dish in her left hand and grasping a sprig of laurel with her right. This dish may have contained black and white beans for prophesy by lots as an alternative to possession. The charge for inspired services was far more costly than that for lots, and the charge for a city's inquiry was higher still. An example of the fees comes to us from a man named Croesus of Lydia who paid what would have amounted to nearly one billion dollars by modern standards. To exact such amounts, Delphi must have had a remarkable reputation.

There are stories of testing the different Grecian oracles' abilities. One involved Cyrus the great. This king sent six messengers to six different oracles to ask the same question at a predetermined time, "What is the king doing?" At that moment, Cyrus purposefully went about doing something very unkingly. He prepared his own dinner. Only the oracle at Delphi responded correctly.

The Norse had a long tradition of consulting a prophetess known as the *velda*, or seer. In thirteenth century Norse literature, two other names for the visionary were given: *spakona*, literally meaning "women of prophesy", and *volva* for "seeress." During the divination rite, the *velda* sat on an elevated seat, not unlike that of the Delphic oracle, called a *seiohjallr*. From this position, she could see what is usually hidden from mortals, and prophesy accordingly. Singers stood around the *seiohjallr*, chanting whatever spells were required for augury. The singing and chanting was believed to attract spirits who could then be queried for their knowledge.

These seers commanded a great deal of trust. They were even consulted in difficult religious questions. For example, in A.D. 1000, Icelanders sought a "lawspeaker" for advice on the mounting pressure for them to convert to Christianity. This pagan lawspeaker advised that the Icelanders should accept the Christian faith, and those who wished could continue to practice the old ways in private. The people heeded the wisdom in order that Iceland could have one law and one faith.

In neighboring lands, the Celts consulted specially trained bards called *awenyddion*. The bards used a trance state to divine answers to questions. In later years this ability was considered a type of possession by spirits, whose messages came through the *awenyddion*, akin to a modern channeler.

While all this oracular activity went on in the West, the East had its oracles and seers, too. In Japan, a supernatural being who had greater knowledge than the whole of humanity borrowed the body of a medium to respond to questions about the community. In pre-Buddhist days, the medium was frequently a woman who used many techniques to induce the trance state, including sacred dance. Later in history, the woman played a more passive role with a male Buddhist aesthetic tend-ing to the magic that brought the entity, posing the questions, and then dispatching the spirit being back to its realms.

Another type of medium in Japan was the village oracle, *takusen maturi*, commonly a farmer or fisherman who manifested the gift spontaneously or through the aid of drums, loud chanting, or recital of the Heart Sutra. Sadly, this tradition has disappeared in recent years. At last count in 1960, there were only six *takusen maturi*.

After the growth of Christianity around the world, instances of mediumship came and went with the prevalent trends in society. During the Victorian Era, for example, numerous people were fascinated by the spirit world, so automatism and mediumship were very common. Again, in the late 1960s when an interest in the occult and other spiritual systems grew, channeling became a popular form of divination.

• ORDEALS

Various societies used ordeals as a way of divining the judgment of the gods in a specific matter. In Arabia, for example, one way used to divine if a child was legitimate was to have it crawl through an opening in a natural rock formation. If the child could crawl through without getting stuck, it was considered to be of proper birth.

A means to divine the guilt or innocence of a prisoner in Arabia was called *Bish'ah*. A red hot knife would be taken by the arbitrator and flicked against the tongue of the accused. If the accused was burned, he or she was considered guilty. There is evidence to indicate though that this was a measure of last resort, the threat of the trial usually being enough to bear out the truth.

Similarly in Babylon, people were tossed in the river to determine their guilt. This seemed to be a gentler form of omen reading, as a person was guilty only if they sank. This particular rite of divination developed in this region because water was considered sacred by desert dwellers. It was felt that such a substance's spirit would not lie or deceive humankind.

In China, an accused person was required to spit out a mouthful of rice, the patterns of which determined guilt or innocence. In Germany, suspects had to pull a hot poker from a fire. If they were burned, guilt was indicated.

• ORNITHOMANCY

(see Birds)

•OUIJA

Ouija is a board game whose name literally translates as "yes yes." It consists of a lettered board that also has spots for "yes" and "no" answers. A pointer is placed on top of this board, and the querent's fingertips lightly rest on it while questions are posed. It is believed that spirits move the pointer and provide the answers.

Ouija could have had several ancient ancestors. First was a Hittite form of logographic divination called Kin. This was a game board with two fields and various symbols inscribed in the fields. Some object or item was placed on or near the board and allowed to move of its own volition. An old woman, who was also skilled in magic, presided over the reading and provided interpretations.

A second ancestor of our modern *Ouija* board originated in Greece around A.D. 371. This tool consisted of a tripod of laurel wood, a round metal plate with Greek letters on the rim, and a ring suspended by linen thread. The ring was set in motion and the letters read off. This tool was popular enough to be used in determining the name of future emperors.

The Romans, Chinese, Mongols, and even some Native Americans had versions of the *Ouija*. Around 500 years ago the Native Americans used a painted board with special emblems. This tool was called *Squdilatc*, and it spelled out the querent's response symbolically instead of literally.

Related Systems: Automatism, Pendulum

Adaptation: As mentioned in Chapter One, I do urge caution if you decide to try this system for yourself. Mass-produced boards are still readily available at stores, but you can make serviceable ones yourself using a piece of cardboard or smooth wood and a glass. Paint the letters of the alphabet on the surface chosen, along with the words "yes" and "no." The glass goes in the center of the board, which you touch with only the very tops of your fingertips while pondering a question.

Try making a system something closer to the Grecian-styled board so that no human hand can taint the unbiased nature of this oracle. Please consult the *Ouija* with great care, taking proper spiritual precautions against any spirits who may not have your best interest in mind.

• PA KUA

The *Pa Kua* consists of the eight main trigrams used in Chinese divination. Each features a combination of three solid or broken lines. Coupled, these become the foundational hexagrams for *I Ching* and many geomantic systems. The symbols and their basic correspondences are:

UPPER / LOWER	Ch'ien	Chên	K'an	Kên	K'un	Sun	Li	Tui
Ch'ien	1	34	5	26	11	9	14	43
Chên	25	51	3	27	24	42	21	17
K'an	6	40	29	4	7	59	64	47
Kên	33	62	39	52	15	53	56	31
K'un	12	16	8	23	2	20	35	45
Sun	44	32	48	18	46	58	50	28
Li	13	55	63	22	36	37	30	49
Tui	10	54	60	41	19	61	38	58

THROWING BY COIN

The result of the first throw is the bottom line of the hexagram.

—X—	3 tails	(3 x 2)	=	6*
——	2 tails, 1 head	(2 x 2) + 3	=	7
— —	2 heads, 1 tail	(2 x 3) + 2	=	8
—O—	3 heads	(3 x 3)	=	9*

*Indicates a moving line

Related Systems: Earth, Geomancy, *I Ching*, Ifa

Adaptations: Place these emblems on disks or wooden rods and cast them in a twelve circle. Consider the placement of each piece as it relates to the others, and its position within that circle. Depending on your outlook, locations on the circle may represent the numbers 1 to 12 like a clock face, the months, or seasons and elemental directions. In all cases, the closer a symbol lands to the center, the more important it is to you personally and to your question.

• PALMISTRY

Palmistry is based on the belief that hands hold the secrets of what you were and truly are. This may have originated with the reverence and trust placed in the hands of ancient healers. The earliest verified records of palmistry date to 2000 B.C.E. in India, and 384–322 B.C.E. with Aristotle. Both records document an oral history for this art prior to those dates.

Most palm readers look to the strong hand of a querent first, observing the whole shape, then noting details. The overall shape tends to influence minute factors in the reading of the lines. For example, if the overall shape is one of generosity, then each quarter of the palm and the lines therein are interpreted with generosity in mind. The upper right part of the palm determines matters of relationships and sexuality, the upper left indicates social matters, the lower left signifies personal energy and creative potential, and the lower right reveals subconscious issues.

A diagram of palm lines is given on page 208. Please note, however, that these are far clearer than those you will find in your own hand, so be patient with this art. If you find yourself having a lot of difficulty seeing lines, try making an ink print of your hand and work from that instead.

The Lines

Headline: The length of the head line equates with intelligence and understanding. When straight, it indicates a good memory, curving upward, effective self-expression, and curving downward, an overactive imagination.

Heartline: The length of the heart line equates to a person's capacity for giving and receiving love. When straight, it signifies emotional reserve. With many branches, the querent has several romantic interests. If it begins at the headline, it portends a working partnership.

PALMISTRY

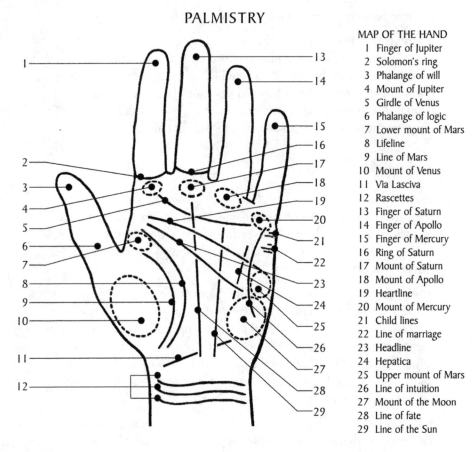

MAP OF THE HAND
1 Finger of Jupiter
2 Solomon's ring
3 Phalange of will
4 Mount of Jupiter
5 Girdle of Venus
6 Phalange of logic
7 Lower mount of Mars
8 Lifeline
9 Line of Mars
10 Mount of Venus
11 Via Lasciva
12 Rascettes
13 Finger of Saturn
14 Finger of Apollo
15 Finger of Mercury
16 Ring of Saturn
17 Mount of Saturn
18 Mount of Apollo
19 Heartline
20 Mount of Mercury
21 Child lines
22 Line of marriage
23 Headline
24 Hepatica
25 Upper mount of Mars
26 Line of intuition
27 Mount of the Moon
28 Line of fate
29 Line of the Sun

Fate line: If there is no fate line, a person will have a calm, rather uneventful life. If there, but it's broken, it portends sudden changes. When this line begins at the top bracelet, the person had many responsibilities in their youth. Ending on the heartline is a sign of sacrifice made for love.

Lifeline: A long, unbroken lifeline shows good health and vitality. One with breaks reveals periodic sickness. Small branches reaching downward portend financial setbacks, and those curving upward foretell prosperity.

Sun line: When the sun line doesn't appear, it is a sign of setbacks. A clear, straight sun line suggests good fortune and charisma. A sun line that begins at the life or fate line and moves up is an omen of success from one's talents.

Girdle of Venus: Lack of a Girdle of Venus line is a sign of self-regulation. One that is very distinct indicates the need for attention and an overly emotional nature. A short girdle reveals sensitivity toward others.

Rascettes: Parallel rascettes show a life filled with health and peace. Those with a chainlike appearance portend a troubled life that eventually yields joy.

Marriage line: A strong marriage line indicates a strong relationship over a fair number of years. The longer and straighter the lines are, the longer and happier the commitment.

The Mounts

Venus: A high firm mount of Venus reveals sexual energy and passions.

Mars, Lower: An underdeveloped or flat lower mount of Mars reveals fear.

Jupiter (base of forefinger): A large mount of Jupiter reveals pride, leadership ability, and ambition.

Saturn (base of middle finger): A large mount of Saturn reveals a wise, prudent individual.

Apollo: An average-sized mount of Apollo indicates an upbeat personality.

Mercury: A large mount of Mercury shows good humor and practicality.

Mars, Upper: An average-sized upper Mars mount reveals moral courage.

Moon: A high firm mount of the moon symbolizes an abundant imagination.

• PAPER

At one time paper was a very valuable commodity, and like most precious things it was used as a "magical" tool in various settings. The ancient Chinese had a form of paper scrying called *yuan kuang fuchou*, which was most often used in cases of robbery. For this, the diviner hung up a piece of paper, uttered a spell, and had a young boy gaze at the paper until he saw the visage of a thief. This practice had become illegal by the 1800s. In Arabia, a diviner would put a blot of ink in the center of a piece of paper to act as a focal point on which to fix his or her gaze. The Arabs applied this divinatory approach to many kinds of questions.

One type of paper divination still used today is that of choosing a slip out of a hat for decision making. Another has you write five potential actions on five equally sized papers and roll each tightly. These are placed in a steamer tray, and the first to open from the heat and moisture advises the best course of action.

Related Systems: Burnings, Hat, Lemon Juice

•PATIENCE GAMES

Patience games, card games so named due to the length of time it took to complete them, were sometimes used for divinatory purposes. The querent would pose a question before shuffling the cards for a game (like solitaire or its derivatives), then proceed to play. Since the odds of winning such a game are low, successful completion is considered a positive answer to the query.

Some patience games use thirty-two cards instead of fifty-two, eliminating the cards numbered 2 through 6 in each suit. This allows for a shorter playing period.

Related Systems: Cartomancy, Tarot

•PEARLS (MARGARITOMANCY)

Place a pearl on the floor before a warm fire, and put a clear bowl over it (so that the pearl is not touching any of the sides). Voice yes-or-no questions. If the pearl moves and touches any of the sides, causing the bowl to sound, the answer is affirmative.

Related Systems: Bowls or Dishes (ringing of), Rings

•PEBBLES (PESSOMANCY)

Pebbles and stones appear in several different divination systems, but frequently their effects are observed after being tossed in water. The number of rings formed or the shape of the patterns become the foundation of the interpretation. Looking for patterns allows for broader interpretive values.

Alternatively, in Africa a system called *An Bere* uses a handful of small pebbles tossed into the air with the left hand. The querent snatches as many as possible before the pebbles fall to earth. The stones make patterns similar to the *I Ching* and other geomantic systems.

Related Systems: Crystals, Gems, Stones

Adaptation: Find a small flat stone like shale and hold it in your hands while thinking of a question. Skip the stone over a calm body of water and count how many times it skips. An even number means "yes," an odd number means "no." If the stone does not skip at all, this is a sign that whatever you're doing should wait a while for better timing.

• PEDOMANCY

Pedomancy is a system of divining personality types and a person's future from the lines in the feet. This originated in China and bears strong similarity to palmistry.

Related Systems: Ears, Eyes, Facial Features, Feet, Fingers, Hands, Palmistry

• PEGOMANCY

(see Water (fountains))

• PEITHYNEN FRAME

There is a claim that a divination method using the Peithynen Frame was devised by Welsh bards, though some historians doubt its authenticity. The method has a tremendous random element and ease of construction that could function very well in a modern setting. The original frames were said to be made with five rods, each of which had four surfaces inscribed with ogham letters. The rods were set in a frame, one above the other, and spun. The ogham letters that faced outward at the end were read for their values.

Related Systems: Ogham, Rods, Wands

Adaptation: Build a frame for yourself, and mark the rods with whatever emblems are personally meaningful to you. The five rods can represent the five elements of Earth-Air-Fire-Water-Spirit. Or perhaps one rod can represent the Self and the others the four seasons or directions.

• PENDULUMS

The Romans appear to be the first people who used pendulums for divination, specifically to determine the outcome of forthcoming battles. The pendulum was not always observed by itself. Sometimes a diviner placed the point in the center of a circle of letters to be able to literally spell out responses.

Among the Koryak, there are special stones for pendulum divination called *anapel*. The father of a newborn child uses this tool to determine what deceased relative's soul has been reincarnated in that child. When the stone moves more quickly than when it began swinging, this indicates the right name has been spoken.

A pendulum is a handy divinatory device that has numerous applications, like determining foods that are good for you, regions of sickness or disease, personality traits, locations of underground waters or metals (like a divining rod), and significances of ambiguous signals. You can use it in finding lost items, uncovering polarity, and foretelling events.

Pendulum use is considered a branch of dowsing, in which the movements of the device indicate specific things. For example, some individuals seek out the earth's sacred energy centers using the pendulum, but people so doing may interpret their findings differently. This is because each individual interacts with spiritual energy uniquely. (This is also what makes divination an art, not a science.)

Numerous objects have been used as pendulums, ranging in shape from the spiral (like a seashell) to the traditional conical (which may be formed with sprigs of herbs, too). The best materials for the art are thought to be brass, amber, silver, and copper, suspended from a natural fiber string of cotton, wool, or linen.

To discover if you have a knack for using pendulums, attach eight to twelve inches of string to a plain ring (like a wedding band). Hold the free end between the thumb and index finger of your stronger hand (the one you write with). Place this over the palm of the opposite hand and ask the pendulum if you are male. Wait fifteen minutes. If it does not begin swinging, try again after a break, this time holding the string with different fingers. If the pendulum starts to swing clockwise, this is an affirmative answer; counterclockwise is negative. If this result does not match your gender, try several more times before giving up, noting that intense personality traits may influence the pendulum, too.

If the pendulum swings accurately for you, then you can try more exacting experiments. Begin by drawing a circle on paper or cloth that is about ten inches in diameter. The background should contrast with the color of your pendulum for easy viewing. Next, place your elbow on the table outside the circle, bending your arm so that the pendulum point is above the circle's center. Try to empty your mind of anything other than the question, including any preconceived notions or bits of wishful thinking. These can sway the results.

Focus only on the pendulum and any movements it makes. Generally speaking, circles are a good answer, portending harmony, joy, improved energy, and intelligence. The power and range of the swing indicates to what degree this interpretation should be taken. Hesitation or bobbing in the pendulum betrays uncertainty or a question that involves conflict between two equally appealing or repelling choices.

In relationships, up-down motions indicate a divide between people, and ellipses reveal a lack of complete understanding or communication. In other questions, ellipses reveal duality in one's desires. Ellipses moving east to west talk of a great capacity for love, and many sensitive people exhibit this with broad sweeping elliptical movements. Along a north and south line, feminine instincts and traits are strongly suggested. Diagonal ellipses warn of depression, questionable ethics, or a lack of assertion in a specific situation.

Vertical strokes indicate a strong ego and will (sometimes to excess), and dominance. Horizontal strokes speak of natural physical urges. If the horizontal stroke is interrupted by jerky motions, this focus is unhealthy. Diagonal strokes reveal conflicts, obstacles, or illness.

If trying to determine the sex of a baby, circles indicate a boy, while ovals indicate a girl.

Related Systems: Botanomancy, Herbs, Needles, Plants, Rings

Adaptations: Change the color of the string used for pendulum divination to better reflect the essence of your question. *A Pendulum Kit* is available through Simon & Schuster. It was devised by Sig Lonegren and includes a brass pendulum, cord, and an instructional guide for numerous applications.

• PESSOMANCY

(see Pebbles)

• PHYLLORHODOMANCY

(see Flowers—Roses)

• PHYSIOGNOMY

Physiognomy is the art of reading character and potential in a person's face and body forms. Physiognomy seems to have origins in China, where references to *shang fa* (face reading) were recorded around 3,000 years ago. The Japanese version was known as *ninso* (person aspect), but both systems bear little resemblance to the interpretations that appeared later in Europe.

The Greeks in particular esteemed physiognomy, often using it in assessing a person's suitability for official office. The study continued throughout history with various scholars, philosophers, and lay people adding their perspectives. In the early 1800s, for example, Sir Charles Bell of Scotland suggested that there was a connection between muscle movements, expression, and the resulting lines in the face. To this day there remains a strong connection between anticipated character and a person's face or body language.

As a divinatory art, physiognomy is quite complex. It takes into consideration many factors, including a person's height, figure, build, carriage, actions, forehead construction, facial features, and hair color and texture. Additionally, any animal resemblances and symbolic facial lines are also considered before making a final assessment. Here are some common interpretations:

Tall: Generous

Short: Cruel, vigorous

Stout: Loving, slow-paced, somewhat weak

Slender: Sentimental, passionate, and vital

Massive: Indulgent, strong

Slight: Average strength

Erect: Morality, prudence

Slouched: Rash, unobtrusive, hard worker

Quick: Firm, direct, sincere, ambitious, courageous, but rash

Slow: Secretive, lazy, insecure, and often jealous

Putting this altogether, if you meet someone who has a small stature, is thin, built slightly, stands erect, and moves quickly, you might anticipate that this person has a high energy level and ambitions that sometimes lead to vicious actions. Nonetheless, they are probably fairly honest, forthright, and amorous in relationships.

To this basic reading, other indicative factors as given under related systems in this book may be added. One word of caution: try physiognomy only for fun. No person should be judged solely on their appearance.

Related Systems: Ears, Eyes, Facial Features, Fingers, Hands, Moles, Phrenology

• PLANTS (BOTANOMANCY)

A few plants with associated divinatory practices include:

Clover with two leaves: Place a two-leaf clover in your shoe. The next person to pass you will bear the name or an initial of a future mate or business partner.

Fern stalk: Cut a fern across the stalk and look at it. The lines in the break will reveal an initial in the name of the person you seek. Finding an image of an oak tree here means that very good luck will be yours.

Holly: Welsh tradition instructs placing a candle on a holly leaf in water. If it floats, it indicates prosperity. Place nine holly leaves under your pillow on Halloween night to receive prophetic dreams (see *Dreams, Holiday Omens and Signs*).

Ivy leaf: Place an ivy leaf in clear water on New Year's night. If it remains green without spots after twelve nights, this portends a year of health for you and your household (see *Holiday Omens and Signs, Leaves*).

Mistletoe: Place a sprig of mistletoe under your pillow to bring prophetic dreams, especially in matters of love.

Myrtle: Myrtle found growing at your door is an omen of happiness and peace for as long as you dwell in that residence.

Peach and pear leaves: If peach or pear leaves fall off the tree in the summer, it is a bad omen for cattle.

Plantain: Pick one sprig of plantain to represent each member of any group or organization. Wrap these in a dock leaf and lay them overnight beneath a stone. If they still appear to be in blossom the next morning, it predicts that your group is of one harmonious mind and will succeed.

Rush: Finding a rush with a green top predicts good luck.

Related Systems: Bay, Botanomancy, Flowers, Herbs, Plantain, Rose, Trees

• PLASTROMANCY

(see Bones and Shells (turtle))

• PODOMANCY

(see Feet)

• POPCORN

Among both the Navaho and Seneca Indians, popcorn was a divinatory tool. Handfuls of the kernels were tossed on a fire and observed. The direction of the kernels' flight and the number that popped both determined the reading's value.

Related Systems: Food, Nuts

Adaptation: Using this method is a fun pastime while sitting around a campfire. Generally, more kernels landing to the right of the querent is a "yes" answer, while more on the left indicate a "no." If you prefer to eat your popcorn, just count the seeds that don't pop when you get to the bottom of the bowl, an even number meaning "yes."

•PRAYER BEADS

Phren-ba or Tring-ba is a Tibetan form of augury that uses a *mala* with 108 prayer beads. They are also employed in daily devotions. To engage the *mala* for divination, the querent holds it, settles his or her mind, and focuses on a question. The querent then grasps the rosary in two random places and counts off beads from each end inward, in groups of four, until the remaining number of beads is between one and four. This process is repeated three times, making note of the final count each time.

Interpretations are as follows:

One: Good fortune, sometimes after a waiting period

Two: Misfortune, adversity, and difficulties

Three: Fast movement for boon or bane

Four: Moderate improvements coupled with complications

The meaning of each number in a reading is augmented by the next one to appear in the sequence of three countings. So if a querent were to get 1-1-1, it could be considered a very auspicious reading.

Related System: Numerology

Adaptations: One might use any set of personally significant beads for this procedure, or perhaps an abacus.

•PSYCHOGRAPHY
(see Automatism)

•PSYCHOMANCY
(see Soul Gazing)

•PYROMANCY
(see Fire)

• RAINBOWS

A commonly recognized emblem of hope from the story of Noah and the Ark, the rainbow has been a significant portent for many cultures. Among tribal cultures in New Zealand, a rainbow appearing on the road ahead warns of danger, and one is not supposed to pass under it. A half-rainbow portends arguments or a brawl, while two rainbows (one appearing on each side of you) indicates a safe voyage. A small rainbow represents blessings, and a white one indicates a visitation by magical beings.

Other rainbow omens include:

• A rainbow appearing around the moon warns of very bad weather, while one that fades quickly predicts quick improvements in the weather.

• In Ireland, people believe that a rainbow appearing on Saturday precedes a week of storms (see *Weather Omens*), and a double rainbow indicates a long dry spell ahead.

• Iranian Muslims feel that a rainbow appearing in the sign of Capricorn when it's located in the eastern sky is an excellent omen, while one appearing in Capricorn in the west means devastation.

• A predominantly red rainbow predicts war, while a predominantly green one presages abundance.

• Malaysians believe a rainbow with a partial arch that ends in water foretells the death of a great leader (see *Death Omens*).

Related System: Aeromancy

• RAISINS

On Halloween in Scotland, raisins become the focus for an old, venerated divinatory game. In it, the raisins are placed in a heat-proof bowl and doused with flammable liqueur. This is ignited, after which participants try to snatch as many raisins as they can until the fire goes out. The number grabbed equates to their fortune, even amounts being favorable, uneven amounts being unfavorable. This game is called "Snapdragon."

Also, eating raisins is said to improve one's capacity for foresight, bringing predictive dreams (see *Food*).

Related Systems: All binary or counted systems, Food, Numerology

• RANDOM DIVINATION

Random divination systems base their interpretive values on something wholly unpredictable to the querent. One excellent example of this comes from Greece. At Hermes' Shrine, a querent paid to whisper his or her question to the Divine image within. The questioner would then plug his or her ears until they left the temple. Immediately upon exiting, the querent unplugged his or her ears and accepted the first phrase heard to be the divine omen. A similar system was used in China during the Feast of the Kitchen God (around January 20). Technically, this type of random divination is known as transataumancy, accidentally seen or overhead events.

Another good example of random omens is in the art of bibliomancy. The querent opens a book, puts down a finger without looking, then reads their fortune in the phrase indicated. In both transataumancy and bibliomancy, the inherent value of random divination is easily discernible. It is very difficult to prejudice a system like this in any way because one cannot easily preordain the results.

Here are a few more illustrations for your consideration:

Bus tickets: If the last digit of the number appearing on your bus ticket or pass is a 7, this indicates that the day will be lucky.

Clergy: Meeting a member of the clergy on the way to a confrontation is a very bad sign. A fight may ensue, or harsh words that lead to regrets.

Dish rag: Dropping a dish rag means that something special is about to happen. Some people interpret this as the approach of a lover, while others believe it foretells dinner guests arriving.

Knife: A knife dropping with its point sticking into the ground is a very good sign for the whole day. Two knives placed accidentally by the same plate reveal that company is coming.

Hand: Accidentally knocking your hand against a piece of wood predicts a love affair, while knocking it against iron warns of treachery.

Milk: Milk boiling over portends trouble in the home (see *Food*).

Pictures: Pictures suddenly dropping out of their frame with no apparent cause is a bad foreshadowing, especially for the person portrayed.

Silverware: Dropping a spoon means a female guest is coming. A fork indicates a man, and a knife, a child.

Related Systems: Books, Breakage, Dressing, Findings

Adaptations: Randomly overhearing a car backfire might portend a project similarly "backfiring." Walking into a photography flash may predict new insight or inspiration. The honking of a horn could mean an important message is coming for you.

•RHABDOMANCY

Rhabdomancy is a type of rod divination in which a number of answers are attached to, or painted upon, an object. A priest or other holy person shoots an arrow into the object, and whichever answer he or she pierces is the correct response to the question.

Related Systems: Arrows, Dowsing, Rods, Wands

•RHAPSODOMANCY

(see Books (poetry))

•RICE

In China, diviners prepare a special dish to aid their prophetic abilities. This meal consists of rice mixed with lychee fruit, cherries, dates, plums, diced lotus flower, cinnamon, ginger, and oranges. When consumed, this is also said to bring visionary dreams.

Related Systems: Food, Ritual

Adaptation: Look through this book, or one on magical herbalism, for edibles that enhance psychic insight. Consume some of these just prior to performing readings for yourself or others.

•RINGS (DACTYLOMANCY)

Rings were used for a type of pendulum divination in the Middle Ages. Different types of rings were chosen, depending on the day of the week, combining the sympathy of the weekday with an appropriate metal and stone to improve results. For questions posed on Sunday, gold and peridot was best. Silver and quartz rings were used on Mondays, iron with ruby on Tuesday, tin or lead with carnelian on Wednesday, tin with topaz on Thursday, copper with emerald on Friday, and lead with onyx on Saturday.

The instructions for ring divination indicated that the suspended ring should be surrounded by letters and set into gentle motion. A sacred fire burned through the suspending thread, allowing the ring to drop to the surface. This was done seven times. Where the ring landed showed the significant letters for the interpretation.

The procedure in Greece varied slightly from this. The diviner suspended the ring in a glass of water and asked yes-or-no questions. If the ring tapped the sides of the glass, the response was favorable. Or alternatively, the diviner dropped a ring connected to a string into water. If it fell to the right side of the glass, the answer was "yes," to the left, "no." If it fell in the middle, directly across from the querent or right next to them, no answer was possible.

In the Victorian Era, and sometimes yet today, young women passed a piece of wedding cake through a ring, then slept with the cake under their pillow to dream of whom they would someday marry (see *Marriage Omens*).

Related Systems: Gold, Keys, Pendulum

Adaptation: For the first system mentioned, use symbols around the ring instead of letters.

•RITUALS

While not a primary focus today, ritual played an integral role in divination's past. Many diviners were also priests or shamans in their communities. Consequently, this art was combined and integrated with religious rituals that honored and invoked a divine or semi-divine presence. Such actions would hopefully succeed in coaxing a god or goddess to help with the matter at hand.

The order and content of rituals changed depending on the era and culture in question. Many included chanting, singing, dance, prayer, meditation, and offering as principal components. Others, like those found in Gaelic Scotland, entailed very specific actions that evoked the desired sign, omen, or vision.

In one Scottish ritual known as *Taghairm*, the diviner wrapped him or herself in bull hide and slept near a waterfall (see *Calfskin*). Waterfalls were regarded as having beneficent indwelling spirits who would whisper the requested knowledge to the diviner as they slept. An example of *Taghairm* is found in the Mabinogion, "The Dream of Rhonabwy," where a warrior sleeps on a yellow skin and dreams of King Arthur's court.

Whatever the approach, the diviner used ritual as a means of not only contacting or channeling divine energies, but also as a way of self-preparation for interpreting the sign, omen, or portent he or she received.

Related Systems: Chanting, Dance, Drums, Fire, Incense, Intoxicants, Offerings, Song

Adaptations: See Chapter Two: Personal Preparation.

• RODS

"And their rods give them oracles."

—Hosea 4:12

Ancient people equated rods with rulership and authority, often conferred by the Divine on a leader. This symbolism eventually led to their use in fortune-telling. One interesting example of rod divination occurs in the Old Testament of the Bible, in which Moses lays out twelve rods in the Tabernacle, each bearing the name of one of Israel's tribes. This was how he discerned which tribe would head all the others.

The Saxons used a seven-rod system made from three short pieces of wood and four long. One of the four long rods had special decorations and was placed on the ground oriented along a north-south axis. The querent held the other rods while thinking of a question, allowing all the rods but one to fall from about one foot above the north-south indicator. Any rod that contacted the north-south indicator was a sign that no answer will be given. If some rods rested on others, no certain answer was available. If all sticks pointed toward the north-south rod, it meant the querent was able to solve the question using sound reasoning. If the rods were parallel to the indicator, fate's hand was at work. A majority of rods in the eastern quarter revealed a positive outcome, while in the western quarter, negative.

A closely related system that offers greater interpretive value is that of the Druid Rods. These seem to have more modern origins, but were based on Druidical geomantic symbols. Most often the Druid Rods are designed from the wood of fruit-bearing trees or from oak. A simpler alternative is to fashion them from four popsicle sticks!

Paint each of the four flat sticks with two circles on one side and one on the other (see below). This creates sixteen potential patterns. Hold these in your hand, mixing gently, while you think of a question. Toss them on a cloth, and cover them with one hand to straighten them out (the one closest to you is the bottom of the pattern). The resulting pattern provides the interpretive value. Note that this system very closely resembles some ancient forms of African geomancy in which a querent made random holes in dirt or sand for the diviner to interpret.

Following is a list of the possible readings:

PATTERN	NAME	MEANING
	Via (The Way)	Movement, travel, action, or sometimes hermetic retreat. Opportunity based on ability.
	Caput Draconis (Dragon's Head)	A beginning, so stay alert. Service to others balanced against personal need. Faith in one's actions.
	Puella (The Girl)	Feminine characteristics emerging, including nurturing and insight. Good relations with women.
	Fortuna Major (Major Fortune)	Victory; symmetry; happy occasions or blessings. Good efforts and kindness returning threefold.
	Puer (The Boy)	Masculine characteristics emerging, including strength and leadership, but with a warning to harness them.
	Acquisitio (Gain)	Advancement and improvement. Money problems abate, allowing for increased focus on the spiritual.
	Carcer (Prison)	A closed door or barrier places life on hold. Negative emotions holding you back. Doubt brings bondage.
	Tristitia (Sadness)	Hopes dashed; foreboding or sadness from unexpected loss. Efforts result in disappointment.
	Cauda Draconis (Dragon's Tail)	Bad luck, decline, or setbacks lead to an ending. Prepare for difficulty, and meet it bravely.
	Conjunctio (The Union)	Unity, love, kinship, friendship. Good communication and careful thought lead to beneficial unions.
	Amisso (Loss)	Technical or financial trouble. Conflict causes financial loss or misunderstandings.

PATTERN	NAME	MEANING
	Albeo (White)	Temperance and patience are called for to bring life into balance. Moderation leads to personal growth.
	Fortuna Minor (Minor Fortune)	A little serendipity and success comes from honesty, humility, and frugality.
	Rubeo (Red)	Don't let emotion overpower you. Take a break from life's hectic pace to think and heal.
	Laetitia (Joy)	All good things: love, health, joy, peace, prosperity, creativity, harmony, and fulfillment.
	Populus (People)	Those people in and around your life, and the messages they bear. Social involvement.

An alternative way of casting the Druid Rods is to throw them nine successive times, then interpret the patterns by adding in the significance of traditional Celtic numerology. Here, the first pattern represents the individual in the question. The second pattern represents matters requiring discretion, especially in relationships. Pattern three equates to communication, your ability to express yourself effectively, and be understood. Pattern four reveals how competently you reason and act. The fifth pattern speaks of liberation, things that will free you or from which you need to free yourself. Pattern six symbolizes matters at home and your responsibilities. The seventh pertains to spiritual pursuits. The eighth relates to money/material matters and the ability to balance one's dreams with reality. Finally, the ninth speaks of your ability to give and receive love, charity, and tolerance. Note that some readers use the ninth pattern as the "outcome."

Related Systems: Castings, *I Ching*, Lots, Ogham, Runes, Wands

Adaptations: Try substituting burnished metal or finished wood for longevity (note that the Druid Rods need to be flat on both sides). In a pinch, even cardboard will suffice. To increase the divinatory value of the rods, you can paint them different colors or add more symbols. Note that any unfinished wooden medium should be treated regularly with oil (like lemon oil) to keep it from drying and cracking.

•ROOSTERS (ALECTROMANCY)

Alectromancy began with the Etruscans around 2,000 years ago, then found its way into many other cultures, including those of Greece, Rome, and eventually America with minor variations. Alectromancy is the interpretation of a rooster's pecking. Several piles or kernels of corn are placed at points in a specific pattern, often a circle. The points at which the rooster eats spells out a message, through emblems or letters placed at those locations. Just before the bird sets to this task, the querent should begin focusing on his or her question and not stop until the rooster has walked away from the grain altogether.

Another method of Alectromancy is based on when and where a rooster crows. For example, one crowing in the middle of the night forewarns the listener that bad news is approaching.

Related System: Animal Omens and Signs

• ROSES (PHYLLORHODOMANCY)

In a rather unique type of divination, a rose petal is placed in the left hand, then snapped with the right. The sound portends the answer, a loud noise being most favorable. This system began in Greece where the rose was an emblem and sacred flower of the Goddess Athena.

There are other ways that roses figure into fortune-telling techniques. For example, pick three equally open roses at the same time. Designate which one represents "yes," which one "no," and which one "maybe" while focusing on your question. The one to last the longest without water represents your answer.

If a rose blossom seems to fade while you hold it, anticipate misfortune in the next year. If its petals begin to fall off, sickness is forecast or trouble in relationships.

• RUNES

The actual origin of runes is the subject of some debate, but most scholars on the subject agree that they have roots in both literary and magical traditions. The predecessors of runes, symbols called *Hallristningar*, which dated to the Bronze Age, were used for lot casting. Later the *Hallristningar* were incorporated into the names and meanings of the runes. Additionally, the Scandinavian tradition of runemal is 2,000 years old, and it appears to have been passed along to Italian, German, Danish, and Druidical traditions.

Runes have shown minor variations depending on the era and region of use. Three of these variants—the *Elder Futhark*, used by northern Germanic peoples, the Anglo-Saxon *Futhore*, and the *Younger Futhark* from Danish regions—are the foundational emblems used for modern rune sets. Of these, the *Elder Futhark* bears the strongest resemblance to sets on the market.

In using the runes for divination, one may either lay out the runes, like a Tarot deck, or cast them in a circle like lots. If using a layout, any pattern you've seen in Tarot books will work. One of the easiest layouts begins with four runes placed as shown below:

1

2   3   4

In this layout, position 1 represents the querent, position 2, past influences, position 3, an action called for, and position 4, the outcome. Your layouts can become far more complex, even to the point of using all the runes. Alternatively, some querents draw one rune each morning to determine the overall energies for that day.

Tacitus mentions that the Romans sometimes scattered runes on a white cloth, then chose three at random. These were read in no particular order but were considered together as the answer to a question. Alternatively, the diviner might read only those runes that landed face up in the casting. The closer the upright runes were to one another, the more they influenced each other and the situation. Any rune landing off the casting cloth was not read, and from what we can tell most rune readers did not see a rune as "reversed" when the carving landed upside down.

Today runes are still either cast or drawn, and their abbreviated correspondences are as follows:

RUNE	NAME	MEANING
	Feoh, Fehu	Wealth, power, status, fortune, accomplishment
	Ur, Uruz	Strength, stamina, health
	Thorn, Thurisaz	Necessary transitions in progress
	Os, Ansuz	Messages or guidance; be receptive
	Rad, Raido	Active pursuit of a goal; success from tenacity
	Ken, Kaunaz	Improved understanding; enlightenment
	Gifu, Gebo	A gift; balance and generosity
	Win, Wunjo	Happiness; joyful opportunity
	Haegel, Hagalaz	Loss, difficulty, disruption
	Nyo, Nauthiz	Obstacles, perseverance

RUNE	NAME	MEANING
$\vert$	Iss, Issa	Constraint, halting; the solitary self
$\diamondsuit$	Ger, Jera	Harvest; reaping earned rewards
$\int$	Eoh, Eiwaz	Planning with care; long-term outlooks
$\Kappa$	Perth, Peord	Mysterious potential; unexpected events
Ψ	Eol, Algiz	Safety, protection; be aware
ζ	Sigil, Sowelu	Success, creativity, the sun
$\uparrow$	Tir, Tiwaz	Fighting for beliefs; action brings victory
β	Beork, Berkana	Growth, evolution, maturity
M	Eh, Ehwaz	Progress from hard work
$\bowtie$	Man, Mannaz	Humility; understanding the self
Γ	Lager, Laguz	Hidden influences; adaptation
$\otimes$	Ing, Inguz	A righteous path results in strength
$\bowtie$	Daeg, Dagaz	Hope; positive change
$\diamondsuit$	Ethel, Othalaz	Tradition, heritage
	Blank*	The unknown; potential
$\digamma$	Ak, Akaz*	Stability, commitment, trust
$\digamma$	Yer, Yeraz*	Practice makes perfect
$\digamma$	Aesk, Aska*	Shelter and protection
$\curlyvee$	Eyar, Eyaruz*	Endings and beginnings
χ	Ian, Iaro*	Meet challenges with flexibility

Note: These are not used in all contemporary runic systems.

Related Systems: Castings, *I Ching*, Lots, Shells, Stones

Modern Alternatives: One unique alternative offered by Scott Cunningham is the use of *Scrabble* letters. Take one of each tile and place it in a bag as you would the runes. Shake the bag while thinking of your question and pour out the letters. Look at those facing upward and see what words/messages form.

Some on-line services offer rune readings.

Take symbols that correspond to the runes and place them randomly on the spokes of a bike (or around any other turning wheel). Think about your question, and when the wheel stops moving take note of which symbols meet the ground, interpreting from that foundation.

•SALT (HALOMANCY)

One type of halomancy bases its interpretations on the reaction of a fire when salt is cast on it. Alternatives to this include:

- In Greece, a method based on geomantic techniques uses a tray full of salt. While thinking of a question the querent lightly taps on the edge or the bottom of the tray. The resulting shapes create the foundation for interpretation.

- If the salt in the house turns moist and is difficult to pour, this is a sign of rain soon to follow (see *Weather Omens*).

- Every grain of salt spilled portends a day of sorrow, and knocking over a salt shaker foretells the breaking of a friendship.

Related Systems: Fire, Random Divination, Sand, Spilling

•SAND (AUTONOGRAPHY)

In China, there is form of autonography called *Fu Kei*. In it, the querent sits down with a T-shaped peachwood device that has a cross bar and a vertical stick. The end of the stick rests in a bed of fine sand, and as it moves it draws strokes or emblems. Navajo Indians employ a similar approach, substituting a stick for the T-shaped tool.

This type of divination is very relaxing and holds tremendous potential as a meditative tool as well. Find a wooden box about three inches deep and fill it with well-sifted sand. Sit before the box with a wooden stick, close your eyes and begin centering your attention on your question. Allow your hand to doodle in the sand until you feel done, but for no longer than two to three minutes. When you open your eyes, first look for obvious symbols in the patterns, like a letter "Y" for yes. Small circles talk of intimate energies, such as receiving news from a friend or a fellow employee. A triangle indicates your efforts will be successful, it also might portend a business improvement. Lines speak of travel or one's path in life. Squares symbolize foundations and possible obstacles. A heart relates to love, crosses indicate barriers, and flowers suggest a new beginning of some sort (see Appendix B).

An alternative to the above approach is mixing other natural items into a bowl of sand, like shells, small stones, driftwood, and feathers. Ponder your question and pour out the sand mixture on a flat surface. Let your instincts guide you as to when to stop. Scry the patterns made by the sand and objects for your interpretation.

Related Systems: Automatism, Scrying

Adaptations: Children's toy stores sell colored sand for projects. Randomly take pinches of this sand and sprinkle it on a damp surface, then scry your future in the resulting pattern. Alternatively, wipe a thin coating of glue on a sturdy paper surface, then sprinkle the sand on it. Keep this afterward as a decorative meditation poster.

•SANDALS

In Kenya, a shaman or fortune-teller known as the *murogi* tosses his or her sandals in the air. Omens are derived by the manner and directions in which the shoes fall.

Related Systems: Arrows, Blocks, Clothing, Drumstick

•SCAPULIMANCY

(see Bones, Shells)

•SCARFS

To divine if a lover is faithful, toss a lightweight scarf on a pool or other source of moving water. If it moves toward the north, your love is true.

Alternatively, a silk scarf was used in a Tibetan ritual held once every three years. For this the presiding Lama walked the ritual fire, putting a silk scarf, salt, wine, and sulphur into a suspended pot of burning oil. If the eruptions of this mixture brought bright blue-yellow flames, it signaled the banishing of old evils and a future filled with joy and prosperity.

Related Systems: Feathers, Fire, Floating, Flowers, Oil, Rituals, Salt, Water, Wine

•SCIOMANCY

(see Shadows)

•SCRYING

Scrying is gazing upon crystals or other surfaces in search of prophetic patterns. It comes from the English word *descry*, meaning to discover. A large diversity of scrying systems were developed by the ancients, including ones that used crystals, mirrored surfaces, flames, and the sky. Studies were done on scrying techniques in the late nineteenth and early twentieth century. This resulted in a theory that a scryer brings on a self-induced trance by focusing on the medium. This change in awareness allows symbolic pictures to appear in the medium, such as swirling clouds. These symbols are then interpreted for their meaning.

Some people seem to have an innate talent for scrying. Many such individuals suggest that it is best to purify oneself before attempting this procedure. Specifically, they may fast or bathe, then meditate before doing a reading.

Related Systems: Blood, Crystals, Fire, Hydromancy, Ink, Lithomancy, Mirrors, Pyromancy, Sky, Stones (polished), Water, Wax

Adaptations: Try scrying soap bubbles or film in a sink full of water. A blank TV and computer screens also work well, because you already subconsciously anticipate seeing something on them, making them easier to use.

•SCYPHOMANCY

(see Cups/Glasses/Vases)

•SEASHELLS

Many shells have been used in casting systems, but by far the most popular one in West Africa is the cowrie shell. Four of these are tossed in a basket, then their pattern is interpreted by a shaman. This method of divination is known locally as *Dilogun*. Before divination, the shells are cut in such a manner that they have two definite sides, one of which reveals a spiral representing female energies, and the other signifying male. In yes-or-no questions, four male sides facing up indicate a definite "yes." Three male sides up suggest that further exploration is necessary. Two male, two female sides indicate that things will go well, and the querent will gain much spiritual understanding from this situation. One male side up portends instability, and four female sides up is a definite "no."

Related System: Ifa

Adaptation: In Tibet and China, people hold a seashell to their ear and interpret the sounds they hear in response to a question. The conch shell most commonly used for this is still readily available in many gift shops. Generally, a loud roaring response is positive, silence is negative, and the echo of a quiet wave means a waiting period is necessary.

•SECOND SIGHT
(see Clear Sight)

•SEEDS

Depending on the time period and region, seeds were either planted and observed or scattered for divinatory purposes. In the case of the former, the first seed to sprout or blossom symbolically indicated the best course of action or most likely future. In scattering, the patterns of the seeds provided the foundation for a reading. For example, in Madagascar, a querent casts acacia seeds several times on a grid of nine circles to create patterns. They call this technique *Sikidy*, and the patterns are nearly identical to those formed by Druid Rods with the exception that the interpretive values are more negative, likely reflecting the harshness of life in this region.

Related Systems: Apple Seeds, Drums

•SEIDE

In Lapland, *seide* were sacred stones used for divination. The stones appeared to have a human or animal form naturally, and sometimes they were given in offerings to aid divinatory practices. The information on the stone's exact application is incomplete, but there may have been some connection here to totemism or animism, in which the image formed by the stone provided clues to its meaning.

•SELENOMANCY
(see Moon)

•SENET

Senet was an Egyptian game that modeled its patterns on the moon's monthly cycle. Boards have been discovered dating back to 1500 B.C., and they show various emblems combined with "good" or "risky" indicators over 30 squares. Along with the moon's movements, each square had some associations with the next life and various obstacles that impeded a beneficial reincarnation. This suggests that the game may have been undertaken during times of serious illness, especially since the final square was marked with the emblem of Horus, portending a successful rebirth for the winner. There are also some corollaries to the Egyptian calendar, meaning the game may have had other prognosticative applications that were lost to time.

Related Systems: Day Signs, Go

• SERPENTS (OPHIOMANCY)

In ancient Rome and Greece, people, especially in the noble classes, often kept serpents in special pens and observed them for insights into the future. A snake entering one's home was considered a very lucky omen, while one leaving portended trouble. Other than this, little information exists on ophiomancy.

Related Systems: Animal Omens and Signs, Bird Augury, Horse Omens

• SHADOWS (SCIOMANCY)

Divination based on the appearance of a person's shadow, sciomancy likely grew out of Celtic shadow magic, which was often used as propitiation in place of an actual sacrifice. One tradition states that if a person's shadow has no head on New Year's, they will not live to see the year's end, and a faint shadow portends sickness. In numerous traditions, a person without a shadow is regarded as having no soul. Having a buzzard's shadow touch your own is an omen of death, sickness, or disaster (see *Birds*).

• SHAMANISM

Shamanistic traditions retain a holistic view of the cosmos, and through a shaman's relationship to it, the cause of problems or sickness may be divined. Many shamanic traditions employ a trance to contact spirits for information. To achieve this, costumes, music, dance, or chanting might be used. In this altered state of awareness, they become intermediaries between worlds. They share their vision and its interpretation when normal awareness returns.

Besides visionary information, shamans often seek animal or plant spirits to aid their task, often through possession. Before such a rite, purification of both the holy person and the querent is considered essential. Then, through ritual, the nature spirit awakens in the shaman to share the requested information, much of which comes in symbolic or allegorical verse. One example is the *balian* in Indonesia who is a medium-priest. The *balian* consults the spirits to learn how to protect or aid people and property in his or her community.

Related Systems: Dance and Movement, Gyromancy, Meditation, Oracles

• SIDEROMANCY
(see Straw, Hay)

• SIGNS

By definition, a sign is anything that provides a hint or indication of something else. Consequently, signs can come from numerous sources, including overhead conversations, a slip of the tongue, peripheral vision, songs, dreams, the media, the environment, pets, and coincidences. Exactly what each person or cultural group accepts as a significant positive or negative sign and exactly how that sign is interpreted varies tremendously.

Experts in sign watching and interpretation often recommend that a person keep a journal of signs and omens, similar to a dream journal. Mark down when the sign occurred, the conditions under which it occurred (place, weather, etc.), your immediate impressions, and any perceived interpretive value. In time, this diary will become a strong indicator of what occurrences in life should be thoughtfully pondered.

Numerous signs are provided by topic throughout this book, but here is a sample listing:

- An ant near your door presages new social activity.

- Finding a bed bug portends nuisances.

- Having a bee land on you, but not sting, is a good omen for leaders, and also indicates forthcoming news.

- Finding a bird's egg intact is very favorable, as it means trouble averted and new beginnings. If it is broken, however, beware of mishaps.

- Seeing a balloon above you either indicates a time when you will be subject to the winds of change or new liberality.

- Hearing a canary sing is a sign of coming joys.

- A feather falling in front of you is a message from the Universe to be more aware of the signs in your life.

- A grasshopper appearing in your home advises you to enjoy living in the moment, but never cease preparing for the future.

- Finding a key is a sign that a solution is forthcoming.

- A light going on by itself indicates new ideas and improved awareness will soon be yours.

- Finding a stray piece of metal is a sign to gather your strength and courage for a coming storm.

- In Tibet, a dry tree suddenly sprouting leaves or branches portends arguments in the region, often over land matters.

- Also in Tibet, when traditionally hot and cold weather patterns are reversed, it indicates a year filled with harmful events.

Related Systems: Animal Omens and Signs, Birds, Findings, Insects, Random Divination

Adaptation: While driving, think of a question, then watch to see what advertisements or street signs you pass. For example, a yellow light might be a sign to slow down and be cautious. A yield sign says to pass up this particular opportunity; something's not quite safe here. A sign for "Hope Avenue" might portend improved spirits.

• SKY SCRYING (TSHO)

Tsho is a Tibetan form of meditative divination similar to *Me-lon*, as discussed in Crystal Scrying. This form of divination begins by staring thoughtfully at a clear sky. This is the method Tibetans used to find the present incarnation of the Dalai Lama.

Related Systems: Forms of Aromancy, Scrying

• SMOKE (LIBANOMANCY, CAPNOMANCY, THURIFUMIA)

Observations based on smoke from a fire is called libanomancy, from an object placed in a ritual fire is called capnomancy, and from incense, thurifumia. Two Babylonian clay texts mention the technique of throwing cedar shavings, poppy seeds, sandalwood pieces, or incense on a fire, and the subsequent observation of the shape and direction of the smoke. This was regularly practiced as a family tradition, the secrets of which were passed on as an oral tradition. To begin, the diviner placed a censer on his or her lap, then added the wood pieces. While a complete text of divinatory meanings could not be found, generally, shapes moving to the right were favorable while those going left were not. If the smoke moved east and dispersed near the diviner, this indicated that the querent would prevail over obstacles.

In Greece, a slightly different version of capnomancy entailed observing the smoke from food offerings (see *Food*). In Malaysia, fires were observed to determine the relative security of a location. If the smoke rose up without wafting, it indicated the region was safe from tigers. Additionally, dark or dense smoke was an evil omen, indicating overwhelming odds against you.

Armenians use smoke for divination every year during the festival honoring *Mihr*, a fire god. If the smoke from the ritual fire blows to the east, this presages a good harvest; if the smoke blows westward, drought and famine.

Related Systems: Burning, Candles, Fire, Scrying, Torch

Adaptations: Pass a three-by-five card through candle smoke three times quickly, and read the carbon deposits as if they were ink blots. Or simply watch the smoke after the candle is extinguished. Rising straight up is good sign, while lingering near the wick is negative.

The smoke from incense cones and sticks is also excellent for scrying. Choose the aroma so it corresponds with your question.

• SNEEZING

At one time a sneeze was thought capable of expelling the spirit from a person's body, which is why, to this day, we say, "God bless you." This association may be the reason that sneeze observation became a divination system. The Chinese felt it was a very bad omen to sneeze on New Year's (see *Holiday Omens and Signs*). According to historical records the Greeks trusted in sneezing omens so much that about 2,000 years ago a single sneeze stopped an entire battle.

Plutarch, a Greek scholar, felt that one could answer questions by observing head movements when a sneeze occurred. Sneezing toward the right was a positive indicator. Later in history, sneezing while dressing meant that one should go back to bed for the day! In Germany, if you sneeze while putting on your shoes, it is an omen of bad luck for that day. Additionally, the day of the week on which a sneeze came meant specific things, as follows:

Monday: Health may be in danger.

Tuesday: You will receive a kiss and improved finances.

Wednesday: A sign of luck or a letter.

Thursday: An omen of loss followed by improvements.

Friday: Sorrow.

Saturday: You will have no luck in love the following week.

Sunday: Misfortune.

At dinner: You will be healthy.

2 times: A wish will be fulfilled.

3 times: A gift is coming.

5 times: You will receive something silver.

6 times: You will receive something gold.

•SORTILEGE

Sortilege is the practice of interpreting the symbolic elements from any assemblage of items. This comes from the Latin *sous*, meaning a lot, and the term may be applied to all divinatory systems that use a specific collection of tools as a focal point.

•SOUL SCRYING (PSYCHOMANCY)

Indirectly related to past life readings, soul scrying is an intuitive divinatory talent requiring no tools. A person with this ability simply "knows" the future of individuals by attuning themselves to that person's auric energy.

Related System: Clear Sight

•SPEAKING

Words have tremendous power, which is why a curse was taken so seriously by our ancestors. In terms of divination, here are some samples of how words are thought to affect our future:

- If your speech rhymes without intending it to do so, you will receive a gift within a month.

- Among some Native American tribes biting one's tongue while speaking means that a gift of sweets or pleasant news is on its way.

- When two people say the same thing at the same time, they will both soon fulfill a wish.

• SPILLING

Spilling is another form of random or spontaneous divination, suggesting that instead of "crying over spilt milk," one should scry over it! If you spill ink, it portends petty annoyances; salt, bad luck. Spilling wine during a toast foretells health and happiness. In Greece, people believed that any wine spilling was a lucky omen.

Related Systems: Breakage, Falling, Random Divination, Smoke

• SPODOMANCY

(see Ashes)

• SPONTANEOUS DIVINATION

Spontaneous divination arises out of the images or omens in unforeseen events interpreted on the spur of the moment. Historically, this type of divination has occurred all over the world and in so many situations that it is nearly impossible to record or track thoroughly. For example, if a cup of wine spills during a conversation in which someone is trying to track down a thief, and the spill seems to indicate a specific direction, this may be interpreted as a sign to seek out the thief in that direction.

Related Systems: Breakage, Findings, Omens, Random Divination, Signs

Adaptations: If you have a question weighing heavily on your heart and you spill milk, salt, or anything else that can make a pattern, scry the pattern before cleaning it up. Alternatively, take a look at broken objects before sweeping. Do the pieces point inward or outward? Inward pieces indicate the need for reflection, while outward ones counsel that you act. Another example is examining the components of a burned dish of food. For example, if you burn a strawberry pie, this might reveal anger or too much passion in a relationship (see *Food*).

• STAFFS

In Rome, augurs carried a staff called a *lituus* as a sign of their office. The *lituus* had to be totally smooth (e.g., no knots or blemishes) so that mystical energy could flow through it freely. This staff was also important to the divinatory rite, possibly a focal point. For example, some accounts talk of bird augurs inscribing circles in the sky with their staff, marking the region they would watch for omens.

Related Systems: Rods, Wands

• STARS

*"What stars should best the heralds be of seasons to
Mankind?"*

—Aratus; Third Century B.C. Greece

The most popularized form of star divination is astrology, covered under its own heading. However, astrology was not the only way that these "night mariners" were used for prognostication. For example, in Egypt the rising of Sirius predicted the Nile's flood cycle. In almost all cultures a "falling star" was considered the harbinger of disaster (see *Comet*).

In India, star lore was based on the Vedic hymns, the most important stars being those that the moon seemed to move across in its path. An Indian expert in star divination is called *jyotisa*, whose work centered on matters effecting the whole community. Later in history the *jyotisa's* practice became the Indian version of astrology with similar houses and meanings.

Other star-related methods include:

• Over seven nights go out and look at a set of seven stars. On the last night of observation you will receive a prophetic dream. Alternatively, stare at the brightest star in the sky and wink three times while thinking of your question. The answer will come that night in your dreams.

• If a falling star's tail looked like a flute, the Roman scholar Pliny felt this predicted a period of artistic success for humankind.

• In both China and Rome, people believed that falling stars appeared just before hurricanes.

• In England, a woman who spied a falling star was ensured of fertility or marriage.

• Go outside and voice a binary question to the sky. If you see a shooting star within fifteen minutes, your answer is "yes." If clouds cover the sky or no star appears, your answer is "no."

• If you make a wish on the first star appearing, and dream of that wish that same night, it is a sign that your wish will be fulfilled (see *Dreams*).

Related Systems: Astrology, Celestial Omens, Meteorites, Moon, Sun

•STEAM

Place a bowl of steaming water before a mirror. Gaze at the mirror while focusing on your question. As the water condenses on the mirror's surface, watch for images to emerge that answer your question in symbolic or literal terms. Very often this results in the formation of letters or pictures (see *Mirrors*).

Related System: Smoke

•STOLISOMANCY

(see Dressing)

•STONES (PESSOMANCY)

Among the Celts, stones were believed to have indwelling spirits and were quite popular for divinatory purposes. One approach involved tossing a marked stone onto a fire and leaving it until the next day. If the stone was found again, luck was forthcoming. These rocks were sometimes carried as talismans of good fortune.

The *Book of Fferyllt*, an ancient Welsh text, recounts another type of divination from what are called "sky stones." To begin you need a gold or yellow-colored stone (pyrite, tiger's eye, citrine), a silver or white-colored stone (hematite, soapstone, or marble), and a black-colored stone (obsidian, onyx). If you can't find these, paint stones instead, or substitute marbles. The yellow/gold stones represent dawn, the silver ones, twilight, the black ones, midnight. While thinking of a question, cast the stones onto a flat surface. The stone that lands closest to the black one indicates your response. Gold means "yes," silver means "no."

To diversify this system a little, consider the interpretive value for the times of day each stone represents (or alternatively, the colors). To try this, add a fourth stone of your choosing to represent self. Cast the stones and look to see which one lands nearest you. "Dawn," the gold stone, indicates a reason for hope and is an excellent foreshadowing for any new project. "Twilight" reveals that the time for action may soon pass, so a decision should be made quickly. "Midnight" suggests waiting or an unknown. This may also portend a transition phase.

If two stones are very nearly the same distance from self, this can be a sign of two equally inviting choices, or it may simply define your answer more specifically. For example, having silver and gold both equidistant from self symbolizes needing to act soon on an opportunity offered before the door closes. Black combined with gold says that hope is just around the corner, so be patient.

A second form of pessomancy uses thirteen black or brown stones and thirteen white or light-colored stones of approximately the same size. Put them in a cloth bag and shake the bag three times asking your question each time. Grab one handful of stones without looking and put them on a table. If you have more light-colored stones, the omen is positive. More dark-colored stones are negative. An even number of each indicates that there is either no answer presently or that the odds could go either way for you.

Alternatively, choose one set of thirteen stones and mark each with a word or emblem. Toss the stones in a one-foot circle. Those that land outside the perimeter or with the blank side up are not read. Scott Cunningham's *Pocket Guide to Fortunetelling* (The Crossing Press) suggests the following words or emblems and interpretative values:

Sun: Hope, activity, energy, enlightenment on an issue

Moon: Fantasy, dreams, secret matters, change

Mercury: Thinking before you act or speak

Venus: Matters of love, compassion, and other intense emotions

Mars: Anger or danger

Jupiter: Matters pertaining to finances or your job

Saturn: Difficulty with one's health (mental, spiritual, or physical)

Home: Family structure or conditions of living environment

Love: Relationships

Money: Employment, bills, and financial security

News: Messages and communication

Travel: Journeys or other movement

Health: Wellness

The stones that land near each other combine for enhanced meaning. For example, Saturn near Love might mean that the health of a relationship is at stake. Or Mercury near News might suggest careful thought before acting on a message that will soon come your way.

Gypsies used a third type of stone system very similar to the preceding one. Twelve different stones were cast or drawn, each of which had a different meaning depending on where it landed. The basic stones and their correspondences included:

Agate: Good news or a pleasant surprise

Amethyst: The loss of something you value

Bloodstone: Unpleasant news or events

Quartz: Business advancement

Dark green stone (any): A secret admirer

Dark blue stone (any): Karmic retribution, reaping what you sow

Sardonyx: A wedding, union, or partnership

Amber or Topaz: Caution

Turquoise: A journey

Plain stone: The querent or individual in question, either placed at the center of the casting circle or tossed with the rest

Finally, the *Sacred Stone Oracle* is a relatively new system based on many earlier ideas and bits of lore regarding stones. This system has fifteen tumbled stones of approximately the same size and a casting cloth. The cloth depicts the four directions and seasons and a center point for the self and present circumstances. When a querent casts the *Sacred Stone Oracle*, where each stone lands, its relationship to other stones, and its proximity to the center are all considered in the reading. This system is available through Blue Pearl (1-800-822-4810).

Related Systems: Castings, Lots, Pebbles

Adaptation: The Incans used dried corn kernel of different colors like colored stones. For our purposes, try colored popcorn kernels or candies. More than two colors can expand your divinatory interpretations.

• STORM SIGNS AND OMENS

(see Weather Omens)

• STRAW, HAY (SIDEROMANCY)

Divination with hay or straw is related to other forms of botanomancy. Here are some examples:

- Pinch one end of a strand of straw while concentrating on your question. Pinch again, right next to it saying "yes," then again farther along saying "no." Repeat this until you reach the end. The last spoken word is your answer.

- Place a few strands of straw on a hot, flat skillet. While focusing on your question, watch the movements for revealing pictures or symbols. These may also appear in the smoke (see *Smoke*).

- During the Victorian Era, having a cart filled with hay or straw cross your path was an excellent omen of forthcoming abundance. This association likely occurred because of the importance of harvest crops in agrarian communities (see *Omens* and *Signs*).

Related Systems: Bay, Burning, Fire, Flowers, Herbs, Plants—Plantain, most binary systems

Adaptations: The base medium for the first two techniques can be almost anything natural. Examples include a length of string or thread, a fallen twig, and a broom handle (use your whole hand for this last one).

•SUN

As the most visible object in the sky, the sun was once regarded as a god or goddess in its own right. Chaldeans, Greeks, Egyptians, Persians, and numerous other cultures worshipped the sun for its life-giving energies. Over time this veneration included observing the sun for portents, most of which had to do with weather (see *Weather Omens*). Some others are given below:

- If the sun shines on St. Paul's Day (January 25), it foretells a peaceful year (see *Holiday Omens and Signs*).

- The sun shining on any special occasion, like a wedding, is a very fortunate sign for the future of those involved. It indicates divine favor.

- In the sixth century B.C., two Greek armies stopped fighting because of a solar eclipse. They took this as a sign of divine displeasure over their actions.

- If you have a question on your mind and the sun suddenly breaks through the clouds, this portends encouragement coming from people around you in regard to that question (British).

- The sun is said to dance for joy on Easter morning (see *Holiday Omens and Signs*). If you see this phenomena, it foretells a year filled with good health and luck.

- In Incan tradition, if the sun shone on September 20, considered the sun's birthday, it was a very positive omen for the entire year.

Related Systems: Aromancy, Astrology, Celestial Omens, Comets, Moon, Stars

• SYCOMANCY

(see Fig Leaves, Leaves)

• SYMPATHETIC MAGIC

Diviners of the Middle Ages and earlier often used sympathetic magic to divine the identity of a bandit. One technique involved saying prayers while inscribing various letters on a piece of bread, then making all the suspects eat from it. The one who could not swallow was considered guilty. Another means was to draw an eye on the wall, and if tears began to well up in the right eye of a suspect, that one was considered guilty. Or if a nail was driven into this eye, it was believed that the guilty party will cry out as if it were actually piercing his or her body. This type of justice seems to be very old indeed.

Related Systems: Bread, Ordeal

• TABLE TIPPING

> *"All the world is much interested—not to say excited—with the newly developed force as manifested in table moving."*
>
> —*The Illustrated Magazine of Art, 1854*

Table tipping was a type of automatism and necromancy in which a table becomes like a *Ouija* board. The participants placed their fingertips on it while focusing on a question. The fingers were spread so that each person's pinkie touched the next participant's. A spirit was believed to move the table in specific ways in reply to questions. The movement's interpretive value was often predictated to the spirit by a person organizing the event. For example, they might ask a question, adding that movement to the left would indicate a negative response.

Related Systems: Automatism, Necromancy, *Ouija*

• TABLES, TABLETS

The Egyptian Magi used tablets inscribed with letters for fortune-telling. The querent picked letters by chance, each of which corresponded to a mystical number (see *Numerology*) and was interpreted accordingly. Similar in form and function, small books appeared at the turn of the nineteenth century that included "fateful tables," sometimes called Arabian squares, that anyone could easily use to "tell" the future.

Some tablets were extremely complex. One prepared by Cornelius Agrippa (see Bibliography) included lists of questions for the querent to focus on and different interpretations for each randomly chosen sign depending on the question. In his writings, Agrippa strongly recommended that questions should not be posed to the oracle more than twice a day. He also believed that certain dates were not auspicious for working with the oracle. The unlucky dates included: 1/2, 1/6, 1/10, 1/20, 1/22, 2/6, 2/17, 2/28, 3/24, 3/26, 4/10, 4/27, 4/28, 5/7, 5/8, 6/27, 7/17, 7/21, 8/20, 8/22, 9/5, 9/30, 10/6, 11/3, 11/29, 12/6, 12/10, and 12/15. No specific reason was provided for these dates, but one may conjecture that numerology may have been a factor.

The tables below are but a few examples of those that have appeared throughout history. To use them, simply close your eyes and place a pencil point down at random on the paper. Compare the letter or number closest to the pencil and read its corresponding interpretation. For more specific results, think of a question and mark three points on the chart, indicating the past (point 1), present (point 2), and future (point 3) of the question at hand.

General Future

25	6	8	22	2	11
15	13	17	3	24	
5	7	1	12	4	
14	18	9	23	20	
16		10	19	21	

1. For a man: a good marriage or better finances; children and a long life. For a woman: faithful relationships.

2. Loss of friendship or failure in legal battle; bad faith.

3. An unexpected turn for the better, often stemming from news received.

4. Financial setbacks.

5. Secret matters that may cause you trouble, especially if you're the one hiding something.

6. The failure of efforts.

7. A devoted marital partner or lover with financial security.

8. Success; fulfillment.

9. Sudden marriages or other types of partnerships.

10. A traveling friend bringing a wonderful gift for you.

11. Infidelity, mistrust, and falsehood.

12. Victory in your endeavors; successful outcome of plans.

13. Do not borrow any money right now.

14. An elderly man marrying and having a child, or becoming less available to you.

15. Friends showing that they care for and respect you deeply.

16. Travel on the horizon; possibly a new friendship.

17. A fall from grace; loss of status.

18. A new, and advantageous, friendship that may require some work to develop, but be worth it.

19. A potential misuse of someone's charitable nature.

20. Irresponsibility causing problems or setbacks in business or a project.

21. News, often regarding money matters.

22. Depend on yourself and be true to your heart.

23. No values given for interpretation; hidden or unknowable things.

24. No values given for interpretation; hidden or unknowable things.

25. Beware of negative aspects in your personal character; remain upright to avert trouble.

For Matters of Love

E	K	A	I
N	G	D	L
H	C	P	B
F	O	J	M

A) You have found a true love.

B) It is a time of waiting or setbacks.

C) Listen to your instincts.

D) Be sure of your line of reasoning.

E) Stop worrying; everything's fine.

F) Your own actions may cause a separation.

G) If you are not happy, stop blaming others. This comes from you.

H) Jealousy is a terrible characteristic; weed it out.

I) Your mate is very devoted.

J) Someone is thinking of you fondly.

K) There are a few rough spots, but the problems will pass.

L) Expect an altered course or changed outlook.

M) Your attention is in the wrong place, but on the right topic.

N) There is no reason for uncertainty; relax.

O) Words are powerful; beware of what you say.

P) Yes, but be sensible.

For Matters of Insight, Fertility, and Maturity

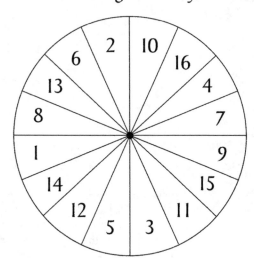

NOTE: This tablet may be spun on a pin while your eyes are closed to improve randomness.

1) Learn the virtue of patience.

2) You are your own obstacle right now.

3) Stop worrying about what others say and think; listen to your heart.

4) Learn to give and receive love freely.

5) Your heart has run away with your head.

6) Wishing and doing are two different things; build foundations for your dreams.

7) A light-skinned person has the answer you seek.

8) Wait; your timing is bad.

9) Things will not go as you might hope.

10) Bide your time and think this through.

11) Don't listen to gossip; find the truth.

12) Seek the aid of a friend.

13) Stand up for what you believe and contentment will follow.

14) Completion and fulfillment are here.

15) Your desire will manifest if you trust yourself.

16) A time alone to think is well worth taking.

For Matters of Logic, Learning, and Leadership

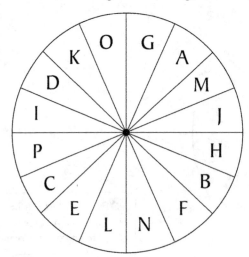

NOTE: This tablet may be spun on a pin while your eyes are closed to improve randomness.

A) Think this move through carefully.

B) Stop doubting yourself; trust in your ability to adapt.

C) Consult a nearby friend for good advise.

D) Speak up before you burst!

E) Something's hidden here; look further.

F) Your misgivings are unfounded.

G) Be careful who you trust with this concept.

H) What you "think" is right isn't.

I) An improvement is just around the corner.

J) Chances are slim.

K) Be discreet and discerning; balance logic with insight.

L) Opportunity's door is slightly ajar; act quickly.

M) You can find a solution, but it won't be easy.

N) Let your conscience guide you and all will be well.

O) In this case, it's your own fault.

P) Everything will work out; stop worrying so much.

• TAMBOURINES (TYMPANA)

In the Victorian Era, mediums sometimes used sound-sensitive items like a tambourine to convey the messages from the spirit realm. The number of times the instrument sounded indicated positive or negative responses from the spirit contacted.

Related Systems: Automatism, Drums, Necromancy, Oracles

• TAROT CARDS (CARTOGRAPHY)

The Tarot can be traced back to Italy in the Middle Ages, although its true origins remain unknown. It may have come from Egypt by way of Gypsies, but this is uncertain. Either way, cartomancy was in use in Europe during the fourteenth century. This type of divination combines casting with symbols.

THE FOOL. | THE MAGICIAN.

THE HIGH PRIESTESS | THE EMPRESS.

The first known Tarot decks were comprised of twenty-two cloth cards, hand paint-ed and slightly larger than modern decks. Later this deck was combined with a fifty-six-card deck that originated in China to make the seventy-eight-card deck of modern usage. Around A.D. 1540, a book appeared in Italy describing cartomancy, dealing specifically with the Suit of Coins in the Tarot.

Today there are literally hundreds of thematic Tarot decks from which to choose. The interpretive value of each card in a deck will vary slightly depending on its theme and makers, as will the layouts offered. However, the fundamental corre-spondences based on the Rider Waite system are as follows:

Major Arcana

There are twenty-two cards of the Major Arcana, which represent major life principles.

The Fool: A beginning; potentials. Reversed: Beware of foolish behavior or hasty actions.

The Magician: Understanding; progress that leads to mastery. Reversed: Don't wait too long or have unreasonable expectations.

The High Priestess: Intuition, wisdom, and psychism. Reversed: Don't let your heart rule your head; use logic.

The Empress: Fertility, stability, and growth. Reversed: Beware of insecurity or setbacks.

The Emperor: Success, personal authority, and power. Reversed: Don't surrender to timidity.

The High Priest: Spiritual authority; a wise, creative, and learned person. Reversed: Watch for deception or delusion.

The Lovers: Good relationships. Reversed: Beware of making the wrong choice.

The Chariot: Movement and progress. Reversed: Don't be so focused on the goal that you run over people.

Justice: Balance and sound thinking. Reversed: Watch for unfair judgments.

Hermit: Reflection and evaluation. Reversed: Listen to good advice; don't be inflexible.

Wheel of Fortune: Fate; changes that must come. Reversed: Prepare for bad luck; a difficult situation gets worse.

Strength: Courage, morality, and tenacity to overcome. Reversed: Act positively to overcome obstacles.

Hanged Man: Risk and sacrifice leading to better things. Reversed: Look further, the truth is hidden; be flexible.

Death: Transformation; failures that bring understanding. Reversed: Let go of old pattern, or trouble will make for an unhappy ending.

Temperance: Balance between the mundane and spiritual. Reversed: Beware of disharmony; it causes setbacks.

Devil: Selfishness; untamed impulses. Reversed: Don't allow shortcomings to overwhelm positive attributes.

Tower: The shattering of hopes and dreams; painful lessons. Reversed: Realize that this is a situation caused by your own doing.

Star: New opportunities, possibly in a whole new direction. Reversed: See the forest for the trees.

Moon: Intuition; psychic awareness; danger from indulging your fantasies. Reversed: Don't be stagnated because of fear.

Sun: Enlightenment, wholeness, triumph. Reversed: Superficial success.

Judgment: Reprisal; the weighing of ones actions. Reversed: Beware of regrets and retribution.

World: Fulfillment; reaching higher goals. Reversed: Learn from total failure or the inability to progress any further.

Minor Arcana

The fifty-six cards of the suits make up the Minor Arcana, which relate to everyday circumstances of life.

Suit of Cups

Cups relate to one's emotions, matters of inventiveness, love, fertility, and relationships. The suit's element is water.

Ace: Prosperity and abundance; possibly a baby

Two: A blossoming friendship; good relationships

Three: The joy of true love

Four: Happiness that may put you off balance

Five: Loss followed by anger or resentment

Six: Reveling in good memories from days gone by

Seven: Well-considered goals

Eight: Dissatisfaction or frustration

Nine: Harmony, wholeness, peace with self

Ten: Tranquillity that comes through achievement

Page: A thoughtful young person

Knight: An upbeat lover or friend

Queen: A person (often female) of creativity, insight, and love

King: A person (often male) of attainment and worldly wisdom

Suit of Coins/Pentacles

Pentacles relate to worldly goods, money, business, security. The suit's element is earth.

Ace: Prosperity; affluence

Two: Financial difficulties

Three: Success at work or with a business

Four: Victory; attainment of a difficult goal

Five: Poverty; a possible fall

Six: Help on its way and new foundations

Seven: Improvements requiring cautious movement

Eight: Rewards from hard work

Nine: Unexpected riches

Ten: An inheritance

Page: A young person of advanced wisdom and caution

Knight: A honorable young person

Queen: A generous person (often female) with wealth

King: A pragmatic person (often male) with position

Suit of Swords

Swords represent opposing energies, finding order, energy, progress, leadership. The suit's element is fire.

Ace: Reaching a goal successfully

Two: An advantage in the present adversity

Three: A path finally clearing for the better

Four: Calm after a storm

Five: Struggle that could go either way

Six: Overcoming your difficulties; a good omen for travel

Seven: Moving cautiously, carrying courage in your pocket

Eight: A difficult time requiring patience

Nine: Failure that only *seems* disastrous

Ten: Dismal prospects, the undermining of all achievements

Page: An astute, shrewd young person

Knight: A warrior spirit in a young body

Queen: A single person (often female) who is strong and assertive

King: A lone person (often male) who is ruthlessly authoritarian

Suit of Wands/Rods

Wands signify mental activity, ideas, knowledge, will, and aspirations. The suit's element is air.

Ace: A new beginning from an inspired thought

Two: An improvement in your fate that comes by your own hand

Three: Bold actions bringing reward and gain

Four: Social favor; success

Five: Meeting a barrier with tenaciousness

Six: Good news

Seven: Difficulties mingled with interesting possibilities

Eight: Slow but steady progress

Nine: Hindrance and adversity, but only temporary

Ten: Running into a proverbial brick wall

Page: An energetic coworker or young person

Knight: A lively young person, met during travel

Queen: A person (often female) of pragmatic outlooks

King: A person (often male) of determination

Sample Tarot Layout

This layout is called the Celtic Cross, and it is one of the most popular layouts used in Tarot practices. "S" equates to the self or the situation. Card one talks of the general circumstances around the question or the querent. Card two represents obstacles or aids. Card three shows the querent's goals, card four, his or her subconscious fears, card five, the immediate past, and card six, the immediate future. Card seven portends the querent's conduct. Card eight signifies other important people in the situation, and card nine, hopes and fears. Finally, card ten is the outcome card.

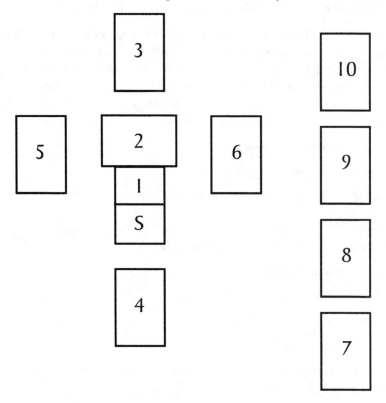

Adaptations: Tarot readings are now available through computer programs and on-line services.

• TEA KETTLES

As the water in the kettle warms, meditate on your question. When the kettle whistles, a broken whistle is a negative response, while a slow steady whistle is positive.

• TEA LEAF READING (TASSEOGRAPHY)

The predecessor of divination by coffee grounds, tasseography is most easily traceable to Gypsy traditions. It reached its height of popularity during the Victorian Era. This particular system may have some ancient roots in people's belief that specific beverages had indwelling spirits. Effectively, the reader consults the spirits of the beverage's source plant for symbolic answers. Exactly what types of tea are chosen for tea leaf reading vary from reader to reader, but most prefer a large-leafed mix for clarity. Sometimes the type of tea relates directly to the question at hand or is a personal blend whose scent improves awareness and insight.

At the start of a tea leaf reading, the querent holds the cup in his or her left hand. Then, while thinking of a question, the querent swirls the tea in the cup clockwise three times. The cup is placed upside down on a saucer, allowed to drain for a minute or two, then righted. The shapes suggested by the leaves and liquid remaining in the cup create the basis for interpretive values, some examples of which follow. Please note, however, that interpretations vary from resource to resource.

Acorn: Success or victory is yours.

Anchor: You will soon be putting down roots.

Arrow: A disagreeable letter or money is soon to arrive.

Bat: Beware of false friends.

Bear: You are in danger from ignorance of a situation.

Bell: An announcement is forthcoming.

Bird: Birds bring messages, often in the form of letters.

Butterfly: Don't be trapped by vanity.

Candle: Good deeds are in the offing.

Cat: Beware of disloyalty or fickleness. Alternatively, expect a whole new beginning (based on the superstition of cats having nine lives).

Clock: There is a potential for sickness, or the need for timely action.

Clouds: After momentary darkness comes a breakthrough.

Clumps: Beware of barriers or delays.

Cup: A sacrifice on your part will bring advancement.

Dice: Beware of a gambling loss.

Dog: A faithful companion has good advice.

Door: Opportunity is about to knock; be prepared.

Ear: Scandal is afoot.

Eye: Look at this situation very carefully.

Fire: Watch out for hasty actions.

Fork: You face a dilemma.

Glass: Fragile situations require you move carefully.

Hammer: Stress and anxiety are building up.

Hat: New endeavors are beginning.

Horse: There is a new love, or the rekindling of a relationship. Be forewarned, however, that if a horse is startled, it can easily run off carrying your heart with it! Alternatively, the horse portends news and movement.

Ivy: A loyal friendship is blossoming.

Kite: You have high ambitions.

Letters: Letters indicate initials of important names having to do with the question. Certain letters like a "W" may be interpreted in reverse (as an M). Letters like "S" are also very close to numbers in shape. It is up to the querent to decide which symbol has meaning for them.

Lock: There is an obstacle to progress.

Mountain: Ambition will be met with challenges.

Mouse: Prepare for financial difficulties. The length of the mouse's tail indicates how drastic these problems will be or the length of time over which they will endure.

Nail: Malice is aimed in your direction.

Path: A path or trail of leaves speaks of a forthcoming trip. If the path is broken, there may be trouble along the way.

People: New partnerships are indicated.

Pillar: Support or strength is needed.

Question mark: You are faced with the unknown or uncertainty; fate's hand is at work.

Ring: Expect good will and friendship.

Scales: A judgment of some type is imminent, often legal.

Shoes: A messenger's approaching.

Snake: A snake may represent evil or malice. Alternatively, it indicates sexual energy and encounters, health-related matters (because of Hermes' staff), or change (due to the snake shedding its skin as it grows).

Stems (floating in the cup): Strangers will be arriving.

Tears: Several drops of liquid (or "tears") around the cup portend sadness within a very short time.

Tent: Take cover and prepare for a storm.

Tree: A wish will be fulfilled.

Umbrella: Protection from trouble will be offered to you.

Volcano: Beware of unbridled passion.

Web: It is an entangling situation; watch your step.

Wheel: Patient, paced progress is called for.

•TEETH

(see Facial Features)

•TEPHRAMANCY

(see Ashes, Wind)

•THRESHOLDS

If you stumble over the threshold going out of your house, this portends the need for forbearance in business endeavors. For travelers, this bad luck omen indicates that it might be best to hold off on your planned departure.

If you stand on your threshold as the clock strikes twelve on All Hallow's Eve, you may hear the names of people destined to die in the next year. Similarly, if you sit on the threshold of England's St. Mark's Church on St. Mark's night (April 24 and 25), between the hours of 11 P.M. and 1 A.M., you may see doppelgangers of those fated to die within the next year (see *Holiday Omens and Signs, Death Omens*).

•THUNDER

The Egyptians, Greeks, and Romans all believed that thunder represented divine rumblings, so it is no wonder that it was used in divination systems. For the Greeks, thunder was the creation of Minerva, the Goddess of wisdom. Zeus could turn the tide of battle by throwing thunderbolts at the enemies of his people. In this tradition, if thunder came from your left, it was a bad omen, and even more so if you happened to be a member of an opposing army!

No matter what the setting, thunder was rarely a positive sign. In the Bodleian Library of Manuscripts at Oxford University, there is a fourteenth century chart that classifies the effects of thunder based on the month in which it occurs. It is an omen of death in most months. The exceptions are thunder that comes in January, which indicates wind and abundant fruit, and that which comes in December, which indicates a good harvest to come.

According to old English tradition, thunder on Sunday foretold the death of an important person. On Tuesday, it was a sign of plentiful grain, on Thursday, of bountiful corn in the fall. On Saturday, thunder was an ill omen of sickness or blight.

•TILES

In Ancient Rome, the Praeneste temple was dedicated to the Goddess Fortuna who, as her name suggests, presided over matters of luck and fate. There was a special set of tiles at the temple with predictive statements on them. A child was enlisted to choose a tile in answer to a question, because only a child could ensure a "pure" answer.

Related System: Bamboo Sticks

•TIN

A late 1800s collection of Charles Godfrey Leland's writings included a unique divinatory application for tin. You place three rose seeds, three nettle leaves, two rue leaves, and three cumin seeds on a tin plate with a small piece of lead. At midnight, in the light of two yellow candles, you melt the tin plate with all its contents over the fire. You pour this entire mixture into water and scry the cooled shape for an interpretation. The cooled shape may also be carried afterward as a talisman.

Related System: Lead

• TIROMANCY

(see Cheese)

• TOPS

Siamese Brahmans used spinning tops to predict the future. This system employed three tops representing Vishnu, Brahma, and Siva, each of which was made from nine metals. The nine metals represented the nine planets known to rule humankind's destiny. Each top was wound with a silken cord, then spun. Its movements were then observed for prognostications.

Related Systems: Chain, Gyromancy, Rings

Adaptation: A dreidel could be substituted here, using the symbolic correspondences of Hebrew letters as the foundation for interpretive value. Spin this within a circle of letters or symbols for improved insight.

• TORCHES (LAMPADOMANCY)

Lampadomancy is strongly related to other forms of pyromancy, except that in this case the nature of the torch's flame becomes a focus, interpreted as follows:

One point: Good omen

Two points: Negative omen; division

Three points: Very good future

Going out: Disaster on the horizon

Related Systems: Burning, Candle, Fire, Incense, Smoke

• TRANSATAUMANCY

(see Random Divination)

• TREES AND BUSHES

The groves were the gods' first temples. From humankind's earliest histories, people have always venerated trees for their strength and other positive symbolisms. By far, the most tree-loving people were the Celts, who went so far as to fashion a calendar after various trees. This calendar became the foundation for at least three divination systems of which I am aware: the Celtic Tree Oracle, the Ogham, and the one given here.

For this technique you will need to travel to a wooded spot with a variety of trees. One possibility for city dwellers may be a greenhouse or arborium. Walk around for a little while, allowing the tensions and worries of the day to leave you. Focus only on your question. Close your eyes and visualize your question in symbolic or literal form while carefully turning your body clockwise. Listen to your instincts. When they tell you to stop, open your eyes and look to see what type of tree is before you. Relate it to the correspondences given below.

For broader interpretive value, also look to see what condition the tree is in. If it is barren or sickly, this is a contrary sign and the interpretation should vary accordingly. For example, a bug-infested oak could reveal that the querent has ignored custom or taken an exorbitant risk that could prove quite disastrous.

If you cannot find a suitable location for this exercise, gather a good quality leaf from each of these trees, wax or laminate them, and then randomly draw one in answer to your question. Common tree associations are:

Birch: Potential that comes from a strict regimen; reliable associates. In love, a time of solitude.

Rowan: Secrets revealed, possibly through a vision or oracle. The need to protect one's freedom and maintain control. In love, a slowly developing, unromantic relationship.

Ash: Triumph over overwhelming circumstances through pragmatism. Compassion and charity aiding recovery. In love, an impractical relationship that may cause confusion.

Alder: Enduring a trying time courageously; impatience or fear leading to strife. In relationships, the need for more love or affection.

Willow: A decrease in pain as wisdom, intuition, and tenacity grow. Your emotions overcoming your reason. In love, a close relationship.

Hawthorn: An unfortunate turn, often a result of anger. Change with new ideas, interests, or occupations; a positive leadership role. In love, an unsteady relationship.

Oak: The honoring of history and tradition. Slow, consistent growth. An enterprising idea with some risks that will bring improved finances. In love, a good relationship, but also one with blind spots.

Holly: Longevity of efforts or personal causes, with integrity and quiet support. Firm personal values and characteristics without dogmatism. In love, good partners and affectionate friends.

Hazel: Wisdom and discernment within; seeing the truth. The need to gather knowledge, then act. In love, an indulgent relationship.

Vine: Enthusiasm without thought. Staying cool in the face of difficult odds; showing mercy and fairness. In love, friction caused by possessiveness.

Ivy: A very "toxic" situation filled with manipulation or immorality. The need for loyalty, stamina, faith, and humor. In love, a very emotional relationship.

Reed: Successful leadership that comes from a firm purpose and wise use of power. In love, a passionate but difficult relationship, in which fights regularly erupt.

Elder: A mysterious, heated romance or love affair with a project. The need to use constructive approaches and discipline to gain respect. In love, a casual relationship that may uncover some type of scandal.

Here are a few other omens, signs, and portents of trees and bushes:

Bay Laurel: In Greece, bay withering and dying, especially on your property, was a terrible omen of troubles, including death.

Bush: Getting your clothes caught on a bush predicts financial increase.

Cherry: In the Orient, one wishing to know the number of years they would live shook a cherry tree. Each falling cherry symbolized one year.

Fir: If you spy a fir tree growing in an odd location, this indicates a time of trouble or obstacles in the near future.

Oak: Take the oak apple from an oak tree and cut it open. If you find a spider, this is an omen of pestilence. An ant indicates a good year for rain, and a small worm foretells plenty.

Mulberry: In western England, people believe that once the mulberry bears its leaves there will be no more frosts until fall (see *Weather Omens*).

Pine: When pine cones are wide open they indicate a day of fine weather (see *Weather Omens*).

Related Systems: Dendromancy, Flowers, Herbs, Ogham, Plants

• TUG-OF-WAR

In Inuit tribes, tug-of-war becomes a symbolic ritual every fall, often around the equinox. One side of the tug represents winter, and it is made up of only individuals born in the winter. The other side has those born in the summer. If the winter side wins, it portends plentiful food.

Moroccans play a similar game during their New Year's observance (early October). The men tug against the women, and the winners in this tug-of-war indicate which sex will have the upper hand all year!

Related Systems: Ritual, Sympathetic Magic

• TWITCHING

In the Maori tradition of New Zealand, body twitches are signs of things to come. The interpretation depends on where the twitch occurs. For example, a twitching nose that refuses to stop portends an untimely death or perhaps another type of ending.

In Guatemala, a Chorti diviner looks to twitching in his or her right calf as an affirmative response to a question. Many Guatemalans believe that a spirit dwells in that part of the body. Before consulting the spirit, the leg is ritually rubbed with a mixture of saliva and tobacco, possibly as an offering of sorts.

Related Systems: Itching, Sneezing

• TYMPANA

(see Drums, Tambourine)

• UROMANCY

Uromancy is divining the future based on the appearance of a person's urine. This practice originated during the early history of humankind when all bodily excretions were considered somehow magical, especially saliva. These days, in the "magic" of medicine, urine is tested regularly to determine a patient's prognosis.

• VICTORIAN FLOWER ORACLE

A cartomancy system based on the Victorian Language of Flowers, the flower oracle recommends making your own cards from plants, or from pictures of plants,

261

choosing from the seventy-one flowers, herbs, and trees detailed in the book *The Victorian Flower Oracle* (Llewellyn Publications, 1994). The layouts in this system portray natural cycles or images, including the winds, the elements, and a full flower spread. The interpretation of each card is based on the depicted flower and where it lands in the reading. An overview of the flowers' meanings follows. Note that if any card appears in a reading reversed, the meaning is likewise contrary.

Buttercup: Monetary improvement

Carnation: Admiration

Chrysanthemum: Reward of hard work

Clove: Success; the hand of fate

Cowslip: Pensiveness

Daisy: The inner child

Dandelion: Messages; communication

Foxglove: Ambition

Geranium: Remembrance

Hollyhock: Decision making

Honeysuckle: Fidelity, honesty, integrity

Hyacinth: Reliability

Iris: Promises; improvements

Jasmine: A mystery with a favorable outcome

Lavender: An answer or a resolution

Lemon blossom: Discretion and trust

Lilac: Innocent love

Lily: Purity; being true to self

Lotus: Virtue in word and deed

Marigold: Hardship, misfortune, sorrow

Nasturtium: Public service; community spirit

Orange Blossom: Sincerity and devotion

Orchid: Spiritual understanding and insight

Pansy: Consideration and courtesy

Peony: Wealth and honor

Primrose: Harmony; symmetry

Rose: Matters of the heart

Snapdragon: Presumption or arrogance

Tansy: Hostility; conflict

Tulip: Insight and wisdom

Violet: Tenacity and steadfastness, reaping rewards

Wisteria: A stranger who may become a friend

Related Systems: Bay, Botanomancy, Flowers, Herbs, Plants—Plantain, Roses, Trees

Alternatives: All of nature has a language for us to read, if we just look. Any pictures of plants, stones, animals, and the like, may be placed on sturdy cards for a similar system of your own devising. Some places that sell Tarot decks also sell blank cards as media for such projects.

•WANDS

Tacitus tells us in the tenth chapter of *Germania* about the various means of German augury. The first method is similar to Witan wands, discussed later under this heading. In it, slices of a branch of a fruit-bearing tree were marked with divinatory signs. After a prayer to Odin, the slices were randomly tossed onto a white cloth. Either the father of the family with the question, or, if a public inquiry, the priest of state, offered another prayer, then picked up three of the slices while looking up at the sky. The divinatory meaning was determined from the markings on the gathered slices.

It is very plausible that these markings were runes, or their forerunners. Runes were closely linked with Odin. They have been traced to the third century when they were used to write names, inscriptions, and even spells on wood, stone, and metal. These runes, being very specific in nature, would lend themselves perfectly to this type of casting.

Another version of wand divination is very simplistic, yielding a yes-or-no response. The bark is peeled off one side of each of two branches. The querent rolls these branches on the ground while voicing a question. If both peeled sides land upward, the answer is "yes." If both land downward, the omen is negative. One of each is an unknown or uncertain response.

A third method of wand divination comes from the Saxons. For this you will need seven wands: three nine-inch wands, four twelve-inch wands. Mark one of the twelve-inch wands in a special manner. This is the Witan wand, which acts as a signifier. Lay the Witan wand in front of you, extending left to right. Hold the other wands in your hands and think of your question. Take all the wands with your right hand and randomly grab one with your left, allowing the rest to fall to the ground. Interpret the results as follows:

More long wands than short: Yes

More short wands than long: No

Wands touching the Witan wand: A very definite answer either way.

Wands resting on other wands: No definite answer can be given; consider any indicators as very "iffy."

All wands point toward Witan wand: The querent plays a very important role in the outcome of this question.

No wands point toward Witan wand: A matter that is out of the querent's control.

Related Systems: Lots, Rods

Alternative: Try pick up-sticks, adding the colors of the sticks into your interpretive values.

•WATER (HYDROMANCY, ELAEOMANCY)

Numerous forms of water divination exist. Included among them is pegomancy, or divination by spring water, and hydatoscopy, divination by rain or spring water. Some rather famous people have trusted this method, including Biblical seer Joseph who used a silver goblet specifically for water scrying, and Nostradamus who looked into a water bowl for his predictions. Here are just a few specific approaches to water divination:

- *Nam-mkh* is a Tibetan system that uses the still waters of a lake as a source of visions. The diviner first makes an offering to the spirit of the lake, then prays or performs a mantra while waiting for a vision to come.

- In Arabia, people listened to the "murmuring" of water, believing that the jinni often lived in water, and would communicate messages this way.

- In New Zealand, people listen to the "mood" of neighboring rivers, lakes, and streams to determine the flow of the future (see *Geomancy*).

- In China and Greece, people looked upon their image in a quiet pool of water to discern the future. If the image remained clear, it was a sign of hope. Broken images foretold trouble.

- Pegomancy is a type of water divination that uses the sounds made by natural fountains for its interpretations.

- The ancient Greeks filled a vessel with water at night and placed a torch nearby. They voiced invocations, then a chaste boy or pregnant woman read any images that appeared on the water's surface (see *Torch*).

- The Irish consider great waves as harbingers of important events like the death of a king. Such waves are thought caused by the sea fairies or other spiritual powers trying to communicate.

Related Systems: Ink, Scrying, Wine

•WAX (CEROMANCY, CARROMANCY)

Ceromancy originated in ancient Rome and continued to be popular until the Renaissance, resurfacing again in the 1700s in Spain. It was also used widely in Mexico, Puerto Rico, and Haiti, where remnants of the art can still be found. Burn a red candle that remains untouched while you consider a question. Then, holding the candle about eight inches above a dish of water, continue to think about a question and let the wax drip into the water. The resulting shapes may be interpreted like ink, coffee grounds, or tea, using any of the symbol guides in Appendix B. Other forms of ceromancy include:

- In Tibet, *The-bon* instructs the diviner to consult a thumbnail painted red and dipped in wax to create a shiny surface. All lights are dimmed except for a butter lamp, which gives off enough light for scrying.

- In Irish tradition, candles are often used to determine matters of love. Light a candle and watch how the wax drips off it. If the wax falls to the left, your answer is "no." If it falls to the right, the answer is "yes." If it forms a winding path, the answer is uncertain, or in some instances people felt this indicated a death was on the horizon.

- Melt some wax in a brass pot and pour it into cold water or onto a flat surface. The patterns and shapes created may then be interpreted as symbolic omens of the future (see *Lead, Tin*).

Related Systems: Candles, Fire, Ink, Torches, Water

Adaptation: Save your candle ends and pieces from various magical workings. Melt these one at a time and let them drip onto a surface. When dry, scry the results.

•WEATHER OMENS

Weather divination can be separated into two distinct categories. The first is the observation of omens and signs to predict forthcoming weather conditions, and the second is the observation of distinctive weather conditions for omens and signs in themselves.

The Celtic culture provides numerous examples of weather prediction. For example, when January was predominantly sunny, they anticipated very bad weather in February and March. Winds arriving in March were a good harbinger for crops, and cold weather in April bode well for the harvest of hay. When August started out damp, it portended heat before the end of the month. Sun in October signified a damp winter, while storms in early November symbolized a long, difficult season. Finally, a green Christmas was the forerunner to a white Easter (see *Holiday Omens and Signs*).

Examples of Predicting the Weather To Come

- Mist at sunrise means it will be clear for two to three days.

- Fine clouds coming from the northwest along with higher clouds indicate a short span of pleasant weather.

- Lightning without thunder after a fair day means the weather will continue to be fair (see *Lightning, Thunder*).

- Mists on a flat field early in the morning are a sign of fair weather.

- A dark gray sky combined with a southerly wind brings frost and cold.

- Dark, heavy clouds at sunset means rain on the following day.

- Winds changing from west to south indicate wetness.

- If the North Star is seen flickering, it means rain is coming (see *Stars*).

- Sailors say, "A wet Friday means a wet Sunday."

- Spiders working webs during the rain predict clearing.

- If the oak tree buds before the ash, a wet summer is forecast.

- If it storms on the first Sunday of a month, it will do so all month (see *Days*).

- When snowflakes are small, the storm will last a long time.

- When walnut trees produce a lot of nuts, expect a long winter (see *Nuts, Trees*).

- A greenish horizon precedes warm wet weather.

- A red moon on the rise with clouds will be followed by rain within twelve hours. Red spots on the moon portend high winds. When the weather on the fourth and sixth day of the moon is the same, the rest of the month will follow accordingly. If the new moon is far to the north, there will be two weeks of cold. Two full moons in one month precede a flood (see *Moon*).

- Butterflies appearing early in the morning indicate sunshine, as does chickweed opening first thing after dawn and bees flying late at night.

- Biting flies, cows with their tails in the air, cackling hens, hissing geese, and busy ants portend rain (see *Animal Omens and Signs*).

- If it rains before 7 A.M., there will be sun by 11 A.M.

- Porpoises playing by a ship in good weather warn of a storm coming (see *Animal Omens and Signs*).

- Clouds in the west at sunrise that quickly disappear foretell a fine day.

- If the sky is tinged sea green during a rain storm, the rain will increase.

- Seeing lots of falling stars on a summer night portends thunder (see *Meteors, Stars*).

- In rural America, dry morning grass portends rain by nightfall.

- Marigolds staying shut after 7 P.M. mean that rain is coming (see *Flowers*).

- When the wind changes to the north or northeast, anticipate cold; a south to southwest change conversely indicates warmth.

Examples of Weather as a Prognosticator

- Short, sharp rain showers are called "sacred footsteps" in New Zealand. They suggest that important guests are coming.

- In Africa, a person who is hit by lightning is considered cursed by the gods for the rest of his or her life. In ancient Greece, however, it was a more positive omen. Where lightning struck often became a sacred site, as if god had pointed a fiery finger there (see *Lightning*).

- Ask a numerical question at the outset of a storm. The number of hours the storm lasts is the answer either specifically or symbolically (see *Numerology*).

Related Systems: Animal Omens and Signs, Lightning, Moon, Rainbow, Sun, Thunder

• WELLS

In Europe, wells were once thought to have indwelling spirits that could be convinced by offerings to grant various favors. This is how we come by the tradition of tossing coins into wells, and very likely why divination using wells developed. Some examples include:

- Toss a pebble into a well with your question. Count the number of bubbles that rise to the surface. Even number is "yes." Alternatively, throw in objects with different shapes and count the number of rings made by each. Each shape should be symbolic of a different element of your question to which a binary answer will be useful.

- At either dusk or dawn gaze into a well and look for a symbol. When the image comes, then disappears, toss a rock into the well. If you hear an echo of the splash, the divinatory image was true.

- Place the shirt of an ailing person on top of the water in a well. If the shirt floats, the patient will recover. Alternatively, take a cup of water from this well to the patient's room. If the water moves clockwise in the presence of the inflicted, their chances of recovery are good. These two traditions come from Europe, where sacred wells dot the countryside.

• WHEELS (CYCLOMANCY)

Cyclomancy is divination based on the random stopping point of a wheel. This form of fortune-telling became the basis of modern roulette wheels and other similar gambling wheels. In the Tarot, it is inspiration for the Wheel of Fortune card.

An ancient version of wheel divination came from Asia Minor. One of the fortune-telling tools consisted of a bronze table engraved with sacred images, a circular dish, and two rings that were spun like the roulette wheel. The symbols at which the rings stopped indicated the interpretation.

Related Systems: Gyromancy, Rings, Tops

• WICKS

After the Tibetan ritual of divining by butter lamps, the reader called a *mapo* also takes advantages of any signs left in the wick of the lamp. When the wick burns down into a shape resembling a lotus, the flower that represents enlightenment, it portends a gain. When the wick burns away, the future is clear for movement and advance. A wick that falls over into the candle means difficulties await you, and when the butter puts out the wick, it portends losses.

Related Systems: Burning, Butter Lamps, Candles, Fire, Torch, Wax

Adaptation: All of these interpretations may be applied to the wick of a wax candle.

•WIND (AUSTROMANCY, TEPHRAMANCY, CERAUNOSCOPY)

Wind was considered the breath of the gods among many ancient peoples. Hot winds were sometimes associated with malevolent forces like demons, but this occurred in regions where heat was a terrible enemy, like the desert. Among certain New Zealand tribes, people listen to the wind's "mood" to determine omens.

Divinatory methods using wind as a portent usually depend on the direction the wind blows and its intensity, north and west generally being positive responses. The wind has also been a birth omen. Among the Celts, for example, a child born during a north wind was destined to be prosperous, but only after much hardship (see *Birth Signs*). The east wind brought a life of comfort, love of the arts, and land, while the west brought one sustained by fundamental labors like fishing or sewing. Southerly winds brought difficulties and intense feelings to a child, whereas no wind whatsoever portended foolishness.

Wind behavior was regularly used to predict the weather, too. At Winter Solstice, if winds blew from the north, they portended that the remaining season would stay cold and damp. Eastern winds foretold of snow, southern winds, of a harvest of fruit, and western winds, of an excellent fishing season ahead. In China, this system varied slightly, the west wind indicating a good harvest of grain, the north wind, general bounty, the east wind, calamity, and the south wind, an increase in crop prices.

Related Systems: Aromancy, Clouds, Weather

•WINE (OINOMANCY, OENOMANCY)

The ancient Greeks used wine at least three ways for divination. The substance gained a positive reputation for divination due to its connection with the god Dionysus, who provided inspiration and foresight. One technique instructed a scryer to illuminate the surface of wine with a candle and gaze at the liquid. A second approach involved drinking a glass of wine to inspire prophetic dreams.

The third technique is more interesting. It was part of an ancient game called *Kottabos*, in which a glass of wine was tossed back and forth between players. If the cup dropped, the spilled wine was scried like an ink blot for signs.

Related System: Food

•WOOD (XYLOMANCY)

Zylomancy has many different approaches. One seer might read the signs created by wood-eating animals, while another may observe woodpecker's markings in the forest, and another still may pick up a random piece of wood and "read" its shape for interpretive values. The Scandinavians specifically divine information from the manner in which sticks lay across their path in the forest, and the Baltic Slavs use wood chips with dark and light sides in a type of lot system.

Related Systems: Earth, Trees

•WREATHS AND GARLANDS

In Germany, young girls make pine and straw wreaths on September 21 as part of St. Matthew's day festivals. These are mixed together in a pile and left until dark. Then each person randomly chooses a wreath. A pine wreath portends joy and prosperity, while the straw one predicts sickness or difficulties for the rest of the year. Pine likely has a positive association in this tradition due to its evergreen nature (see *Trees*).

Morovian girls make garlands during Midsummer festivals, fashioning them from nine different flowers. This garland is tossed into the window of the house, then placed beneath a pillow to bring prophetic dreams, especially about love.

Related Systems: Botanomancy, Flowers, Plants, Trees

Adaptation: Make a special wreath, using a form from a florist's shop. Loosely attach symbolic items to the wreath before a ritual gathering. Blindfold each person, have them think of a question, then randomly "pick off" their fortunes.

•WRINKLES

(*see Facial Features*)

•XYLOMANCY

(*see Wood*)

•ZOOMANCY

Zoomancy involves the prediction of future events based on reported sightings of fabled beasts such as the Loch Ness monster.

PART THREE

Appendices

Gods and Goddesses of Divination

*"Chance is but the pseudonym of god for those par-
ticular cases in which he does not chose to subscribe
openly with his own sign manual."*

—Coleridge

Ancient people customarily called upon facets of the Divine for the information received in a reading. After all, the gods could see the past and future, and if approached and appeased they might share that insight. Not all gods and goddesses were credited with oracular abilities, however. Below is a brief listing of some beings under whose dominion divination came. This information is provided as an interesting aside, but may also prove useful to your own divining arts.

If you pray before working with your tools, for example, there may be a god or goddess here that you would like to call upon for aid. If so, make sure you understand the cultural context of the Divinity, and pronounce his or her name correctly. Honor that visage in a fitting manner in your Sacred Space, and approach the god or goddess with all due respect, knowing that All are One.

Akuj (African): Supreme god who governs divinatory arts.

Apollo (Greco–Roman): God of prophesy who oversaw the oracle at Delphi.

Artemis (Greek): Goddess who presides over psychic insights.

Brigit (Celtic): Goddess of inspiration and metaphysically obtained knowledge. Especially useful to call upon for aid with pyromancy.

Carmenta (Roman): Goddess of prophesy whose sisters' names mean "looking forward" and "looking back." Her festival dates are January 11 and 15.

Chang Kuo (Chinese): A patroness of the arts who used bamboo tubes and rods to evoke the souls of the dead for communication. Call on her to bless any necromantic efforts, or those that use rods or bamboo sticks.

Daughter of Voice (Hebrew): An oracular goddess who was called upon to provide verbal clues to a problem's solution. The first word or phrase the querent heard after invoking this goddess was considered the answer.

Demeter (Greek): Mistress of magic who is best called upon for divinations that use corn, seeds, grain, or earth. She is also suitable to call upon for answers to questions about love.

Dione (Greek): Homer calls her the mother of Aphrodite. This goddess was the patroness of the oracle at Dodona, and is appropriate to call upon when using trees, lots, or a channeler for divination.

Ea (Mesopotamian): God of oracles and fortune-telling by water.

Egeria (Roman): An oracular goddess whose central element was water.

Fa (Benin): The god of destiny. In Benin tradition, one's future is fixed within a certain limit, and therefore Fa will know it.

Faunus (Roman): God of soothsaying.

Fortuna (Roman): A goddess of fate and fortune, sometimes depicted as a wheel and therefore might be best suited to divination methods that use a wheel.

Freyja (Norse): Goddess of foresight, best called upon when using cats, water, the moon, or flowers as tools or focals.

Gabriel (Biblical): The angel of revelation and truth, who presides over clairvoyance and water scrying.

Gaia (Greek): The Oracle at Delphi originally belonged to her before Apollo's occupation. Gaia as a prophetess was invoked with oaths and offerings of fruit, grain, or a black ewe.

Graiae (Greek): Considered the Mothers of Greece, these spirits had all seeing eyes. Call upon them in visually aided divination such as scrying.

Hecate (Greek): The patroness of prophesy, especially those techniques that use the moon or a key.

Hiisi (Finnish–Ugrian): Spirits of necromancy.

Ida (Italian): The vital force located in the heart, and who presides over matters of divination.

Ishtar (Assyro–Babylonian): A divinatory goddess who was the personification of Venus. As such, she is best to call upon in questions centered on love and romance.

Isis (Egyptian): Goddess of good advice and divination, especially methods that utilize knots, string, or woven items.

Janus (Roman): The gatekeeper of beginnings and endings, this god has two faces, one of which looks to the future. Especially suited for divining information on the outcome of a situation.

Katunda (East African): God of oracles.

Kuan Ti (Chinese): God of fortune-telling. Honor him in your sacred space with red and green candles.

Kusor (Phoenician): God of magic formulas and divination.

Li (Chinese): A Taoist immortal called upon to aid magicians in necromantic procedures.

Masaya (Nicaraguan): An oracular goddess of the volcanoes, she is best invoked for fire divination.

Mati Syra Zemlya (Slavonic): Goddess of divination, especially geomancy.

Merlin (Wales, Britain): Great Druid and prophet. Best called upon when using crystals in divination.

Michael (Biblical): The prince of wisdom and angel of divination, especially pyromancy.

Mithra (Persian): God who presides over clairvoyance and prediction, especially divinations involving the sun.

Nerus (Greek): God of the sea and water who is credited with creating the divinatory art of hydromancy.

Nina (Chaldean): Goddess of oracles, especially those of water.

Norns (Teutonic): The three fates who weave tapestry of a person's life. For prophetic insight, Skold was the fate of the future (Wyrd was of the past, and Verdandi, of the present).

Odin (Norse): Chief god who originated the divinatory arts, specifically runes.

Orunmila (Africa): A Yoruban prophet whose spirit is consulted for *Dafa*.

Pan (Greek): God of soothsaying and natural omens.

Sakunadevatas (Hindu): The goddesses of all good omens.

Selene (Greek): Full moon goddess presiding over all lunar divinations and magic.

Shait (Egyptian): A god of destiny.

Shamash (Sumerian–Babylonian): God of divination, specifically methods employing the sun or rods.

Shaktis (Hindu–Tibetan): An aspect of the supreme force, one aspect of which is called Inanashakti, who governs clairvoyance and other divinatory talents.

Shamash (Assyro–Babylonian): An all-seeing sun god upon whom the *baru*, a local soothsayer, called to reveal the future. The *baru* first prepared an offering to the god, then either poured oil on water in a sacred tub, or read celestial signs for the querent. This approach flourished especially in the region known as Sippar.

Siduri (Sumerian): Oracular goddess who gave utterances to the prophets. A suitable offering for her is beer.

Svantovit (Slavonic): A god of plenty, war, and prosperity. He has four heads, each of which sees in all four directions. His emblems include the bow and a drinking horn.

Tezcatlipuco (Mexican): God frequently called upon for visions and visionary answers, specifically those obtained by using a magic mirror.

Themis (Greek): The Greek goddess of sound counsel and oracles. Her festival date is February 28.

Thoth (Egyptian): God of divination and prophesy, especially numerology.

Tlazolteol (Aztec): Goddess of magic and divination, especially those methods centered on earth, like geomancy. A suitable offering for her is maize.

Viracocha (Incan): God of oracles, especially water-related ones.

Zaqar (Assyro–Babylonian): God who brings prophetic dreams.

Zervan Akarana (Zoroastrian–Persian): God of time and one's destiny.

Zeus (Greek): The oracular center at Dodona was dedicated to him, as were the sacred oaks that were observed for omens and signs.

Symbols and Pictographs

"Nature speaks in symbols and signs."
—John Greenleaf Whittier

Symbols are very important to the diviner's art. They visually represent the shapes of power, cosmic law, and universal truths that words cannot always convey adequately. The experienced diviner learns to identify these emblems, even when only partially formed, and interprets them accordingly. Nonetheless, the sheer volume of symbols that may appear and the different ways they might be construed by each individual makes it difficult for even an adept reader to decipher them all.

Say, for example, that someone asked a question regarding a move under consideration. The resulting picture of a bird on the wing or in a tree could be deciphered as a "yes" or "no" answer, respectively. On the other hand, the tree could represent a firm foundation in a new locale, or the bird could metaphorically symbolize a "flighty" decision. A lot depends on the diviner's instincts, the question, and the outlooks of both the reader and the querent at the given time.

Additionally, there are times when a design seems to have no meaning at all, like a random doodle on the Universal chalk board. Or times when the design, while recognized, is confusing to the reader when juxtaposed against the question at hand. In these moments, I recommend that the diviner share the imagery with the querent. He or she may immediately understand the likeness because of its personal significance. Even if not, this allows the querent to stay intimately and actively involved in receiving and comprehending the messages from the Universe, be the symbols immediately discernible or not. Remember, some symbols that arise in a reading may remain unclear for days, weeks, and even years, so note such odd occurrences somewhere in your personal diary and see what the future brings!

Following are some symbols and pictographs and their common associations that may help you with particularly elusive emblems.

SYMBOL	NAME	MEANING
☉	Air	Spirit; the mind
	Bow	Wealth; improved stature
	Cinquefoil	Secrets; physicality
	Diameter	Lower and Higher Self; division
	Egg, Lozeng	Femininity; motherhood; potential; fertility
	Horseshoe, Yoni	Luck; self-awareness
∞	Infinity	Completeness; dualism
	Island	Isolation; haven
	Spiral	Cycles; path; womb
	Trefoil	Triune nature
	Triple ring	Thought; word; deed
	Wheel	Time; movement; seasons; cycles
	Wishing well	Hope; prayer; offerings
	World triad	Time; providence
↑	Arrow	Directions; messages
	Obelisk	Male phallic emblem
	Tipple Arrow	Virility; unity
	Trident	Water element; fertility
	Trisula	Law

SYMBOL	NAME	MEANING
	Ladder	Ascension; enlightenment
	Mural crown	Victory
	Rectangle	Proportion; good structure; logic
	Throne	Truth; justice; judgment
	Aries	Aggression; impulse
	Taurus	Steadiness; personal flair
	Gemini	Versatile skills
	Cancer	Emotions
	Leo	Style; dominance
	Virgo	Prudence; detailed
	Libra	Grace; logic; balance
	Scorpio	Life's stingers; secrets
	Sagittarius	Charity; idealism
	Capricorn	Organization; authority
	Aquarius	Diplomacy; communication
	Pisces	Empathy; obscurity
	Cauldron	Womb; feminine principle; wisdom and inspiration
	Comb	Weather control; woman's magic
	Fish	Luck

SYMBOL	NAME	MEANING
	Feather	Truth; lifting burdens
	Flag	Strong characteristics
	Key	Knowledge; openings
	Lotus	A windfall
	Tree	Success; fame
	Wood	Stability; luck
	Dragon's eye	Protection; ancient wisdom
	Double triangle	Creation
	Fate	Destiny
	Triple Alpha	Successful beginning
	Ab	Heart; truth
	Ako-Ben	Caution; alarm
	Ankh	Life; fertility; abundance
	Aya	Bravery
	Epa	Restraint
	Fofoo	Self-restraint; control
	Kramuh	Discrimination
	Kuntinkantan	Modesty; meekness
	Nssa	Safety; security

SYMBOL	NAME	MEANING
	Shuti	Awareness; enlightenment
	Sma	Union
	Uat	Renewal of energy
	Urs	Vitality; energy
	Usekh-T	Liberation
	Usr	Culpability
	Wawa Aba	Beginnings
	Anchor cross	Protection in a storm; faith
	Crossroad	Change; decisions
	Lunate cross	Safety; shamanic awareness
	Shepherd's cross	Leadership; plenty
	Tau cross	Life and luck
	Vesta	The sacred hearth
	Androgyne	Yin-yang balance
	Athene	Self awareness; loyalty
	Ceres	Results; nature
	Hermes	Occult interest and insight
	Isis-Hawthor	Cycle of death and rebirth
	Juno	Light; life; health; fertility

SYMBOL	NAME	MEANING
	Spring	Beginnings; hope
	Summer	Maturity; socialization
	Fall	Harvest from hard labors
	Winter	Frugality; rest
	Earth	Order; law
	Jupiter	Humor; generosity
	Jupiter rex	Health and healing
	Mars	Warrior spirit
	Mercury	Commerce; illusions; trickery
	Moon	A gentle, insightful nature
	Pluto	Abundance; financial increase
	Saturn	Wiles; festivity
	Sun	Great fortune
	Venus	Passion; love; beauty
	Double furka	Strength; motivation
	Solar swastika	Progress, usually over a year
	Star	Fifth element; wishes
	Universe	Greater perspectives

Bibliography

Agrippa, Cornelius. *The Ladies' Oracle*, Farrar, Straus and Giroux, NY, 1983.

Blackerby, M. *Cosmic Keys*, Llewellyn Publications, St. Paul, MN, 1991.

Blum, Ralph. *The Book of Runes*, St. Martin's Press, NY, 1982.

Broekman, M. *Palmistry*, Prentice Hall, Englewood Cliffs, NJ, 1972.

Buckland, Ray. *Secrets of Gypsy Fortune Telling*, LLewellyn Publications, St. Paul, MN, 1988.

Cavendish, Richard. *A History of Magic*, Taplinger Publishing, NY, 1977.

Chambers, H. V. *An Occult Dictionary*, Award Books, NY, 1966.

Chaundler, Christine. *Everyman's Book of Superstition*, Philosophical Library, NY, 1978.

Complete Book of Fortune. Crescent Books, NY, NY 1936 (no noted author or editor).

Conway, D. J. *Ancient Shining Ones*, Llewellyn Publications, St. Paul, MN, 1993.

Cunningham, Scott. *The Art of Divination*, The Crossing Press, Freedom, CA, 1993.

_____. *Crystal, Gem and Metal Magic*, Llewellyn Publications, St. Paul, MN, 1988.

_____. *The Encyclopedia of Magical Herbs*, Llewellyn Publications, St. Paul, MN, 1988.

_____. *The Magic in Food*, Llewellyn Publications, St. Paul, MN, 1990.

deGivry, Grillot. Witchcraft, *Magic & Alchemy*, Crown Publishing, NY, (no year given).

Delsol, Paula. *Chinese Astrology*, Warner Books, NY, 1976.

Diagram Group. *Predicting Your Future*, Ballantine Books, NY, 1983.

Edmonds, I. G. *Second Sight*, Thomas Nelson Publishers, NY, 1977.

Ellis, Arthur. *The Divining Rod*, U.S. Department of the Interior, Washington Government Printing Office, Washington, D.C., 1917.

Faraar, Janet and Stuart Faraar. *The Witch's God*, Phoenix Publications, Custer, WA, 1989.

_____. *The Witch's Goddess*, Phoenix Publications, Custer, WA, 1987.

Fatunmbi, Awo Fa'lokun. *Iwa Pele, Ifa Quest*, Original Publications, NY, 1991.

Ferm, Vergilius. *Lightning Never Strikes Twice*, Gramercy Books, NY, 1989.

Guiley, Rosemary Ellen. *Moonscapes*, Prentice Hall Press, NY, 1991.

Hutchison, R. and Adams, R. *Every Day's a Holiday*, Harper and Brothers Publishers, NY, 1951.

Kieckhefer, Richard. *Magic in the Middle Ages*, Cambridge University Press, NY, 1989.

Krupp, Dr. E. C. *Beyond the Blue Horizon*, Oxford University Press, NY, 1991.

Kunz, George F. *Curious Lore of Precious Stones*, Dover Publications, NY, 1913.

Leach, Maria, ed. *Standard Dictionary of Folklore, Mythology and Legend*, Funk & Wagnall, NY, 1984.

Leek, Sybil. *The Book of Fortune Telling*, MacMillan Co., NY, 1969.

Linn, Denise. *The Secret Language of Signs*, Ballantine Books, NY, 1996.

Lorie, Peter. *Superstition*, Simon Schuster, NY, 1992.

Loewe, Michael and Carmen Blacker, eds. *Oracles and Divination*, Shambhala Publishing, Boulder, CO, 1981.

Lyle, Jane. *Secrets of the Zodiac*, Harper, San Francisco, CA, 1993.

Mathews, John, consultant editor. *The World Atlas of Divination*, Bulfinch Press, Hong Kong, 1992.

Maven, Max. *Book of Fortune Telling*, Prentice Hall, NY, 1992.

Melville, John. *Crystal Gazing and Clairvoyance*, Weiser Books, York Beach, ME, 1974.

Murray, Liz and Colin Murray. *The Celtic Tree Oracle*, St. Martin Press, NY, 1988.

Noss, John B. *Man's Religions*, Macmillan Publishing, NY, 1969.

Oesterley, W. O. E., DD. *The Sacred Dance*, Dance Horizons, Brooklyn, NY, 1923.

O Hogain, Daithi. *Irish Superstitions*, Gill and Macmillan, Dublin, Ireland, 1995.

Oken, Alan. *Pocket Guide to Astrology*, The Crossing Press, Freedom, CA, 1996.

_____. *Pocket Guide to Numerology*, The Crossing Press, Freedom, CA, 1996.

_____. *Pocket Guide to the Tarot*, The Crossing Press, Freedom, CA, 1996.

Opie, I. and Tatem, M. *Dictionary of Superstitions*. Oxford University Press, NY, 1989

Paterson, Helena. *The Celtic Lunar Zodiac*, Charles E. Tuttle Co., Boston, MA, 1992.

Pennick, Nigel and Nigel Jackson. *The Celtic Oracle*, Aquarian Press, London, England, 1992.

Pennick, Nigel. *Rune Magic*, Aquarian Press, London, England, 1992.

Pennick, Nigel. *The Secret Lore of Runes and Other Ancient Alphabets*, Rider & Co., London, England, 1991.

Pollack, Rachel. *Teach Yourself Fortune Telling*, Holt & Co., NY, 1986.

Reid, Lori. *The Chinese Horoscope*, Ward Lock Books, London, England, 1992.

Ross, Anne. *Folklore of the Scottish Highlands*, Barnes & Noble Books, NY, 1976.

Sams, Jamie and David Carson. *The Medicine Cards*, Bear & Co., Santa Fe, NM, 1988.

Secrets of the New Age, Bell Publishing, NY, 1989 (no noted editors).

Stuart, Gordon. *Encyclopedia of Myths and Legends*, Headline Book Publishers, London, England, 1993.

Telesco, Patricia. *Folkways*, Llewellyn Publications, St. Paul, MN, 1995.

_____. *The Language of Dreams*, The Crossing Press, Freedom, CA, 1997.

_____. *Kitchen Witch's Cookbook*, Llewellyn Publications, St. Paul, MN, 1994

_____. *Seasons of the Sun*, Samuel Weiser, York Beach, ME, 1996.

_____. *Victorian Grimoire*, Llewellyn Publications, St. Paul, MN, 1992.

_____. *Witch's Brew*, Llewellyn Publications, St. Paul, MN, 1995

Thompson, C. J. S. *The Hand of Destiny*, Bell Publishing, NY, 1989.

Viemeister, Peter E. *The Lightning Book*, Doubleday & Company, NY, 1961.

Visions & Prophecies, Mysteries of the Unknown Series, Time Life Books, Richmond, VA, 1988.

Walters, Derek. *The Fortune Teller's Mah Jongg*, Viking Books, NY, 1988.

Waring, Philippa. *Dictionary of Omens and Superstitions*, Chartwell Books, Secaucus, NJ, 1986.

Webster, Richard. *Omens, Oghams and Oracles;* Llewellyn Publications, St. Paul, MN, 1995.

Wilhelm, Richard and Cary F. Baynes, trans. *The I Ching*, Princeton University Press, Princeton, NJ, 1967.

Zolar. *Encyclopedia of Ancient and Forbidden Knowledge*, Nash Publishing, Los Angeles, CA, 1970.

Listing of Entries

BOOKS BY THE CROSSING PRESS

Other books by Patricia Telesco:

The Language of Dreams

Patricia Telesco outlines a creative, interactive approach to understanding the dream symbols of our inner life. Interpretations of more than 800 dream symbols incorporate multi-cultural elements with psychological, religious, folk, and historical meanings.

$16.95 • Paper • 0-89594-836-2

Wishing Well:
Empowering Your Hopes and Dreams

Blending folklore, magic, and creative visualization, author Patricia Telesco explains how reclaiming the practice of Wishcraft can create our reality exactly as we wish it to be.

$14.95 8 0-89594-870-2

Spinning Spells, Weaving Wonders:
Modern Magic for Everyday Life

This essential book of over 300 spells tells how to work with simple, easy-to-find components and focus creative energy to meet daily challenges with awareness, confidence, and humor.

$14.95 • Paper • 0-89594-803-6

Related books of interest:

A Woman's I Ching

By Diane Stein

A feminist interpretation of the popular ancient text for diving the character of events. Stein's version reclaims the feminine, or yin, content of the ancient work and removes all oppressive language and imagery.

$16.95 • Paper • 0-89594-857-5

BOOKS BY THE CROSSING PRESS

Casting the Circle:
A Women's Book of Ritual
By Diane Stein

A comprehensive guide including 23 ful ritual outlines for the waxing, full, and waning moons, the eight Sabbats, and rites of passage. It also contains a wealth of information on developing, planning, and leading personal and group rituals.

$14.95 • Paper • ISBN 0-89594-411-1

Experiential Astrology:
Symbolic Journeys Using Guided Imagery
By Babs Kirby

Explore astrology in a more personal way without an interpreter. Guided imagery is an innovative technique that will translate the astrological symbols into a more personal set of images, offering a better understanding of what these symbols actually mean to us.

$14.95 • Paper • 0-89594-798-6

Healing with Astrology
By Marcia Starck

Bring balance and energy to your life using the correspondences between your horoscope and a wide range of natural healing systems—vitamin therapy, herbs, music, color, crystals, gemstones, flower remedies, aromatherapy, and unification rituals

$14.95 • Paper • 0-89594-862-1

Pocket Guide to Fortunetelling
By Scott Cunningham

Pocket Guide to Fortunetelling is a complete guide to determining your past, present, and future. With detailed instructions of over 100 techniques, we find that this ageless art is a powerful ally in reshaping our lives.

$6.95 • Paper • 0-89594-875-3